GENDERED SITUATIONS, GENDERED SELVES

THE GENDER LENS SERIES

Series Editors

Judith A. Howard
University of Washington

Barbara Risman
University of Illinois, Chicago

Joey Sprague
University of Kansas

The Gender Lens series has been conceptualized as a way of encouraging the development of a sociological understanding of gender. A "gender lens" means working to make gender visible in social phenomena, asking if, how, and why social processes, standards, and opportunities differ systematically for women and men. It also means recognizing that gender inequality is inextricably braided with other systems of inequality. The Gender Lens series is committed to social change directed toward eradicating these inequalities. Originally published by Sage Publications and Pine Forge Press, all Gender Lens books are now available from The Rowman & Littlefield Publishing Group.

BOOKS IN THE SERIES

Judith A. Howard and Jocelyn A. Hollander, *Gendered Situations, Gendered Selves: A Gender Lens on Social Psychology*

Michael A. Messner, *Politics of Masculinities: Men in Movements*

Judith Lorber, *Gender and the Social Construction of Illness*

Scott Coltrane, *Gender and Families*

Myra Marx Ferree, Judith Lorber, and Beth B. Hess, editors, *Revisioning Gender*

Pepper Schwartz and Virginia Rutter, *The Gender of Sexuality: Exploring Sexual Possibilities*

Francesca M. Cancian and Stacey J. Oliker, *Caring and Gender*

M. Bahati Kuumba, *Gender and Social Movements*

Toni M. Calasanti and Kathleen F. Slevin, *Gender, Social Inequities, and Aging*

Judith Lorber and Lisa Jean Moore, *Gender and the Social Construction of Illness, Second Edition*

Shirley A. Hill, *Black Intimacies: A Gender Perspective on Families and Relationships*

Lisa D. Brush, *Gender and Governance*

Dorothy E. Smith, *Institutional Ethnography: A Sociology for People*

Joey Sprague, *Feminist Methodologies for Critical Researchers: Bridging Differences*

Joan Acker, *Class Questions: Feminist Answers*

Oriel Sullivan, *Changing Gender Relations, Changing Families: Tracing the Pace of Change over Time*

Sara L. Crawley, Lara J. Foley, and Constance L. Shehan, *Gendering Bodies*

Yen Le Espiritu, *Asian American Women and Men: Labor, Laws, and Love*

Scott Coltrane and Michele Adams, *Gender and Families, Second Edition*

Manisha Desai, *Gender and the Politics of Possibilities*

Jocelyn A. Hollander, Daniel G. Renfrow, and Judith A. Howard, *Gendered Situations, Gendered Selves: A Gender Lens on Social Psychology, Second Edition*

GENDERED SITUATIONS, GENDERED SELVES

A Gender Lens on Social Psychology

Second Edition

Jocelyn A. Hollander, Daniel G. Renfrow, and Judith A. Howard

ROWMAN & LITTLEFIELD PUBLISHERS, INC.
Lanham • Boulder • New York • Toronto • Plymouth, UK

Published by Rowman & Littlefield Publishers, Inc.
A wholly owned subsidiary of The Rowman & Littlefield Publishing Group, Inc.
4501 Forbes Boulevard, Suite 200, Lanham, Maryland 20706
http://www.rowmanlittlefield.com

Estover Road, Plymouth PL6 7PY, United Kingdom

British Library Cataloguing in Publication Information Available

Library of Congress Cataloging-in-Publication Data

Hollander, Jocelyn A.
  Gendered situations, gendered selves : a gender lens on social psychology / Jocelyn A.
Hollander, Daniel G. Renfrow, and Judith A. Howard. — 2nd ed.
    p. cm. — (Gender lens)
  Includes bibliographical references and index.
  ISBN 978-0-7425-6351-3 (cloth : alk. paper) — ISBN 978-0-7425-6352-0 (pbk. : alk.
paper) — ISBN 978-1-4422-0864-3 (electronic)
  1. Social psychology. 2. Sex role. 3. Personality and situation. 4. Social exchange. 5.
Symbolic interactionism. 6. Social perception. I. Renfrow, Daniel G. II. Howard, Judith
A., 1947– III. Title.
  HM251.H72 2011
  305.301—dc22   2010028852

∞™ The paper used in this publication meets the minimum requirements of American
National Standard for Information Sciences—Permanence of Paper for Printed Library
Materials, ANSI/NISO Z39.48-1992.

Printed in the United States of America

For Felix and Fiona Violet, with the hope that they may grow up into a less gendered world. And for Chris, who helps create that world every day.
—*Jocelyn*

For Donnie and Judy, for seeing beyond gender.
—*Dan*

For Chris, and for our animal family, Maggie, Tucker, Emma, and our late beloved Chambon, all five of whom turn the concept of gender on its head each and every day. I count on that, and on them.
—*Judy*

Contents

Acknowledgments

ACKNOWLEDGMENTS PROVIDE A rare opportunity to thank in print the people who sustain you. For each of us, these are our friends and families. Dan thanks especially Teresa Ciabattari, Joanna Gregson, Anna Leon-Guerrero, Jan-Martijn Meij, and Alicia Suarez. Jocelyn thanks her family: her parents, brother, aunts, uncles, cousins, and especially her grandparents, who are greatly missed. Judy thanks especially Carolyn Allen, Jerry Baldasty, and Pat Novotny for their steadfast friendship; she will always miss the wit and the warmth of Phil Blumstein. Judy joins Jocelyn in thanking also our longtime fellow sociologists and dear friends Rachel Einwohner and Toska Olson.

Kathleen Crittenden, Chris Halaska, David Newman, Barbara Risman, and Michael Schwalbe provided incisive and thoughtful readings on the first edition. Janet Yale has provided considerable help with many of the details involved in this revision, and we are grateful to her. We thank the various editors with whom we have worked—Mitch Allen and Peter Labella on the first edition, and Sarah Stanton on this revised edition. We reserve a special thanks for Alan McClare, our Rowman & Littlefield editor for the series and the early stages of this revision, and mourn his untimely passing as this revision was under way. All of them have shown unswerving support for our project. We are especially grateful to our Gender Lens *madrina*, Joey Sprague, who read multiple versions of every chapter and offered wonderfully tactful and dead-on comments on this project from the moment it was an idea in our heads through this revised edition.

In the acknowledgments to our first edition, we noted that "the main thing that happens when you write a book is that everything else in your life takes a back seat." A lot of life has happened in the years since Judy and Jocelyn wrote the first edition. Back seats are no longer really possible. When you write a book, you are juggling many balls, and inevitably, some of them drop. With this in mind, Dan thanks Doug, and Jocelyn and Judy both have their respective Chrises to thank for gracefully picking up those dropped balls. Jocelyn also thanks her children, Felix and Fiona Violet, for the delight, beauty, and daily silliness they have brought to her life.

Finally, we thank each other. Collaboration is a risky endeavor; it can be wondrous or disastrous, and we feel fortunate that ours continues to be a great pleasure, even though it is now long distance. Judy and Jocelyn are especially grateful to Dan, who joined this collaboration in the formation of this revised edition. We're now a triumvirate, and grateful for that.

1

Defining Social Psychology and Gender

A NUMBER OF SOCIAL PSYCHOLOGY textbooks begin with the following story:

On the night of March 13, 1964, at about 3:20 a.m., a woman named Kitty Genovese parked her red Fiat in the lot of the Long Island Railroad Station. She lived nearby in Kew Gardens, a quiet middle-class residential area of Queens. As she began the short walk home, sensing something wrong, she started running along a well-lit major boulevard. Milton Hatch heard the first scream. He looked out and saw Kitty Genovese kneeling on the sidewalk, a man standing over her. She screamed, "Help me! Oh God, he's stabbed me!" Hatch leaned out the window and shouted, "Let that girl alone!" Other windows opened and lights went on. The assailant fled in his car. No one called the police. No one went outside to help. She dragged herself along the street, but within ten minutes the assailant drove by again, looking for her. He got out and stabbed her a second time. Still no one called the police. The third and fatal attack occurred in the vestibule of a building a few doors from the woman's own entrance. Onlookers saw the assailant push open the building door. At 3:55 a.m., Harold Klein, a man who lived at the top of the stairs where she was murdered, called the police. The patrol car arrived within two minutes, but Kitty Genovese was already dead.

Why is this violent, disturbing story used to introduce students to the field of social psychology? We[1] begin by defining social psychology and presenting some of the traditional accounts of this murder as illustrations of the social psychological approach to social interaction.

What Is Social Psychology?

Social psychology is fundamentally concerned with the relationships between individuals and their social environments. From the perspective of social psychology, the failure of the thirty-eight witnesses to Kitty Genovese's murder to intervene in the assault or even to call the police reflects the immediate social situations of these witnesses, rather than, for example, a pervasive societal alienation.

For example, one explanation focuses on the effects of social influence on interpreting such situations. Many social situations, even emergencies, are ambiguous. It is not always clear precisely what is occurring and what, if anything, should be done. People look to others to assess whether there is an emergency, and if so, what to do about it. If no one else is doing anything, perhaps it is not an emergency; or, if it is, perhaps there is no way to help. Social influence can occur also through social norms. Suppose the situation in question involves an assault, as in the Kitty Genovese murder, but in this case the assailant is known by the neighbors as Ms. Genovese's romantic partner. Are bystanders likely to intervene? Social psychological research suggests they are not. Social norms prescribe the privacy of intimate relationships, discouraging third parties from intervening in incidents involving family members or romantic partners (e.g., Katz 2006; Shotland and Straw 1976).

Another explanation emphasizes emotional rather than cognitive factors. Social actors are concerned not just about what others might do, but also about what those others might think about them. Bystanders to a possible emergency may feel "evaluation apprehension," concern about how others will evaluate their behavior. If no one else seems to be reacting to the situation in question, they may worry that they will appear foolish or even wrong in intervening. How many of us have hesitated to assist someone in a wheelchair, not sure whether the person needs help or how others might view us?

A third explanation addresses the acceptance of responsibility. Suppose Milton Hatch had seen a man attack Kitty Genovese outdoors in a field, where he and they were the only people present. Would he have done more than call out? Latane and Darley's (1970) theory of the diffusion of responsibility suggests that he might well have. In this situation, the responsibility to intervene would be focused entirely on a single bystander. In contrast, many of the thirty-eight witnesses to Kitty Genovese's murder reported that they assumed others had already taken action; they diffused responsibility to the other bystanders.

Each of these three traditional social psychological explanations concerns the relationship between individuals and their social environments. Social influence, whether informational or normative, refers to the effect of other people's behavior on one's own decisions and actions. Evaluation apprehension refers to concern about the reactions of other social actors to one's own actions. The diffusion of responsibility points to the influence of a simple but significant feature of social environment—the number of other actors present—on individual action.

Other potentially relevant sorts of factors are overlooked by these traditional explanations, however. One of the most obvious social patterns is that Kitty Genovese was a woman and her assailant a man. Could this sex composition shape how witnesses responded? Would they have been more likely to intervene if both had been women? Or men? The sex category of the witnesses themselves may also have been relevant. Interviews with the witnesses revealed one persistent pattern in their reactions. When the residents of an apartment were a woman and a man, the man was the one who decided whether to take action (or at least this is what the woman and man reported). Another potentially relevant factor is the socioeconomic circumstances of the neighborhood in which this occurred. Does an assault in a quiet, isolated, middle-class area evoke different responses from witnesses than an assault in a more lively, busy, commercial or working-class neighborhood? Or do the class backgrounds of the witnesses shape the sorts of responses they are likely to consider? The racial identities of the actors might also matter: Would the witnesses have responded differently if the assailant had been white and his victim black? Or if he had been black and she had been white? Would the racial identities of the witnesses complicate these patterns?[2]

In raising such questions, we are asking whether the social structural positions of the actors (i.e., their location in the various social hierarchies of race, gender, or socioeconomic status) have anything to do with their responses in this situation. Because social psychology, more than many disciplines, sees human behavior as rooted in social context, these are crucial questions. Nevertheless, many social psychologists have explored such questions in only the most limited way, if at all. This volume presents an analysis of social behavior that highlights the social structural characteristics of situations and human actors, focusing particularly on gender. We believe that gender is invoked by virtually all social behaviors and situations; therefore, gender must be a central component of theories and empirical research on social behavior. At the same time, however, we believe that it is impossible to analyze gender in isolation from other significant social positions such as race, social class, sexual orientation, or age. As a simple example, imagine yourself walking down a deserted street near your home late one night. Suddenly you notice that there is someone else walking toward you. How would you feel if this person were an older white woman dressed in dirty clothes and pushing a shopping cart? What if she were young, Asian, and carrying a small child? What if she were wearing gang insignia? Would your reaction be different if this person were a man? What if the man were black, middle-aged, well-dressed, and carrying a briefcase? What if he were young, white, with a shaved head and heavy boots? What if he were a school-aged child carrying a lunch box?

As these hypothetical transformations show, it is impossible to analyze any one social position without considering others. No one has only a sex, or only a race, or only a class; our various social positions coexist, in our own experiences, in our perceptions of other people, and in their perceptions of us. Thus, while we focus on gender in this book, we consider it in the context in which other social statuses are played out.

We devote the rest of this chapter to introducing the key theories in social psychology and the key terms used to discuss gender. In the next chapter we combine these emphases, discussing how gender has been conceptualized within social psychological theory and research. Later chapters present more detailed analyses and evaluations of the major social psychological theories, with a particular focus on how individuals and situations are shaped by gender, race, and social class.

Before we begin, however, it is crucial to point out an important distinction within the field of social psychology. Social psychology obviously concerns both social and psychological issues. But the theories, key questions, empirical research, and applied utility of the scholarship and knowledge generated by social psychologists diverge on the basis of whether those social psychologists work within a psychological or a sociological framework. The *psychological* approach takes the individual as the primary unit of analysis, evaluating differences in behavior as a function of personality, emotional makeup, and aptitude. Psychological studies of helping behavior, for example, have attempted to identify features of an "altruistic personality" or attributional style. The *sociological* approach, by contrast, emphasizes how social dynamics and social contexts shape cognition, emotional experiences, and behaviors. Such investigations view "interpersonal situations as a lens through which broader social forces, properties, and processes can be understood"—a sociology in miniature (Stolte, Fine, and Cook 2001:388). Sociological studies of helping behavior, as we have illustrated, focus on the constraints and opportunities for helping located in particular situations— the number of other people present, the social relationships among those people, their location in social structures, or the prevailing social norms about behavior in those situations. Moreover, psychological treatments of social psychology tend to be more topical and to draw on relatively narrow, specific theories of human behavior, whereas sociological treatments tend to be integrated with more general theories of human behavior. In a practical sense these different perspectives reflect "the bureaucratic structure of the modern American university, including the division of knowledge" into disciplines and departments (DeLamater 2003:ix).

We draw on both perspectives in our analysis of the field, using the sociological theories of social psychology to organize our discussion, and using the rich empirical traditions within psychology to illustrate our points. The key message of both perspectives, however, is the same: social behavior always involves a reciprocal relationship between individuals and their social environments. To understand individual behavior, we must consider individuals in the social contexts in which they act.

Social Psychological Theories

Social psychology proceeds within a variety of conceptual frameworks. Primary among these are social exchange theory (and related theories such as behaviorism and social learning), social cognition, and symbolic interaction. We organize this brief summary of the major social psychological theories around an illustration, the details of which may be familiar to many current and former college students.

Consider the following scenario, which we borrow from David Mamet's play *Oleanna* (1992).[3] A male college professor is on the phone in his office in the late afternoon. A female undergraduate student comes to his office for an appointment he asked her to make with him. He keeps her waiting for a good twenty minutes while he has a long phone conversation with his wife about a house they are trying to purchase. Eventually the professor turns to the student, invites her to sit down, and they discuss the student's poor performance on a recent exam and her confusion about the class material. She emphasizes her difficulties in understanding the main textbook, written by this professor, and the content of his lectures, which focus on all that is wrong with higher education. He stresses the importance of this material and urges her to try harder. She becomes increasingly more emotional and at one point begins to cry. He comes over to the sofa where she is sitting and consoles her. At the end of the appointment, he suggests that he will give her an A for the course if she comes in regularly and works with him on the material.

What is going on here? What would each of these three perspectives have to say about this interaction?

Social Exchange Theory

Social learning and social exchange theories both derive from the key principle of behaviorism: that humans are likely to repeat behaviors for which they are rewarded, and to cease behaviors for which they are punished. We learn behaviors either by enacting them and directly experiencing their consequences or by observing the behaviors of others and the consequences of those behaviors. While social learning theory focuses on individual behavior, social exchange theory applies the principles of social learning theory to understanding social relationships. Every human relationship involves the exchange of resources, whether material (such as money) or intangible (such as status or affection). People tend to remain in mutually rewarding relationships and end relationships that are not rewarding. One key factor in such decisions is the availability of alternatives: people may remain in unsatisfying exchange relationships if the alternatives are even worse.

Social exchange theory would analyze the professor-student interaction in terms of what each actor contributes to and gets from the relationship. The professor is offering to contribute his time and expertise to the student. While on the surface he may not appear to be getting much from the interaction, on closer inspection one could speculate that he gains a great deal. If the student agrees to the exchange, the professor receives the rewards of status enhancement that are implicit in the professor-student relationship. He may also gain personal satisfaction from helping a struggling student. From the student's perspective, the benefits may be more obvious than the costs. The student gains the advantage of individual tutoring, which presumably may help her do well in this class. She may gain some personal understanding from the professor, as well as the promised A. What the student gives to the exchange is her own time and the contribution of subservient behavior—that is, status acknowledgment. Does the professor have alternative sources of status enhancement? Presumably he does: each of his students is a potential source. Does the student have alternative sources of the information she needs to pass this course? Presumably not. Not only is there just a single professor in charge of this course, but the text on which the course relies is written by the same professor. We can predict then that she will accept this exchange.

One important issue in exchange relationships is the operation of power. When one partner has greater control over the available rewards and punishments than the other, that partner has more relative power. Power implies that one partner is dependent on the other; whoever has the least to gain from the relationship is the more powerful partner, because she or he needs the relationship less. The power dynamics of the relationship portrayed in this situation are not straightforward. In the first act, which we have described above, the student is clearly dependent on the professor—for help with the course, for a grade, for her future. By the end of the play, however, the tables have turned, at least on the surface. The student has now charged the professor with sexual harassment, threatening his acquisition of tenure and potentially ruining his career—or so the playwright would have the audience believe. At this point the student holds a degree of power over the professor, who is now dependent on her for the future of his career.

Our more detailed discussion of social exchange theory in chapter 3 will allow the reader to apply the principles of social exchange more thoroughly to this interaction. For now, we note that social exchange theory helps us analyze behavior in the context of social interaction. The answers it offers, however, emphasize situated, individual power. This perspective has tended to minimize the effects of those social structures that endow the professor with more institutional, systematic power than the student, such as the advantages associated with his occupation, his sex, his age, or his socioeconomic position.

Social Cognition

Thought is, of course, necessary for the calculation of exchanges, as well as for the capacity to learn through observation. Social learning and social exchange theories, however, do not fully explore the human capacity for thought. Social cognition, in contrast, emphasizes the ways in which we think about our social worlds. There are two fundamental premises of social cognition. First is the assumption of cognitive mediation: thought intervenes between the environment and behavior. How we think about our environments shapes how we behave. This assumption implies that two different people in the same situation might behave differently, based on how they think about that situation. A second fundamental premise is that human cognitive capacities are limited. Because we cannot possibly perceive or use all of the available information in a given situation, we rely on cognitive shortcuts, attending to and using only a portion of the available information.

This perspective distinguishes between the ways our thoughts are organized and the ways we process social information. Most important among the elements of cognition are social schemas: organized, abstract frameworks of information. The need for cognitive efficiency encourages the development of cognitive categories such as social schemas as a way of organizing information. Repeated experiences with particular people, social roles, or situations allow us to develop what are essentially summaries of their "typical" characteristics and behaviors. We develop schemas about other people and ourselves (e.g., a "Woody Allen type"). We also develop schemas about social positions (e.g., gender or race stereotypes) and social roles (e.g., parental roles). And we develop schemas about various types of social situations, such as shopping at the grocery store, attending a play, or getting married.

The student-professor situation described above activates a number of familiar social schemas. First, an interaction between a professor and a student is itself scripted. Many of the details of this situation are predictable: they meet in the professor's office; the professor sits behind the desk, the student in a chair in front of the desk; the professor can interrupt the student but the student cannot interrupt the professor. All of these are recognizable components of a situational script. Person and role schemas are evident as well. The professor is likely to have a "typical student" script, the student equally likely to have a "typical professor" script. (Indeed, many faculty who have seen the play cringe when confronted with the schemas the general public appears to hold for college professors.) Student and professor are themselves social roles for which there are schematic cultural expectations. And, importantly for this play, the sex and associated gendered expectations of these actors is also the basis for social schemas. In short, there are a host of orderly, well-recognized expectations for the actors and the situation in which they find themselves.

These cognitive elements are used in several key cognitive processes. Most important among these are attention, memory, and social inference. When we enter a situation, we must attend to some things in the environment and, by implication, fail to attend to others. We store some information in memory, and again by implication, neglect to store other information. When necessary, we retrieve some information from long-term memory, bringing it to immediate consciousness, and fail to retrieve other information. We use the available information to make a series of social inferences such as decisions, judgments of probability, evaluations, attributions of causality, or assessments of the characteristics of other people. We use schemas in selecting what to attend to, what information to retain in memory, and what information to retrieve in making social inferences.

Note that people in different social positions and with different social experiences may develop systematically different schemas. Viewers of *Oleanna* who have a schema for sexual harassment presumably process the professor-student interaction quite differently from those who do not. Gender may also be associated with different understandings of the concept of sexual harassment; some (most often, men) may view the situation from the perspective of the person accused of harassment, others (most often, women) from the perspective of the victim. These variations lead to systematic differences in the evaluations and judgments the viewers make about such situations.

Social cognition thus provides the tools to analyze precisely how social structures and social patterns affect everyday situated thought, and in turn the daily behaviors of individuals—and also how individuals both contribute to and undermine social structures. Where this perspective is weak, however, is in specifying the ways in which these cognitive structures and processes are enacted in social interaction. This is the domain of symbolic interaction.

Symbolic Interaction

Symbolic interaction differs from social exchange and social cognition in emphasizing the everyday interactions and negotiations that constitute social life. Interaction relies on the human capacity to use symbols, a capacity that also enables the peculiarly human consciousness of self.[4] Meaning is created through the manipulation of symbols in interaction. In other words, meaning is not inherent in the people or objects a person encounters, but is created by the person perceiving them. This implies in turn that one of the main tasks of social interaction is literally to define the situation, to resolve the contradictions and inconsistencies between actors' individual understandings and interpretations of a situation into a common perspective that facilitates the accomplishment of their mutual goals.

Symbolic interaction also offers a useful framework for analyzing the student-professor situation described above. This is a richly textured interaction, one with a good deal of symbolic gesturing and negotiation. One of the more obvious symbolic gestures is the fact that the professor makes the student wait for more than twenty minutes while he talks on the phone. He may be oblivious to the symbolic meaning of this behavior. Indeed, even the student may be unaware of the effects of this gesture. Nonetheless, this detail contributes significantly to the creation of status in this interaction. That he sits while she stands, that he dictates her moves around the office, are other gestures laden with symbolic meaning.

It is also clear in the second act that the professor and student do not agree on their definition of this situation. From the professor's perspective, he is making a generous offer to a student, one for which she should be grateful. From the student's perspective, he has stepped across some crucial boundaries, behaving toward her in a way that she interprets as sexual harassment. Their interactions are occasionally stilted and often awkward, attesting to the difficulties of negotiating a common framework. How the actors attempt to sustain this fairly involved interaction with these differing interpretations requires more detailed analysis; symbolic interaction provides a framework for this analysis.

Conclusion

Each of these three social psychological perspectives offers a distinct framework for analyzing complex situations. Social exchange theory focuses on the nature of the exchanges between the professor and student. What resources are exchanged between the two actors? What does each actor gain and what does each actor contribute to the relationship? In what ways does each actor have power over or depend upon the other? Social cognition focuses on the perceptions and thoughts of each actor about this situation. What sorts of cognitive expectations do the actors (and the audience) have about this situation and about themselves and each other? How do these expectations shape their perceptions and interpretations of the situation—and ultimately their behavior? Symbolic interaction addresses the actual negotiations that occur between the actors. What symbolic gestures are used in this interaction? How do the actors define the situation, and how do they attempt to reach a common interpretation of what is going on? What happens if they are ultimately unsuccessful?

These three perspectives offer different approaches to the relationship between individuals and their social environments. While they are often set up as competing theoretical interpretations, we believe it is more useful to understand them as different but not mutually exclusive ways of explaining social interaction. Although we maintain that some theories have more to offer than others (as we discuss in more detail in chapters 3–5), we emphasize that all have both strengths and weaknesses, and that in general it is useful to treat them as complementary, rather than competing.

However, none of the three theories explicitly identifies particular features of the social environment as more or less significant. In contrast, we focus throughout this volume on the pervasive effects of gender, in interaction with other key social structural characteristics, in shaping the kinds of situations we find ourselves in, the resources available to us in those situations, and the patterns of behavior that result. In other words, we look at social psychology through a gender lens. Before we begin, however, we must specify what we mean when we talk about gender.

What Is Gender?

Over the last forty years, social psychologists (and others) have become more and more interested in gender. But what exactly is "gender"? When we talk about gender, do we mean the biological characteristics of males and females, such as genes or genitals? Do we mean the social roles men and women play—mother, father, breadwinner, caretaker? Are we talking about personal characteristics, such as aggressiveness or nurturance—or something else entirely?

Another source of confusion is that the relationship between *gender* and other terms is poorly defined. Some writers use the term *gender*, some discuss *sex*, and some examine *sex roles* or *gender roles*. Moreover, some authors use these words interchangeably, while others distinguish carefully among them.

Our goal in the rest of this chapter is to untangle these confusions, and spell out exactly what we mean—and do not mean—by the term gender. In this section, we define gender and compare it with related terms: *sex, gender role, gender stereotype, gender identity, sexuality, and sexual orientation.* We also define two other terms, race and social class, that we use throughout this book. Our discussion will help to illuminate precisely what we mean by a gender lens.

Sex

What is sex? When we fill out official forms, whether applying for a job, a driver's license, admission to college, or a credit card, we are usually asked to declare our sex by checking the box marked "male" or the box marked "female." How do we know which box to check?

The definition of sex seems straightforward: the term is generally used to refer to the biological characteristics that distinguish males and females, such as reproductive organs or chromosomes. Most people in U.S. society[5] think of sex as dichotomous and unchangeable. That is, they assume that there are only two boxes one can check, male and female, and that everyone falls into one (and only one) of these categories. Moreover, they assume that one always falls into the same category: someone who checks the "female" box at age twenty will have checked the same box at age ten, and will check it at ages fifty and eighty-five as well.

However, these assumptions are not always correct. *Intersexed* individuals, for example, are those who are not easily classified as male or female: their reproductive organs and chromosomal structures are discrepant or ambiguous (Fausto-Sterling 2000; Money and Erhardt 1972). A child may be born with sex chromosomes, internal organs, genitals, and/or secondary sex characteristics that are both male and female. Experts estimate that 2 percent of babies are intersexed in some way (Blackless et al. 2000). Which box would these individuals check on official forms? In 2009, this type of ambiguity threatened Caster Semenya's gold medal in the women's 800-meter at the World Championship when officials questioned her sex. Semenya had appeared female at birth, with female external genitalia, and had been raised as a girl and competed as a woman. When a medical examination confirmed the absence of a uterus and ovaries but discovered internal testes, Semenya's sex remained ambiguous. A clear set of criteria for determining sex remained elusive (Yaniv 2009). Indeed, eight months later, the International Association of Athletics Federations (IAAF), the track and field governing body, had yet to decide on appropriate criteria, delaying Semenya's participation in another key racing event (Clarey 2010).

Transsexuals, by contrast, have literally changed their sex—they have been surgically and/or hormonally altered so that they appear to be a different sex from that which they were born. A well-known example is the travel writer Jan Morris, who began life as a boy, James, but who now lives as a woman, Jan. (Transsexuals are distinct from *transvestites*, who wear the clothes associated with the other sex.) Because transsexuals have the genetic structure of one sex, but the physical appearance of another, they are not easily classified as female or male.

Transgender emerged in the 1990s as an umbrella concept widely used to describe these and other individuals (e.g., drag kings and queens, butches, femmes, genderqueers, etc.) who "cross over, cut across, move between or otherwise queer socially constructed sex/gender boundaries" (Stryker 1994:251). Transpeople disturb assumptions regarding the "natural" correspondence among sex, sex category, and gender (Halberstam 1998; Namaste 1996; Prosser 1998). A growing field of trans studies continues to analyze and theorize these identities and practices that make visible

> the normative linkages we generally assume to exist between the biological specificity of the sexually differentiated human body, the social roles and statuses that a particular form of body is expected to occupy, the subjectively experienced relationship between a gendered sense of self and social expectations of gender-role performance, and the cultural mechanisms that work to sustain or thwart specific configurations of gendered personhood. (Stryker 2006:3)

Taken together, transgender individuals—their bodies, actions, and senses of self—trouble the assumption of a static sexual binary.

The belief in two sexes is an example of what Mehan and Wood (1975) have called an "incorrigible proposition": an unquestioned belief that cannot be proven wrong, even in the face of contradictory evidence. In this society, most people believe that there are two, and only two, sexes, and when we encounter a situation that challenges this belief, such as a person who doesn't fit neatly into one of these two categories, we adjust the situation to fit our beliefs, rather than adjusting our beliefs to fit the situation. Consider the case of Thomas Beatie, a transsexual man who gave birth to a daughter in 2008 and a son in 2009. Beatie was born female but had sex reassignment surgery and is now legally male and married to a woman. Because he kept his female reproductive organs, he was able to become pregnant using donor sperm and to give birth "naturally" (Trebay 2008). The national press drew attention to his case, fueling public debate about which sex Beatie "really is." Many people found his claim that he was a man *before, during,* and *after* the pregnancies an affront to related roles of mother and husband. Such responses attest to the resiliency of the sexual binary. In other cases, such as those of intersexed infants, we "correct" the ambiguity by surgical or hormonal means, and/or assign the person to one of our two categories, rather than admitting the possibility of more than two categories.[6]

How do we determine someone's sex? Most people would answer this question by appealing to biology: males have penises and XY chromosomes, whereas females have vaginas, more prominently developed breasts, and XX chromosomes. In everyday life, however, we do not normally use these criteria to distinguish between males and females. Yet we rarely have trouble classifying those we meet as male or female: "When encountering older children or adults for the first time, most of us do not usually examine their genitals to label their sex! Instead, we use their attire, movements, sex-related characteristics such as height or musculature, and their general style of self-presentation as cues to their sex" (Unger and Crawford 1992:17–18). Thus, assigning someone to a *sex category* is as much a social process as the application of physiological criteria. "Sex category" is a phrase we use to denote the two categories into which "sex" is typically assigned. We intend this phrase to denote the social construction processes (see chapter 5) that define "sex." As we shall see in the next section, the way we ascribe sex is deeply intertwined with gender.

Gender

Gender is a slippery term. Most scholars would agree with the statement that gender has something to do with the social behaviors and characteristics associated with biological sex; however, there is substantially less agreement on exactly what this statement means.

Social scientists use the term *gender* in multiple ways. Some use gender interchangeably with sex, suggesting that sex and gender are essentially the same thing. (Indeed, some argue that the term gender is meaningless and should be abandoned, since everything, they believe, reduces to sex.) These researchers might assume, for example, that women care for children (and are nurturing in general) because of their biological ability to bear children. This perspective sees gender as somehow essential to males and females; it is believed to be both innate and unchanging. For this reason, this approach is sometimes called the *essentialist perspective* on gender. Biology is believed to determine the social behaviors and characteristics of males and females.

Other scholars distinguish between sex and gender, using sex to refer to biological characteristics as we have described above, but using gender to refer to the culturally determined behaviors and attributes that are associated with, but not determined by, biological sex. These writers do not assume that the relationship between sex and gender is direct or automatic. Rather, they believe that mediating processes such as childhood socialization and situational expectations, located within particular social structures and institutions that shape socialization and situational expectations, lead individuals to behave in gendered ways.[7] Thus, different cultures may develop distinct notions of gender, which seem natural because they are associated with sex but which are socially, rather than biologically, driven. In contrast with the essentialist perspective described above, this constructionist perspective does not see gendered characteristics and behaviors as innate or unchangeable.

Some scholars see gender as a social structure. In this view, gender is not simply a set of personal characteristics or behaviors. Rather, it is a social system that sorts women and men into two categories, female and male, and then uses these categories to justify the unequal allocation of rewards and resources, both material and symbolic. According to this perspective, gender functions at all levels of social life—individual, interactional, and institutional—and these different levels reinforce each other (Risman 1998, 2004). In this book, we adopt a combination of this structural perspective and the constructionist perspective described above, which focuses on the interactional level of social life.

What does it mean to say that something is *gendered*? In this book, we use this phrase to mean that ideas about gender—assumptions and beliefs on both individual and societal levels—affect the thoughts, feelings, behaviors, resources, or treatment of women and men. Thus, to the extent that women and men dress, talk, or act differently because of societal expectations, their behavior is gendered. To the extent that an organization assigns some jobs to women and others to men on the basis of their assumed abilities, that organization is gendered. And to the extent that a professor treats a student differently because that student is a man or a woman, their interaction is gendered.

Gender as Difference

In practice, research on gender—from any perspective—has tended to focus on differences between women and men. This tendency persists despite the fact that research shows very few significant sex differences (e.g., Fausto-Sterling 1985; Hyde 2005; Maccoby and Jacklin 1974). In fact, social psychological research indicates that sex differences may be "overrated," as distributions of women and men on most characteristics tend to be overlapping rather than separate (Sprecher and Toro-Morn 2002). Nonetheless, many researchers continue to focus on differences rather than on the overwhelming similarities between the sexes, or even on the extensive variations within each sex category. This pattern of research reinforces the essentialist belief that there are large, stable, innate differences between the sexes, and encourages biological explanations for those few differences that are resilient. Thorne, Kramarae, and Henley (1983) write that these studies mistake "description . . . for explanation" (15) and warn that just because studies find differences between males and females does not mean that physiological sex is the *cause* of the differences. For example, one analysis of gender differences in conversational patterns concluded that power, not sex per se, was the source of those differences (Kollock, Blumstein, and Schwartz 1985).

There are a number of reasons why researchers continue to prioritize sex differences. One of these reflects a pattern typical of human cognition. As we noted in the discussion of cognition above, human beings have a tendency to categorize information wherever possible. As an ostensibly dichotomous characteristic with highly visible social trappings (e.g., hair style and apparel) and a central role in human reproduction, sex is a prime basis for cognitive categorization. The pervasive tendency to focus on sex differences rather than similarities thus may derive partly from cognitive processes.

The persistent belief in sex difference in the face of contradictory evidence is also tied in part to the human quest for self-identity; we want to know who we are. This quest has a peculiar character, at least in Western culture: knowing who we are implies knowing who we are not. Gender is one fundamental source of identity. Although there are several contradictory theories of how gender identity is created, most social psychologists concur that children learn at a young age to adopt gender as a basic organizing principle for themselves and the social worlds they are learning about. While very young children may make "errors," children quickly learn to regard gender as bipolar (Cahill 1986). "Children regard a broad range of activities as exclusively appropriate for only one sex or the other, and . . . they strongly prefer same-sex playmates . . . and gender-appropriate toys, clothes, and activities" (Bem 1993:111). Furthermore, children use play itself, as well as the same-sex and cross-sex interactions incorporated within play, to affirm and reconstruct these positions (Boyle, Marshall, and Robeson 2003; Messner 2000). As studies of gender stereotypes among adults reveal, gender polarization does not wane as children grow older. The cultural centrality of gender, together with the susceptibility of gender to a bipolar model, defines the contemporary social psychological approach to gender.

Perhaps as a result of these tendencies, researchers often expect to find sex differences. Social psychologists are not immune from popular essentialist beliefs about gender. These expectations often act as a self-fulfilling prophecy, predisposing researchers to focus on or even to elicit information that confirms their beliefs. Many studies have shown that experimenters' hypotheses affect research findings. According to Weisstein (1970),

> These studies are enormously important when assessing the validity of psychological studies of women. Since it is beyond doubt that most of us start with notions as to the nature of men and women, the validity of a number of observations of sex differences is questionable, even when these observations have been made under carefully controlled conditions. Second, and more important, [these studies] point quite clearly to the influence of social expectation. In some extremely important ways, people are what you expect them to be or at least they behave as you expect them to behave. (215)

The biases that have plagued social psychology were apparent as early as 1910, when psychologist Helen Thompson Wooley commented, "There is perhaps no field aspiring to be scientific where flagrant personal bias, logic martyred in the cause of supporting a prejudice, unfounded assertions, and even sentimental rot and drivel, have run riot to such an extent as here" (Wooley 1910:340; see also Shields 2007; Stewart and Dottolo 2006).

Another reason for social psychology's focus on sex differences has to do with the structure of the field itself. Over the past century, psychology and sociology (like other sciences) have become more and more reliant on statistical tests. These tests are designed to identify significant differences among groups, and therefore shape a search for differences rather than similarities (Unger and Crawford 1992; Unger 1998). Moreover, even if a difference is *statistically* significant (i.e., unlikely to have occurred by chance), it may not be *substantively* significant (i.e., meaningful). For example, Hyde's (2005) meta-analysis of the social psychological literatures on verbal and nonverbal cognitive abilities, communication, social and personality characteristics, psychological well-being, and motor behaviors concludes that the effect size for 78 percent of identified sex differences in this body of research is small or close to zero. Reviews of other sex differences have found similar patterns of statistically, but not substantively, significant effects (Jaffee and Hyde 2000; Deaux 1984; Sprecher and Toro-Morn 2002).

Researchers may also have a difficult time disseminating the results of studies that find no evidence of sex differences. Findings of similarity are not "newsworthy"; academic journals are much less likely to publish such studies. Newspapers and other media are similarly disposed: while reports of sex differences in math abilities garner headlines and newsmagazine cover stories, reports of similarity are relegated to short, unobtrusive articles, if indeed they are reported at all (Eccles and Jacobs 1986). Thus, even if the majority of research projects were to find no significant differences between women and men, *published* research might actually consist of only those few studies that do find differences.

Sex differences research also tends to ignore the fact that *different* often means *unequal*. In other words, such research tends to ignore power relationships (Hollander and Howard 2000). Carrigan and his colleagues write that in the study of gender, "relations have been interpreted as differences. The greater social power of men and the sexual division of labor are interpreted as 'sexual dimorphism' in behavior. With this, the whole question of social structure is spirited away" (Carrigan, Connell, and Lee 1987:75–76). Even when research considers power differences between the sexes, it rarely looks at power differences within sexes—that is, it ignores very real differences among women and among men, homogenizing each category as though sex is the most important differentiating feature (Fine and Gordon 1989).

Research on sex differences also ignores the fact that behavior and self-reports of behavior are specific to situations, depending on factors such as the structure of the social context or the attitudes and expectations of others in that context. For example, one study found that women's behavior in a simulated job interview depended on the perceived gender stereotypes of the interviewer. When the research participants believed the interviewer to hold traditional views of women, they behaved in a more stereotypically feminine manner (von Baeyer, Sherk, and Zanna 1981). These women altered the femininity of their behavior in order to best achieve their goals in the interview. Similarly, Wilson and colleagues' (2002) study of sexual behavior among Latino couples in California found that men reported having had more sexual partners and a history of engaging in sex with strangers when the interviewer was a man rather than a woman. Individuals' behavior may change significantly from one situation to the next, as may the recounting of one's experiences. Consequently, the results of a psychological study may depend on which situation is examined and by whom. Indeed, the experimental laboratory, a staple of social psychological research, affects the expression of gender. Although it purportedly allows scientists to study gender in an objective context, the laboratory is in fact a specific social setting that affects the subject, as do all social contexts. The laboratory is no more neutral than any other situation.

Thus, it is important to exercise caution when interpreting research reports of sex difference. Findings of difference may be due not so much to meaningful differences in the abilities or behavior of women and men as to a host of other factors, including the norms of publishing and research and the biases of researchers. However, just because these reports of sex differences may be misleading does not mean that they should be ignored. The belief that males and females are fundamentally different is widely shared among Americans, and indeed among most peoples of the world. These beliefs, regardless of their validity, influence our identities, thoughts, and behaviors, and may cause men and women to behave differently (gender difference) even if no underlying difference in ability (sex difference) exists. In other words, these beliefs have material consequences regardless of their basis in fact. We contend that sex differences research must be taken seriously—if only to understand how essentialist beliefs shape social psychological research and social life. We suggest that readers keep these issues in mind as they proceed through the next chapters. For now, however, we return to our definitions of key terms.

Gender Role

Another common term in social psychology is *gender role*, which is often used interchangeably with *sex role*. Sociologists use the term *role* to refer to "a set of prescriptions and proscriptions for behavior—expectations about what behaviors are appropriate for a person holding a particular position within a particular social context" (Kessler and McKenna 1978:11). The term gender role, then, refers to the characteristics and behaviors believed to be appropriate for men or for women. People expect that others will behave in accord with their gender role, and punish those who violate these expectations.

Although still in frequent use in psychology, the concept of gender role has been strongly criticized by sociologists. For example, some note that these roles are based on the theorist's ideas of what people should be like, rather than what people really are like (Carrigan et al. 1987; Kimmel, Hearn, and Connell 2004). Most people's lives, in fact, do not conform to what gender roles prescribe. Moreover, talking about "the male gender role" and "the female gender role" also ignores the very real variation among women and among men, and overlooks the substantial overlap in the characteristics and behaviors of males and females.

Perhaps more important, the concept of gender roles ignores issues of power and inequality. Gender role theory describes the relationship between women and men as one of difference and complementarity: the sexes are "separate but equal" and both roles serve important functions in society. But in fact male and female "roles" are not equally valued and are not necessarily "functional" for everyone. The concept of roles masks the fact, for example, that women have traditionally been legally subservient to men in the family. Until relatively recently in the United States, women could not own property or enter into a contract, and men were legally allowed to rape and beat their wives. These are not the hallmarks of an equal relationship, a fact that is hidden by role terminology (Carrigan et al. 1987; Connell 1995; Kimmel, Hearn, and Connell 2004; Lopata and Thorne 1978; Stacey and Thorne 1985). As a result of these critiques, many scholars have discarded the terms sex role and gender role. However, we discuss these terms here because they are still very much a part of both popular and social psychological discourse.

Gender Stereotype

Stereotypes are "strongly held overgeneralizations about people in some designated social category" (Basow 1992:3). For example, many Americans have stereotypes about athletes, professors, or feminists. These beliefs are "not necessarily based on fact or personal experience, but applied to each role occupant regardless of particular circumstance" (Kessler and McKenna 1978:12). Unlike the concept of roles, stereotypes do not imply that individuals should conform to particular expectations for behavior. Nor do they suggest that these beliefs are useful, either for individuals or for societies. Because stereotypes are oversimplifications, they may be inaccurate for a group as a whole, as well as for any particular member of that group. In sum, as Charon argues, "far from arising out of careful and systematic analysis, stereotypes arise out of hearsay and culture, and instead of aiding our understanding of the human being, they always stand in the way of accurate understanding" (2004:251).

Gender stereotypes, then, are beliefs about the characteristics of women and men, including their physical characteristics, typical behaviors, occupational positions, or personality traits. Reflecting the assumption that sex is dichotomous, stereotypes for women and men often involve polar opposites. For example, "traits related to instrumentality, dominance, and assertiveness . . . are believed more characteristic of men, while such traits as warmth, expressiveness, and concern for other people are thought more characteristic of women" (Deaux and Major 1990:95; see also Deaux and LaFrance 1998; Rosenkrantz et al. 1968). Such polarizations serve to increase the perception of difference between women and men, and mask the ways in which they are similar.

This does not mean that stereotypes paint all women or all men as the same. Indeed, stereotypes for certain subgroups of men and women, such as businesswomen, homemakers, or blue-collar working men, are common. Stereotypes may also vary by race, ethnicity, or class, as we discuss further in chapter 4. However, these variations are accommodated as subtypes subsumed under the more general stereotypes of women and men. The fact that we create subtypes rather than modifying our dichotomous view of gender points to our deep investment in the idea of gender difference.

Gender Identity

The term *gender identity* refers to one's inner sense of oneself as female or male; it is a major part of one's self-concept. Gender identity develops during very early childhood, and, once established, it is quite resistant to change (Kessler and McKenna 1978:9). Gender identity tends to be dichotomous—people generally think of themselves as male or female, not something in between. This is probably due to our "incorrigible proposition" that there are two, and only two, sexes. Kate Bornstein, a male-to-female transsexual, writes that "I know I'm not a man—about that much I'm very clear, and I've come to the conclusion that I'm probably not a woman either, at least not according to a lot of people's rules on this sort of thing. The trouble is, we're living in a world that insists we be one or the other—a world that doesn't bother to tell us exactly what one or the other is" (1994:8). Thus, making sense of one's gender identity and presenting it to others can be a precarious enterprise.

Although almost everyone has a gender identity, the salience of this identity may vary among people. For example, women are more likely than men to spontaneously mention gender when asked to describe themselves (Deaux and Major 1990:93). The salience of gender identity may also vary between situations: a woman alone in a group of men, for example, is likely to find her sex to be more salient than when she is in a group of other women (Cota and Dion 1986; see also Fiske and Taylor 2008; Turner and Brown 2007). Indeed, group identity is generally more salient for those in any kind of subordinate position, indicating the relevance of social position and power to identity.

Sexuality

Sexuality is a fuzzy term, often used to refer to a group of related concepts, including sexual behavior (what you do), eroticism (what turns you on), sexual orientation (who turns you on), or desire to engage in sexual activity (wanting to be turned on). A discussion of sexuality may seem out of place in a book focusing on gender and social psychology. Nonetheless, sexuality is often associated with gender, although the two are not equivalent. This association probably results from the popular essentialist belief that gender is the natural outgrowth of biological sex. Because sexuality is also believed to be biologically driven, gender and sexuality are often thought to be directly related (Rutter and Schwartz forthcoming).

As with gender, however, there are other perspectives on sexuality. Like other activities, sexual behavior has social and symbolic components. Consider the activity of a woman baring her breasts. Now vary the social context: how would this action be interpreted if the woman were in her lover's bedroom, her doctor's consulting room, or a public place? Now take the last location, a public place, and vary the reasons for her action: she is participating in a public demonstration, performing at a strip joint, or breastfeeding her baby. It is the social context, not the activity itself, that leads us to impute meaning to the woman's action as being erotic, clinical, political, exhibitionist, or maternal. The meaning of sexual behaviors varies by situation, and we evaluate behavior on the basis of goals and motivations. Meaning also varies by culture: in some societies, women's breasts are always bare, and thus do not elicit the charged interpretations that they do in U.S. culture. Sexual meanings are thus socially constructed, not inherent in an activity.

Similarly, sexuality is not innate in individuals. For evidence, we can point to the fact that expectations for the sexual behavior of men and women vary historically and cross-culturally. Traditional Western dating scripts, for example, expected men to be more physical and aggressive, and women to be more passive and emotional in sexual situations. Contemporary Western couples have reformulated these scripts to accommodate new ways of interacting, such as online dating, speed dating, and "hooking up" (Bogle 2008; Boswell and Spade 1996; England et al. 2009). Although it might appear that expectations have changed (and they have, to varying extents among different social groups and regions), they have not entirely disappeared. Men, for example, are still expected to take the lead in sexual situations, and women who violate gender expectations by being sexually assertive risk being labeled "pushy," "aggressive," or worse. However, other cultures have very different expectations for women and men. For example, Ford and Beach (1951) report that women are expected to be the sexual aggressors among societies including the Maori and the Trobriand Islanders. Sexual behavior is guided by social factors as much as by biology.

What, then, is the relationship between sexuality and gender? Expectations for "appropriate" sexual behavior and characteristics differ by gender; sexuality becomes a way of expressing gender. For example, Lillian Rubin's study of U.S. working-class families (1976) found that women were expected to be sexually passive and inexperienced, whereas men were expected to be more dominant, experienced, and adventurous. And as the next section points out, there are also expectations about whom we perform sexual behaviors with. An important point, however, is that this society's construction of sexuality helps maintain the existing gender hierarchy. The definition of men as aggressive and women as passive reinforces men's power over women and women's dependence on men. Popular culture's ideology of love and romance also reinforces gender inequality. For example, Cantor found that in popular media "women are usually depicted as subordinate to men and passive-dependent. . . . The basic message is that sexual relationships are all-important in women's lives" (1987:190). Thus, when women attempt to meet cultural expectations about heterosexual relationships, they contribute to their own subordination.[8] However, the examples provided by other cultures show us that this pattern is not innate in human beings.

Sexual Orientation

Sexual orientation, the match between one's sex and the sex of one's (desired or actual) sexual partners, is one component of sexuality. Like sexuality more generally, sexual orientation is part of gender expectations. For example, the expectations for a "real man" include heterosexuality. Think of male icons such as James Bond, Indiana Jones, or Jason Bourne: besides being strong and daring, these characters are all attracted and attractive to beautiful women (although the male actors who play such roles are not always attracted to women, e.g., historic film star Rock Hudson). Thus, in this society, "mainstream masculinity is heterosexual masculinity" (Carrigan et al. 1987:83; see also Kimmel, Hearn, and Connell 2004). This version of masculinity is a yardstick against which all men are measured: "The homosexual-heterosexual dichotomy acts as a central symbol in all rankings of masculinity. Any kind of powerlessness, or refusal to compete among men, readily becomes involved with the imagery of homosexuality" (Carrigan et al. 1987:86). A similar argument can be made for women: mainstream femininity entails heterosexuality, and any deviation from feminine norms risks "accusations" of lesbianism (Akeret and McEwan 2004; Blinde and Taub 1992; Rich 1980). Schope and Eliason's (2004) study of homophobia, however, argues that women and girls may have more flexibility in their gender presentations than do men and boys (presumably because female is the less powerful category than male). In other words, some degree of deviation from feminine norms may not lead to perceptions of lesbianism. Nevertheless, sexual orientation is integrally related to gender. Sexual orientation is one of the ways in which gender is performed, while at the same time, gender incorporates and depends on sexual orientation.

Like sex and gender, people tend to think of sexual orientation as dichotomous: one is either heterosexual or homosexual. But sexual orientation is more accurately described as a continuum, with many possible variations between the two poles. Some people (bisexuals) are attracted to people of both sexes. Some people are attracted to people of one sex but maintain relationships with people of another; these people cannot be easily classified. Many people who define themselves as heterosexual, in fact, have had some sort of homosexual experiences (Blumstein and Schwartz 1983; Hoburg et al. 2004). It should be noted that sexual orientation is distinct from gender identity. Although some people think that those who prefer same-sex partners must be "confused" about their own gender identity, this is not the case. In fact "most gay men and lesbian women have no confusion about their gender identity; they simply prefer sexual partners of the same sex" (Vander Zanden 1990:358).

What is the source of sexual orientation? Debate rages in the scientific community and the popular press about whether sexual orientation is genetically or environmentally determined; at the moment, there is no consensus on the answer (Hughes 2006). One thing is certain, however: like sexuality, the meaning of sexual orientation is socially constructed. Homosexual practices are not everywhere as stigmatized as they are in the United States: many past and present societies of the world, including the ancient Greeks and the modern Sambia of New Guinea, condone and practice both heterosexuality and homosexuality in some forms (Ford and Beach 1951; Herdt 1998). Moreover, the meanings of homosexuality and heterosexuality vary depending on the social and historical contexts, even within the United States. Childhood sexual play, for example, is interpreted very differently than adult relationships (Lamb 2004; Rothbaum, Grauer, and Rubin 1997). Or, to give another example, the same man who might never consider engaging in homosexual activity in everyday life might practice it within an all-male prison context. Furthermore, General Social Survey data tracking American attitudes toward homosexuality over the past thirty years indicate that 32 percent of the people sampled in 2006 believe that homosexuality is "not wrong" compared to only 11 percent in 1973 (McKinley 2009). Loftus (2001) attributes these recent increases in tolerant attitudes toward homosexuals to demographic shifts in the population (e.g., increases in levels of education). We would add that social activism about the rights of lesbians, gay men, bisexuals, transgendered, and intersexed people have led to greater societal recognition of their rights (Fetner 2008). These trends are expected to continue, as more and more people who define themselves as heterosexual recognize that friends, coworkers, and acquaintances of theirs are indeed homosexual or otherwise variant from heterosexual norms. Like sexuality more broadly, the meaning of sexual orientation varies depending on social and historical context, goals, and motivations.

Crosscutting Social Positions

We argue throughout this book, following Collins (2000) and other feminist scholars, that gender cannot be adequately understood without analyzing its intersections with other social statuses. We conclude this chapter by briefly discussing two particularly important statuses: race and social class. Ideally, research and writing would consider all of these statuses—gender, race, social class, sexual orientation, (dis)ability, age, national origin, and others—simultaneously, in order to understand how they collectively contribute to an individual's experiences.

Where research allows, we address how they operate as interlocking systems of oppression (Anderson and Collins 2004; Berger and Guidroz 2009). However, social psychology (and the social sciences more broadly) have generally addressed these statuses separately, and so we are forced to discuss them separately at many points in this book. It is our hope, however, that feminist scholars will continue to develop an adequate vocabulary with which to talk about the simultaneous experience of these social positions, as well as research methodologies with which to study them (for examples, see Harnois 2009; Taylor 2009).

Race

Race is "a social definition of a social category of people, typically based on visible physical characteristics, such as skin color, stature, and facial features" (Rothman 1993:6). Racial groups are generally broader categories than *ethnic groups*, a term that refers to people who share a common culture, including language, religion, and customs.

For those of us who have lived all our lives in the extremely race-conscious United States, it may be difficult to imagine a world in which race is not a central defining feature of individuals. But in fact, "race was first employed as a means of categorizing human bodies in the late seventeenth century, and it was only in the eighteenth century . . . that there began to be made what were taken to be authoritative racial divisions of human beings" (Nicholson 1994:85). People did notice physical differences between themselves and others, of course. But these differences were not used "to 'explain' basic divisions among human populations as the concept of race increasingly did from the late eighteenth century on" (Nicholson 1994:85–86).

Race is popularly thought to be a biological attribute based on genetic ancestry and clearly identifiable by physical features: "In the United States, we tend to see race as a simple, unambiguous matter of skin color alone and to judge everyone as belonging to one and only one group" (Healy 1995:24). But when we look more closely at the use of race, the definition becomes less clear: "Skin color, for example, varies in shades from one extreme to the other, and there are no clear or definite points at which 'black' skin color stops and 'white' (or brown or yellow or red) color begins" (Healy 1995:23). And why is skin color so important?

> There are clear physical differences between human beings and some of these differences are inherited. But the question of why some physical differences, and not others, become matters for social discrimination and prejudice has nothing to do with biology. Racial differences, therefore, should be understood as *physical variations singled out by the members of a community or society as socially*

significant. Differences in skin color, for example, are often treated as significant in this way, whereas differences in color of hair are not. (Giddens 1991:301)

Contrary to popular belief, even genetic makeup does not distinguish between members of different racial classifications. In fact, there is more genetic variation within races than between them (Begley 1995). Race is thus a social and political phenomenon, not a biological one.

Racial identity is also malleable, on both a societal and an individual level. As a society, the United States has often seen changes in racial classification. For example, eastern and southern Europeans were not considered "white" when they first began to immigrate to the United States in large numbers; a century later, this classification has changed. Similarly, the U.S. Census has at different times in the past categorized Japanese Americans as "non-white," "Oriental," or simply "Other." More recently, members of this group have been classified as a specific ethnic group under the general category defined as "Asian and Pacific Islanders" (Omi and Winant 1986:3). Another example is the term "Hispanic," which was created by the federal Office of Management and Budget for the 1980 Census and which includes an economically, racially, and culturally heterogeneous group of people who, "far from being unified . . . are divided along ethnic or racial lines" (Forbes 1992:65). Giménez writes:

> For a substantial proportion of these populations this origin makes no sense either in terms of their actual ancestry (which may be Native American, Northern, Eastern, or Southern European, African, or Asian) or in terms of their historical understanding of who they are as citizens of a given country or as descendents of Latin American immigrants. (1992:12)

Census categories underwent further revisions in 2000, and their evolution will likely continue (Kilty and Vidal de Haymes 2004; Nobles 2000). The 2010 Census includes the possibility of 63 racial and ethnic categories, as well as a distinct categorization as Hispanic (or not), leading to a possible 126 racial and ethnic groups. Although official classification schemes such as those of the Census may appear innocuous, they in fact reify the notion of race and shape how scholars build knowledge about race.

On an individual level, people's racial identities can shift based on their situations and experiences. In the post-9/11 context, a light-skinned person of Middle Eastern descent might "pass" for white in certain situations (Marvasti 2005), but claim this regional identity in others (Peek 2005). A Jewish person might consider herself or himself "white" as compared to black people, but Jewish as compared to other whites (Brodkin 1998). According to the Nazis, having a Jewish grandfather was sufficient to brand one as Jewish; Orthodox

Jews, however, would not consider such a person Jewish. In a fascinating analysis, Saperstein and Penner (2010) find that people who are poor, unemployed, or in prison are more likely to be seen—and to identify themselves—as black rather than white, regardless of how they had previously been identified by self or others. Many people—probably most—have a mixed heritage, yet in everyday life they are classified as belonging to only one racial group. Consequently, as one respondent in Renfrow's work on "passing" noted, multiracial individuals often "struggle between two cultures, trying to be both at the same time" (2004:499). (Note the similarity here to gender classification; in both cases, ambiguous persons are assigned to one category that may not accurately represent their own identity.)

Many social scientists have argued that the term *race* is meaningless and should be abandoned. It is indisputable, however, that race has a social and political reality regardless of its scientific status. People believe that race is real, and societies and individuals allocate rewards and power based on racial classification. In other words, "racial distinctions are meaningful because we *attach* meaning to them, and the consequences vary from prejudice and discrimination to slavery and genocide" (Pitchford 1992:1617). As a result, racial classification must be taken seriously, despite its tenuous grounding in biology.

Like gender, racial classification is fundamentally about difference, although in the case of race there are many possible differences, not just the assumed dichotomy associated with sex. Smedley (1993) articulately summarizes the pervasiveness of difference:

> Race in the American mind was and is tantamount to a statement about profound and unbridgeable differences. In whatever context race comes to play, it conveys the meaning of nontranscendable social distance. This sense of difference is conditioned into most individuals early in their lives and becomes bonded to emotions nurtured in childhood. In the United States, it is expressed in all kinds of situations and encounters between peoples. It is structured into the social system through residential separation, differential education, training, and incomes, and informal restrictions against socializing, intermarriage, and common membership in various organizations, including, most visibly, the church. It is reflected in virtually all media representations of American society and in institutional aspects of culture such as music, the arts, scientific research, educational institutions, politics and political forms, businesses, the theater, television, music, and film industries, and recreational activities. It provides the unspoken guidelines for daily interaction among persons defined as of different races, especially black and white. It sets the standards and rules for conduct, even though individuals may not always be conscious of this fact. (21)

As with gender, a focus on differences has guided social psychological research about race. The vast majority of empirical research on race investigates only the possibility of difference and accepts race as the explanation for any differences found between people categorized as belonging to different races. Our discussions of race in the following chapters, in contrast, are premised on the assumption that race (like gender) is a social phenomenon and is something that must be explained, not an explanation in itself. Indeed, the election of Barack Obama to the U.S. presidency in 2008 and the intense reflections about race that his election has triggered indicate powerfully just how social the phenomenon of race is. Social psychological research has not yet caught up to these societal and cultural conversations, but we anticipate that a wealth of new such research is currently under way (and we look forward to discussing all of this in the next edition of this book!).

Social Class

Social class refers to an individual's location in the economic system of a society. Unlike race or gender, it is based in part on a material reality: economic resources. How a person's class position is measured varies but is most often based on factors such as occupation, income, and education. According to Marx (1974), class position is determined by a person's relationship to the "means of production," such as machinery, offices, or money: does the person own the means of production (a capitalist), or does the person sell his or her labor to capitalists in order to earn a living (a member of the working class)? Whereas gender and race are considered ascribed statuses (i.e., based on relatively fixed characteristics of individuals), class is considered an achieved status, based on the individual's own behavior and permitting more mobility between groups. We note, however, that neither of these classifications is definitive. We have discussed above the fact that both gender and race are more malleable than they appear; in contrast, we contend that class is more constrained than is generally believed. Many Americans accept the ideological position that anyone can "pull themselves up by their bootstraps" if they simply try hard enough—what McNamee and Miller (2009) call the "myth of meritocracy." One's class position, however, is driven as much by current and historical family circumstances, structural barriers, and discrimination as by individual ability or effort (Domhoff 2009; Feagin and McKinney 2003; Lareau and Conley 2008; Massey 2007).

Social class is important not only because it determines one's financial position, but also because it influences other factors such as prestige, power and authority, control over resources, and possibilities for advancement. And although class is often discussed as simply a matter of economics, it has important ramifications for self-concept. In "A Question of Class," Dorothy

Allison (1994) describes how her childhood of extreme poverty affected her identity:

> When I was six or eight back in Greenville, South Carolina, I had heard that same matter-of-fact tone of dismissal applied to me. "Don't you play with her. I don't want you talking to them." Me and my family, we had always been they. Who am I? I wondered . . . Who are my people? . . . What may be the central fact of my life is that I was born in 1949 in Greenville, South Carolina, the bastard daughter of a white woman from a desperately poor family, a girl who had left the seventh grade the year before, worked as a waitress, and was just a month past fifteen when she had me. That fact, the inescapable impact of being born in a condition of poverty that this society finds shameful, contemptible, and somehow deserved, has had dominion over me to such an extent that I have spent my life trying to overcome or deny it. I have learned with great difficulty that the vast majority of people believe that poverty is a voluntary condition. (13–15)

Class position is related to race and gender. Racial minority group members are overrepresented in the ranks of the working class and the poor. Women of any race living without a man are also more likely to be poor; association with a man is often what makes the difference between social classes for women (and children). Furthermore, the particular combinations of these statuses—being a poor, white single mother living in the rural South, for example—impact both one's visibility in the real world, and popular and academic interest in understanding these experiences (Callahan 2008).

Before concluding this section, we must make one final point that applies equally to all of the social positions described above—gender, sexual orientation, race, and class. It is obvious that these statuses affect the experiences of those who are in the subordinate categories of each group—women, homosexuals, people of color, poor people. It is much less obvious, however, that these statuses also affect the lives of those who are not subordinate:

> In the same way that both men's and women's lives are shaped by their gender, and that both heterosexual and lesbian women's experiences in the world are marked by their sexuality, white people and people of color live racially structured lives. In other words, any system of differentiation shapes those on whom it bestows privilege as well as those it oppresses. (Frankenberg 1993:1)

Privilege is often invisible to those who enjoy it, because to them it is simply the normal state of affairs. Privilege "makes life easier—it is easier to get around, to get what one wants, and to be treated in a way that is acceptable" (Rosenblum and Travis 1996:139; see also Kendall 2006; Kimmel and Ferber 2003; McIntosh 1990). For example, white people driving a fancy car generally are not suspected of having stolen it, as people of color often are. Men, for the most part, do not consider their safety when deciding whether to walk to the grocery store after dark, as women often do. Heterosexuals do not need to consider whether their jobs or friendships with coworkers will be threatened if they place a photo of themselves with their romantic partner on their desk or in their locker at work, as homosexuals often do. Upper-class people do not have to decide between taking their sick child to the doctor and feeding their families, as poorer people sometimes do. In each case, the advantages of privilege may not be noticed by those who enjoy it—but they are real nonetheless. Thus, each of the social statuses we discuss is in effect a system of hierarchy and difference that permeates the lives of all people—those who are privileged by it as well as those who are not.

A Gender Lens

To conclude this chapter, we return to the metaphor of the gender lens. What do we mean by this term? What can we see through the gender lens that we cannot see without it?

Throughout this book, we emphasize two points. First, we argue that social psychology has simultaneously ignored and been deeply influenced by gender. Social psychologists have assumed that situations and behavior are gender neutral; yet they have nonetheless allowed prevailing cultural assumptions about gender to affect the questions they have posed and the answers they have provided. Most obviously, as we have discussed above, social psychologists have focused on gender differences in personality and behavior and have often assumed that these difference are fixed, stable, and rooted in biological sex.

Our second argument in this book is that although gender differences may exist, they are not the same as sex differences. In other words, just because women and men may appear to behave or think differently does not mean that they have different innate characteristics or abilities. Instead, these differences may be (and, we believe, generally are) constructed through social processes. Thus, in a sense we are arguing that these differences are not as meaningful as people—both social psychologists and laypeople—believe they are.

This does not mean that we should ignore these differences, however. If that were the case, there would be no reason to write (or read) this book. On the contrary, these ideas about gender deeply affect people's thoughts and behaviors and are central to the ways in which resources, power, and status are distributed. In other words, despite its lack of grounding in sex, gender has real, material consequences for people's lives. For this reason it is crucial to

Chapter 1

understand gender and the role it plays in the social world. It is only through such an understanding that we can hope to address the pervasive and deeply damaging social problems (such as discrimination, violence, and injustice) that continue to plague human societies.

Looking at the world through a gender lens, then, means recognizing and analyzing the central role gender plays in social life. More concretely, it implies two seemingly contradictory tasks. First, it means unpacking the taken-for-granted assumptions about gender that pervade social psychology and, more generally, social life. We must show how the terms we use to discuss gender (such as "gender role") naturalize inequality and perpetuate gender difference. We must question the truth of these assumptions and, where warranted, reveal them as the illusions they are.

At the same time, looking through the gender lens means showing just how central these assumptions about gender continue to be to the perception and interpretation of the world, regardless of their grounding in reality. We must show how our unquestioned ideas about gender affect the world we see, the questions we ask, and the answers we can envision. In other words, we must show how deeply the social world is gendered, and how far-ranging the consequences are. Looking at social life through the gender lens means asking where gender is overemphasized and where it is ignored; it means making the invisible visible and questioning the reality of what we see.

In the remainder of this book, we use this gender lens to look more closely at social psychological theory and research. In chapter 2, we present the major social psychological perspectives on gender, elaborating at the same time historical trends in social psychology. In chapters 3–5, we look more closely at the three social psychological theories described above, showing how assumptions about gender have shaped research in each tradition. In the subsequent chapters, we apply these theories, through a gender lens, to the traditional social psychological topics of altruism and aggression, showing the fundamental ways in which assumptions about gender have shaped the questions asked and the theories developed to explain these forms of social behavior.

Notes

1. "We" can be a slippery and ambiguous word. It is not always clear whether it is meant to refer to the speaker alone, to one or more of the social groups to which the speaker belongs, or to all humans in general. In this book, we use the term with caution. Unless otherwise specified, we use "we" to refer either to the three of us as authors, or to human beings more generally. We try to ensure that the context will make clear which of these meanings is intended.

2. For an incisive analysis of the response to this crime, see chapter 2 in Cherry (1995).

3. A film adaptation of *Oleanna* was released in 1994.

4. Research exploring the development of "animal selves," however, is beginning to question the uniqueness of the human self; see Irvine (2004) and Sanders (1999).

5. There is no one U.S. society, no one Western society, but rather different subgroups differentiated particularly by societal inequalities. In using the phrase "U.S. society," we intend to indicate some national common threads of experience, while recognizing that there is no single common or consensual national experience.

6. The occurrence of sexual ambiguities—as well as our tendency toward "correction"—is not exclusive to humans. See Hubler et al. (1999) and Meyers-Wallen (2009) for discussions of intersexuality within other species, including domestic dogs.

7. Indeed, some authors also argue that sex itself is a social construction (Kessler and McKenna 1978; Scott 1988). According to this view, "society not only shapes personality and behavior, it also shapes the ways in which the body appears. But if the body is itself always seen through social interpretation, then sex is not something that is separate from gender but is, rather, that which is subsumable under it" (Nicholson 1994:79).

8. For further discussion outside of social psychology, see Butler (2004) and hooks (2006).

2

Conceptions of Gender in Social Psychology

A S WE NOTED IN CONCLUDING CHAPTER 1, social psychologists have simultane-ously ignored and been deeply influenced by gender. Existing patterns of relationships between women and men have been taken for granted. Until fairly recently, social scientists regarded traditional sex-role arrangements as nonproblematic, often assuming that such patterns were biologically inevi-table. Many studies used only one sex—almost always men—as respondents, and assumed either that the processes being studied were so general that they would apply to all humans or that women's behavior would be the opposite of men's behavior. In either case, male behavior was taken as the norm.

In this chapter we trace and evaluate this social psychological treatment of sex and gender. Our discussion loosely follows the historical development of social scientific theorizing about gender, moving from essentialist per-spectives through socialization to social constructionist and structural ex-planations of gender. These four perspectives underlie contemporary social psychological research, to varying degrees, and cut across the three social psychological theories we present in chapters 3–5. These four perspectives propose radically different explanations of gendered behavior, the causes of gender inequality, and therefore the ways in which these (and other) inequalities might be reduced. As we elaborate below, these perspectives reflect the sociopolitical and historical climates in which they were gener-ated. Because these climates have also shaped prevailing accounts of race, class, sexuality, and other social positions, we weave these accounts together as fully as possible.

Essentialist Approaches

As we discussed in chapter 1, an *essentialist* approach to gender maintains that innate, stable differences between the sexes shape divergent social behaviors. This approach was prevalent among social psychologists (and social scientists more generally) in the first half of the 1900s. Thus, when two psychologists, Helen Thompson Wooley and Leta Stetter Hollingworth, published results in the early 1900s showing that women and men were virtually equal in a broad range of abilities (cited in Bem 1993), others took it upon themselves to refute these findings. Terman and Miles (1936), for example, developed an "M-F Test" that was intended to assess individuals' own masculinity or femininity. The test items were selected explicitly to distinguish between men and women. Respondents earned femininity points for agreeing that they "nearly always prefer for someone else to take the lead," for example, and they earned masculinity points for disliking nursing. (Women who did not score high on the femininity pole of this dimension and men who did not score high on the masculinity pole were thought to have homosexual tendencies; this is another example of stereotypes about social groups.) Underlying this test were the related assumptions that masculinity and femininity are the opposite poles of a single dimension and that masculinity and femininity are virtually synonymous with being male and female. This M-F Test is based on an essentialist understanding of sex and gender. For the next several decades this conviction of natural gender difference prevailed.

Although the essentialist perspective is less explicit in more recent social psychological research, the underlying assumptions are often consistent with essentialism. One example is the common use of sex as a variable representing gender. In these studies, subjects are simply categorized as females or males, and any differences found between the two groups are labeled as "gender differences." This approach treats sex and gender as one and the same; sex/gender is conceptualized as a stable, innate, bipolar property of individuals. Much of this research is unreflective about the nature of gender as a social category. "Sex as variable" research leaves sex differences untheorized and other social and contextual factors unexplored. The implication is that sex itself is a sufficient explanation for behavior—an assumption that is at the heart of the essentialist view of sex and of gender.

Take, for example, the substantial body of research on sex differences in mathematical ability. The conventional belief is that men have greater abilities in math than do women. For many years, empirical research on mathematics skills appeared to confirm this assumption of male superiority; study after study found that men outperformed women on math tests, beginning in the seventh grade. These studies were used to bolster the claim that men have superior cognitive abilities (ignoring the parallel finding that women have superior reading skills during the same developmental period). These studies treat gender differences as sex differences.

When researchers began to consider the social contexts in which these differences occurred, however, the sex difference in math performance all but disappeared. Social factors, such as the expectation that boys will take more math classes than girls and the perceived importance of such classes for future careers, as well as the actual number of math classes taken, provide a more adequate explanation for the observed differences than the relative math abilities of girls and boys (Fausto-Sterling 1985). Sex differences in math performance are very small (Leahey and Guo 2001), vary across ages and nations, and have generally decreased over time (Hyde et al. 1990; York and Clark 2007). In a recent study, Logel and colleagues (2009) find that female engineering students who interacted with sexist men (confederates or otherwise) performed worse on an engineering test compared to women who interacted with nonsexist men. This "stereotype threat" effect did not carry over to an English exam, a subject on which women are expected to do well (see also Dar-Nimrod and Heine 2006). We discuss such stereotype threat effects in more detail in chapter 4. Recent newspaper reports indicate that girls' math and science ACT scores are rising because they are taking more advanced courses in these subjects in high school, underscoring the importance of contextual factors. In their attention to the social context of patterns associated with sex—that is, both the broad social context and the local social situation—these more recent studies *analyze* gender, rather than treating it as an unproblematic variable.

"Sex as variable" research implies that sex and gender are isomorphic. Gender and sex are not identical, however. While sex category is usually constant and dichotomous, gender is fluid and dependent on social contexts. There is substantial overlap between women and men on virtually all personality traits and behaviors. Although dominance is a stereotypically "masculine" trait, for example, some women are more dominant than some men. And in some situations, most women are more dominant than most men (e.g., gendered contexts such as cooking or child care). Using sex as an indicator of gender is thus misleading. Measures of masculinity and femininity are more appropriate indicators of the personality components of gender.

Social psychological research on race, echoing research on gender, also began with a deeply essentialist set of assumptions. Characteristics correlated with racial categories were assumed to be innate and irreversible; this legacy has been most striking in the considerable research on the relationship between race and intelligence. Strains of essentialism continue to the present day (e.g., Herrnstein and Murray's *The Bell Curve* [1994], one of several contemporary books that argue both that racial differences in intelligence do exist and are based in genetic differences). This literature has been criticized on precisely the same grounds as essentialist approaches to gender; interactional, cultural, and structural factors provide more adequate explanations for human behavior (see Fraser 1995).

Thus, many social psychologists have pursued other nonessentialist approaches. We continue to refer to essentialism in the next several chapters, despite these problems, because essentialist assumptions continue to shape some social psychological research, as well as much popular discourse on both race and gender. We turn now to a socialization approach to gender, the perspective that dominated social psychology during the 1960s and 1970s. We devote considerable attention to this approach, as it has been particularly influential in shaping social psychological research on gender, race, sexuality, and class.

Socialization Approaches

Sparked in part by the social movements of the late 1960s, the focus of the social psychological study of gender shifted from biology to socialization. New empirical investigations found that women and men were more similar than different on most social psychological dimensions. Researchers began to consider social processes and factors other than biology that might account for those gender differences that were observed. According to the socialization perspective, children are not innately gendered, but rather learn gendered behavior from their environment through a variety of processes, including modeling and imitation (Bandura 1977), the gender-specific application of rewards and punishments, and/or intrapsychic processes facilitated by parenting practices (Chodorow 1978). (These processes of social learning are discussed in more detail in chapter 3.) Through these processes, children learn to internalize prescriptions and proscriptions (i.e., "dos and don'ts") for being appropriately masculine and feminine according to the norms of their society. These processes result in gendered personalities and patterns of behavior. Thus, gender differences are believed not to be essential but, rather, the result of societal and cultural forces.

Two implications of this approach are notable for our purposes. First, a socialization perspective on gender can more easily account for intragroup diversity than does an essentialist approach. For example, differences in the gendered behaviors of white and black women, or upper-class and working-class men, can be explained by the systematically different socialization environments they may have experienced as children. Second, the socialization perspective suggests that changes in gendered behaviors and personality characteristics are possible, if a society and its members choose to modify socialization practices. Both of these implications stand in stark contrast to the assumptions of essentialism that all women and all men are fundamentally alike as a result of biology and that therefore change in gender patterns is impossible.

From a socialization perspective, gender differences in personality and behavior are created and become ossified in childhood; the implication is that behavior throughout one's adult life follows unproblematically. Gender thus is viewed as operating at the level of individual personality, but in the service of more general social control. Through socialization, girls and boys learn to behave in ways that sustain the social order when they are women and men. In this section, we focus on the adult consequences of this socialization (although there is a substantial literature on the gender socialization of children). We begin by discussing what is learned during socialization—that is, cultural stereotypes about the characteristics of women and men.

Gender Stereotypes

As we noted in chapter 1, *stereotypes* are primarily descriptive; they detail what members of particular categories are believed to be like. Stereotypes also have prescriptive power. Beliefs sometimes shade into normative "oughts" and "ought nots." Stereotypes about gender are particularly likely to carry prescriptive as well as descriptive elements. In addition, members of different groups often differ in their conceptions of selves and of others. Much of what we discuss below concerns the stereotypes held by those in dominant social positions, although where research is available, we address stereotypes held by both dominant and subordinate groups. (Much of the material presented here derives from the social cognitive perspective, which we elaborate in more detail in chapter 4.)

The conceptions of gender we learn through socialization shape both our definitions or senses of self, and our perceptions of others. In the sections that follow, we begin by discussing gendered personality—that is, perceptions of self in terms of gender—and then move into gendered stereotypes about others. Until fairly recently, gender stereotypes have been conceived primarily in terms of personality. Deaux and LaFrance (1998) argue that gender stereotypes are a good deal broader than personality, including role behaviors, physical characteristics, and occupations, in addition to personality traits. Stereotypes include "type of dress and bodily adornment, codes of sexual etiquette, styles of self-presentation, patterns of sexual behaviors, rules for social interaction in various settings" (Spence, Deaux, and Helmreich 1985:153). The variety of social characteristics that compose gender stereotypes attests to the fact that gender is much more than biology.

Personality: Masculinity and Femininity

Personality refers to characteristics of individuals, and is conceptualized as stable and inherent. For this reason, personality is the component of gender stereotypes that comes closest to an essentialist perspective. There has been extensive research on personality correlates of sex, or masculinity and femininity—the traits, behaviors, and interests believed to be associated with males or females in a particular culture.

As we noted above, early measures of personality were based on an essentialist understanding of gender (e.g., Terman and Miles's M-F Test). Later researchers, however, conceptualized masculinity/femininity as socialized characteristics learned through cognitive and emotional development. Beginning in the 1970s, researchers began to demonstrate that masculinity and femininity are two independent dimensions; that is, one's score on a masculinity scale need not be associated with one's score on a femininity scale. Scales such as the Bem Sex Role Inventory (e.g., Bem 1974; Spence, Helmreich, and Stapp 1974) treated masculinity and femininity as separate dimensions, allowing an individual to be categorized as highly masculine, highly feminine, both, or neither.

Those individuals who have high, approximately equivalent scores on both the masculinity and femininity scales are labeled *androgynous.* The concept of androgyny (derived from the Greek roots *andro*—male—and *gyn*—female) captured both academic and popular attention in the 1970s. Some suggested that androgyny was an ideal state: androgynous individuals should have a wider variety of skills and characteristics at their disposal than primarily masculine or primarily feminine people and would therefore be able to deal with a broader range of situations (e.g., Bem 1975). Research showed some evidence of the greater mental health of androgynous individuals (Heilbrun 1973) as well as interactive advantages in group decision-making (Kirchmeyer 1996). Yet many scholars were persuaded to abandon the concept by other studies reporting that androgynous benefits occurred only for the more masculine forms of androgyny and by studies documenting the ineffectiveness of androgynous managers (Pyke 1985). (It is worth noting that these negative effects may have been artifacts of poor measurement.)

In the end, the concept of androgyny (which long predates social psychology) fell out of academic favor. Because it treats masculine and feminine as if they were equal, the concept of androgyny is insensitive to the power differences that mark gender. Moreover, this concept reproduces the very gender polarization it seeks to unsettle, treating masculinity and femininity as conceptual givens; this tendency is characteristic of the socialization perspective more generally. Many contemporary scholars recognize that behavior is determined by situational factors as much as by the traits reported on per-sonality inventories.

Some scholars have attempted to resolve these problems by labeling these dimensions as expressiveness (e.g., aware of feelings of others, expresses ten-der feelings, tactful) and instrumentality (e.g., objective, competitive, makes decisions easily) (see Deaux and LaFrance 1998). As with masculinity and femininity, these traits are related to sex category, but the correlations are small. Carol Gilligan's (1982) research on interpersonal moral orientations and behaviors does show empirical support for gender differences in these behaviors: she finds that women understand their responsibilities to others in the context of specific relationships, while men use abstract rules and prin-ciples as guides to moral behaviors. Gilligan's explanation of these differences relies almost completely on very early childhood socialization. Although Gil-ligan does not explicitly espouse biological determinants of these patterns, much of her own writing and the use of her work in the subsequent research of others come close to an essentialist position whereby these gendered pat-terns are so pervasive and persistent as to seem "natural."

Nonetheless, there is considerable variation within the sexes on both expressiveness and instrumentality; women vary widely in how often they engage in expressive behaviors and men vary widely in how often they engage in instrumental behaviors. Because of this variation, there is also a good deal of overlap between women and men in these characteristics; some women, for example, behave instrumentally more often than some men. Interestingly, even Gilligan's own recent work provides clear evidence that social factors such as contact with family hinder the development of instrumentality in both seventeen-year-old boys and girls, although the effect lessens among girls as they enter adulthood (Sneed et al. 2006). Furthermore, instrumental-ity within finance and romance domains increases for both young men and women as they enter adulthood, demonstrating the fluidity of these traits through life course transitions.

The various measures we have discussed above refer primarily to assess-ments of one's own gender. Stereotypes of the gendered characteristics of others, as we have suggested, are also prevalent. Despite both the variation among women and among men and the overlap between women and men on these characteristics, early empirical studies of gender stereotypes found wide-spread agreement about the personality characteristics of men and women across respondents of different ages, educational levels, religions, sexes, and marital statuses (Broverman et al. 1972; Deaux and LaFrance 1998). Respon-dents rated men highly on instrumental attributes and rated women highly on expressive attributes. Despite the social and political changes that have occurred since many of these studies were carried out, these stereotypes have changed very little (e.g., Smith and Midlarsky 1985; Spence and Buckner 2000; Spence and Savin 1985).

Intersecting Stereotypes

The studies we have described so far imply that stereotypes of women and of men can be described independent of their other structural positions. Other studies, however, demonstrate that this assumption is wrong. Stereotypes about women and men differ on the basis of the race, ethnicity, social class, sexual orientation, disability, and other social locations of both the perceiver and of the target of the perception. Landrine (1985) reports, for example, that middle-class white students rate white women as more dependent, emotional, and passive than black women and rate poorer women as more dirty, hostile, inconsiderate, and irresponsible than wealthier women. Romer and Cherry (1980) observe that black children perceive women and men as fairly similar in expressiveness, in part because these children also describe men as extremely expressive. Social class qualifies these patterns. Black middle-class children view men as more competent than women; black working-class children see women and men as similarly competent, because they perceive men as relatively less competent than do black middle-class children. Combining these perceptions of expressiveness and competence suggests that black children and children from working-class backgrounds perceive fewer gender differences than do white children and children from middle-class backgrounds.

Historical and sociopolitical contexts are important influences on prevailing images of these intersecting social categories. Works by Collins (1990, 2000) and White (1999) comment on the images of black women prevalent at different historical moments in the United States. Images of black women—as mammy (generated through slavery and dominant during the following century, during which black women were disproportionately likely to work as domestic servants), as Jezebel, the sexually aggressive black woman (an image also generated during slavery but which has given rise to the modern club hoochie counterpart), and as welfare mother, or irresponsible breeder (a more recent image constructed in the context of the post–World War II welfare state and set up in opposition to the black lady)—each served symbolic functions in maintaining the oppression of blacks and of women. The Stereotypic Roles for Black Women Scale recently developed by Thomas, Witherspoon, and Spreight (2004) suggests these notions endure; the results for some women include lowered self-esteem due to internalization of these perceptions.

Chow's (1985) analysis of stereotypes of Asian American women also points to historical and cultural influences. Chow suggests that Asian cultures tend to reinforce "feminine" characteristics (as defined by Western norms) for both women and men (a suggestion supported by Fong and Peskin's [1969] empirical findings that Chinese-born American men and women exceed American norms on femininity). An anti-Asian political context prevalent in the United States during the early 1900s and again during World War II also deepened the prevailing perceptions of Asian women as sexual commodities and of Asian men as desexualized (Espiritu 2007).

Thus, it is crucial to recognize the varying perceptions of and about different social groups. Socialization is always only partial, but at the same time, it is the rare individual who is not exposed to and influenced by the values and perspectives expressed by a dominant culture. We can speculate that Japanese Americans, African Americans, or European Americans living in the United States during World War II had different perceptions of the attributes of Asian women and men, for example, and at the same time all of them were likely influenced to varying degrees by media portrayals of these groups.

Although gender, race, and class positions are not separable, they often have been treated quite differently by social scientists. Ferree and Hall (1996) offer an insightful analysis of differential approaches to gender as opposed to race or class in introductory sociology textbooks from the 1980s. They assert that gender has most often been explained in terms of socialization; socialization has been treated not as a reflection of structural sources of gender inequality, but rather as an explanation in its own right.

Race and class, on the other hand, have been treated quite differently. Textbook discussions of race throughout the 1980s emphasized the arbitrariness of racial categories, rather than the essential nature of differences associated with race. To be sure, the concept "culture of poverty," a theory of racial and class differences that relies on socialization, is alive and well in both sociology texts and political discourse. Nonetheless, there has been considerably more debate about the idea of a culture of poverty than about the socialization of gender. Moreover, discussions of race socialization often address the learning of prejudice by dominant group members, not only the learning of subordination by racial minorities. In contrast, there is virtually no discussion of why and how men learn to discriminate against women. Thus, the socialization of gender remained the major explanation of gender difference, and gender was analyzed primarily in terms of difference rather than of inequality. In contrast, race and class were more likely to be analyzed in terms of systematic and structured inequalities.

Manza and Van Schyndel's (2000) analysis of introductory sociology textbooks from the 1990s suggests that discussions of gender are increasingly multilevel, emphasizing the dynamics of social interaction and the organization of institutions in addition to socialization. However, the majority of the discussions of gender they analyze occur in chapters on socialization. Ferree and Hall (2000) suggest that the authors' theoretical paradigm has led them to conceptualize and measure gender in ways that overstate the extent of this change. Within the sex roles perspective utilized by Manza and Van Schyndel, "the emphasis is on 'society' making women and men different kinds of people and on the implications and outcomes of such differences for society" (476). In other words, sex and gender differences are functional. The feminist perspective—the approach guiding Ferree and Hall's analysis—argues that gender "operates in and through macro-social institutions" (476) and produces not only sex difference but also societal inequalities. Consequently, Ferree and Hall conceptualize gender differences as social constructions linked to differential opportunity and power structures. Therefore, they look at textbook passages on the structural bases of inequality, where they see little evidence of change. In another study of gender in introductory texts, Clark and Nunes (2008) analyze 3,085 photographs in twenty-seven textbooks published since 2002. They conclude that the "face of society" presented within current textbooks portrays diverse and intersecting gender and racial statuses. This "face of society" is more often presented as a person of color *and* female than as white or male. Taken together, these studies identify modest changes in introductory textbook treatments of gender, as they continue to discuss gender differences within a socialization framework rather than discussing gender inequalities as the products of social structures and the power differentials within them.

Gender Prescriptions and Gender Roles

Gender socialization is also prescriptive. Gender stereotypes carry prescriptive implications, manifested in gender roles—prescriptions for two opposite sets of behaviors and characteristics, one believed appropriate for women and the other appropriate for men. The male "breadwinner" and female "homemaker" roles emphasized in the United States following World War II, for example, limited men's and women's contributions to particular social spheres and then justified this arrangement as "natural." In chapter 1, we outlined some of the criticisms of the concept of gender role: it ignores the differences within each sex and the considerable overlap between the sexes. Moreover, gender roles are often unrelated to how people actually behave. We do not mean to imply that most people do not conform in various ways to prescriptions about gender; even ostensibly "progressive" parents determined to avoid traditional gender socialization continue to "girl" and "boy" their children in some ways. This speaks to the power of social norms. Nonetheless, some parents also consciously undermine the prescriptions of gender. And people of a wide variety of political orientations often violate the conventions of gender in their everyday behavior.

Despite these critiques, the "gender as role" approach continues to be influential. Why? The concept of gender role reinforces the normative power of gender. Spence and colleagues (1985) note that in marking the differences between women and men, normative expectations of gender preserve (white middle-class) men's generally dominant position over women and their greater access to economic and political resources. The concept of gender role is rooted in a fundamentally functionalist understanding of gender difference as integral to maintaining a smoothly functioning society. The prescription of reproductive tasks such as childbearing and childrearing for women and the prescription of productive tasks such as wage labor for men legitimize a division between private and public spheres that entrenches women's subordination and men's domination (Kimmel 2006).

Stacey and Thorne (1985) offer a telling contrast between gender and other significant social positions, noting the absence of concepts such as "class roles" or "race roles." Presumably sociologists are sufficiently aware of (or at least cautious about) race- and class-based social inequalities to avoid language that would suggest that social order depends on such inequities. The concept of gender role, in contrast, prescribing the allocation of women and men to different types of work, implies that gender inequalities are part of the foundation of social order.

Consequences of Gender Stereotypes and Prescriptions

Gender socialization does have serious negative repercussions for individuals, although few social psychologists have explored these consequences. Bem (1993) maintains that the rigid, polarized conception of gender means that the everyday behavior of women and men often violates these prescriptions. These violations generate deep insecurity, motivating adults to strive to be "real women" and "real men."

Bem speculates that in this androcentric world, the consequences of this rigidity are particularly difficult for men. Joseph Pleck and his colleagues have studied the effects of "masculinity ideologies," "beliefs about the importance of men adhering to culturally defined standards for male behavior" (Pleck, Sonenstein, and Ku 1993: 85; see also Connell 1995; Kimmel, Hearn, and Connell 2004). Believing in the ideal of masculinity can be damaging: endorsement of masculinity ideology is correlated with problem behaviors among adolescent males, including drug and alcohol abuse, educational troubles, being picked up by the police, and coercive sexual behavior (Pleck et al. 1993). As Bem (1993) summarizes,

> It is males who are made to feel the most insecure about the adequacy of their gender. It so thoroughly devalues whatever thoughts, feelings, and behaviors are culturally defined as feminine that crossing the gender boundary has a more negative cultural meaning for men than it has for women—which means, in turn, that male gender-boundary-crossers are much more culturally stigmatized than female gender-boundary-crossers. At the same time, androcentrism provides such an unreachable definition of what a real man is supposed to be that only a few men can even begin to meet it. (149–50)

Ideologies of masculinity are likely to have negative consequences for women as well as men; among the more obvious are violence against women, pervasive wage inequities in the paid labor force, and persistent disparities in the allocation of domestic labor.

Ideologies about femininity can also be damaging. Fox's (1977) work on the "nice-girl" ideal of femininity suggests that adherence to this ideology can be harmful to women: Women are discouraged from being in public alone or without "appropriate" supervision; they are channeled into jobs consistent with the "nice girl" image, jobs that call for nurturance, service, or emotional behavior and that, not coincidentally, are poorly paid. Similarly, Crane and Crane-Seeber's (2003) observations regarding the "good girl" suggest this ideal constrains women within their intimate relationships with men: She should be just smart enough to be interesting but not so smart to suggest she can get by on her own; she must be sexy but not too sexy; and she must limit her demands or risk being replaced by someone younger and/or more compliant. Such ideologies of femininity are likely to harm men as well as women; as one example, if parenting is viewed as something women do, it becomes difficult for men to experience sustained involvement in and commitment to parenting.

At the same time, of course, gender stereotypes and prescriptions significantly advantage some social groups. As we have suggested above, prevailing conceptions of masculinity and femininity allocate a great deal of power and privilege to men. Indeed, gender nonconformity may have more serious consequences for men than for women precisely because it threatens to undermine this pattern of male domination; women's nonconformity is less threatening because women as a group have less social power. These advantages of gender are not shared seamlessly by all men or suffered seamlessly by all women, however; hierarchies of race and class modify the consequences of gender. For example, do cultural ideals of masculinity harm poor men of color differently and possibly more than affluent white men? Do cultural ideals of femininity harm lesbian mothers differently and possibly more than heterosexual married mothers?

In summary, socialization approaches to gender have produced valuable insights into the content and sources of gender. Nonetheless, they suffer from significant problems. This perspective emphasizes that gender is learned, rather than innate, but it continues to define gender in terms of dichotomous difference. The distinction between innate and learned characteristics is in some senses merely semantic; gender socialization is conceptualized as so deep-seated that it persists throughout the life course. Thus, in practical terms, gender is still believed to be internal and unchangeable. These approaches have also overlooked or at least minimized situational and cross-cultural variations in gendered behavior. These concerns are addressed by the next perspective we discuss, the social constructionist approach to gender.

Social Constructionist Approaches

According to social constructionism, social reality is created through human action and the interpretations of those actions. Social phenomena can be interpreted in a wide variety of ways; objects and behaviors do not have inherent meaning. Interaction cannot proceed, however, until those involved agree, at least provisionally, on a common interpretation of the situation in which they interact. Through interaction, we negotiate particular interpretations; that is, we create meaning. Through talk, through participation in the rituals of social interaction, through our active engagement with the symbols and material realities of everyday life, we literally create what we recognize as real. A minimum common understanding of shared rules and realities is necessary to sustain human communication and interaction, and ultimately, societies.

The first analysis to frame gender in this way was Garfinkel's (1967) now classic case study of a transsexual named Agnes, who appeared male at birth but underwent sex reassignment surgery after she began to develop female secondary sex characteristics at puberty. The focus of Garfinkel's analysis was not Agnes's sexual ambiguity, but the ways in which her case illustrated the ubiquitous performance of gender. Because she wanted to "pass" as a woman, Agnes took great pains to appear and behave in feminine ways. Garfinkel argues that Agnes's efforts to become "female" in a social sense reveal the strategies that "real" women use to construct and maintain gender: dressing in an appropriate "feminine" manner, dieting, wearing makeup, holding a "female" job, and so on. In essence, Agnes had to learn in adulthood what most women learn as children: how to manage their self-presentation to appear appropriately feminine. Thus, Agnes's efforts illuminate the strategies of "normal" females, strategies that are taken for granted to such as extent that they are invisible in everyday life.

Garfinkel argues that these strategies revolve around eight "facts," or assumptions, regarding gender in this culture:

1. There are two, and only two, genders (female and male).
2. One's gender is invariant. (If you are female/male, you always were female/male, and you always will be female/male.)
3. Genitals are the essential sign of gender. (A female is a person with a vagina; a male is a person with a penis.)
4. Any exceptions to two genders are not to be taken seriously. (They must be jokes, pathology, etc.)
5. There are no transfers from one gender to another except ceremonial ones (masquerades).
6. Everyone must be classified as a member of one gender or another. (There are no cases where gender is not attributed.)
7. The male/female dichotomy is a "natural" one. (Males and females exist independently of scientists' [or anyone else's] criteria for being male and female.)
8. Membership in one gender or another is "natural." (Being female or male is not dependent on anyone's deciding what you are.) (Kessler and McKenna 1978:113–14)

Garfinkel contends that gender is not "natural," but is instead accomplished through everyday behavior.

Televised interactions offer an unusually pointed example of this process, since they are deliberately designed to be engaging and interpretable modes of communication. In an analysis of the interactions on the 1990s television dating game show *Studs*, Hollander (1998) shows the rich interactional dynamics of performing both gender and sexuality. Some highlights: "Dates" (the women) sit demurely on the stage, whereas "studs" (the men) run onstage and engage in physical clowning; the women's clothing emphasizes feminine curves, whereas the men's emphasizes masculine strength; the women sit with legs crossed and close together, their arms close to their bodies, whereas the men sit with legs wide apart or crossed knee to ankle; the stories they both tell enact the "nature" of women as sexually reluctant and of men as sexually aggressive; their verbal comments on what sort of date they might want establish their heterosexual "normality." In short, they perform gender, and culturally appropriate gender, through a rich repertoire of actions. Their behaviors literally sustain the social reality of gender.

Kessler and McKenna (1978) go even further and argue that not only gender, but the very idea of two distinct sexes, is socially constructed. They note that there are a considerable number of people who do not fit easily into the categories male and female. Examples include intersexed individuals (who are born with both female and male physical characteristics or with ambiguous physical characteristics), *berdaches* and *hijras* (who are physically assignable to one sex but who take on the social behaviors and characteristics of the other), and transsexuals (who move from one sex category to the other). These examples, as we mentioned in the previous chapter, demonstrate that sex is not dichotomous. Our cultural belief in two (and only two) sexes, however, leads us to categorize these people as "really" one or the other sex. Transsexuals might seem to violate Garfinkel's "facts" about gender, but in fact they reaffirm it. By engaging in sex reassignment surgery, they change not gender, but genitals; they alter sex to conform to gender. In a society that tolerated a lack of correspondence between genitals and gender, there would be no need for such surgery.

This approach to gender differs significantly from the essentialist and socialization approaches. Deaux (1984) criticizes these latter approaches for "the static nature of the assumptions—that sex-related phenomena are best approached either through biological categories, via stable traits, or in terms of relatively stable stereotypic conceptions" (113). She suggests that attention "be directed toward more active interaction sequences, toward the processes through which gender information is presented and acted upon" (113)—the choices women and men make and the processes of interaction. Gender is not only something society imposes on individuals; women and men themselves enact gender, and in doing so, choose certain behavioral options and ignore others. This perspective challenges the naturalness of gender difference, maintaining that all significant social characteristics are actively created, rather than biologically inherited, permanently socialized, or structurally predetermined.

In other words, gender is constructed in part through performance. "Doing gender" means behaving so that whatever the situation, whoever the other actors, one's behavior is seen in context as gender appropriate. To be sure, women and men do take actions that contradict norms for their sex; what is important is that the balance of one's actions is perceived as conforming. Although individuals do have agency in constructing their performances, their choices are not entirely free. West and Zimmerman (1987) argue that one driving force behind gender performance is the threat of being held accountable for one's behavior:

> A person engaged in virtually any activity can be held responsible for performance of that activity as a woman or a man, and their incumbency in one or the other sex category can be used to legitimate or discredit their other activities. (136; see also Fenstermaker and West 2002)

Thus, female college professors, for example, are often expected to be more nurturing than male professors in their interactions with their students. When they fail to conform to this expectation—an expectation that has no relationship to their position as college professor—students may express their dissatisfaction through their evaluations of these professors (Sprague and Massoni 2005). To the degree that a society is organized in terms of what it understands as essential differences between women and men (or among the races), doing gender (or doing race) is thus unavoidable.

Erving Goffman (1977) provides an apt example of the ubiquity of doing gender, noting that public bathrooms (at least in the United States) are segregated on the basis of sex. This is despite the fact that "both [ladies and gentlemen] are somewhat similar in the question of waste products and their elimination . . . there is nothing in this functioning [of sex-differentiated organs] that biologically recommends segregation; that arrangement is a totally cultural matter" (315–16). In other words, bathroom segregation creates gender difference for social, not biological ends. Lest one doubt this claim, consider the absence of single-sex bathrooms in most private homes. Every time we enter a women's room or men's room, we do gender. We even do gender when we enter the "wrong" bathroom, if we express embarrassment or otherwise indicate this is not something we would normally do (a not uncommon occurrence during short intermissions when there are long lines outside women's bathrooms and none outside men's bathrooms). Should individuals occasionally lapse, social institutions enforce gender segregation, as Denise Wells learned when police arrested her for using the men's room at a concert in Houston, Texas (*New York Times* 1990).

The social constructionist conceptualization of gender helps reconcile the empirical findings that women and men are more similar than different on most traits and abilities with the common perception that they seem to behave quite differently. Women and men may have the same abilities, but because they face different societal constraints and expectations, they often make different choices from this repertoire of options. Gender expectations can thus act as *self-fulfilling prophecies.* Suppose an employer interviewing a woman for a position in his (or her) firm holds traditional views about women and he (or she) makes these opinions clear in his (or her) behavior. The woman being interviewed is likely to respond by behaving in a "feminine" way, whether or not those behaviors reflect her usual behavior, thus confirming the employer's gender expectations (Snyder and Skrypnek 1981).

These cumulative performances of gender create the gendered institutions of contemporary society. Brines (1993), for example, demonstrates how husbands' and wives' contributions to housework serve as gender performances: "Among couples whose earnings arrangement seriously deviates from the gender norm, housework is used symbolically to reassert [the respective partners'] 'essential' masculinity or femininity" (302, and see chapter 3 of this volume). Individual husbands and wives thus perform gender through their allocation of household work. Summed across the members of a society, these performances reproduce the division of public and private labor and maintain the subordination of women.

Performances of gender are also performances of other intersecting social positions. Pate (2006) shows how seemingly minor "acknowledgment rituals"—the nod of a head or verbal hello when passing a stranger in public— among members of various minority groups simultaneously reinforce both intraminority group solidarity and the boundaries between minority and majority groups. Importantly, these rituals are strikingly more frequent among African American men than among African American women or women and men of other racial groups. These patterns likely reflect the markedly visible and virulent racial discrimination against African American men. Similarly, race marks the performance of other status positions. Harlow's (2003) research on black professors, for example, emphasizes the careful attention they must give to their everyday performances. According to Harlow, black professors must expend more time and energy in emotional labor in the classroom to renegotiate their devalued status as racial minorities.

Doing gender is also doing sexuality. Herbert (1995, 2000) shows the performance strategies of women in the U.S. military as they attempt to avoid being perceived as too masculine, on the one hand, and too feminine, on the other. Over half of the women in her study identified being labeled a lesbian as the primary penalty of being perceived as too masculine. The penalties of being perceived as not masculine enough include career limitations and being judged an inadequate soldier. Similarly, Bemiller's (2005) research on male cheerleaders shows how these men face accusations of being gay despite their being in a rigorous sport requiring close physical contact with attractive women; as a consequence, these men engage in numerous face-saving strategies to repair both their gender and sexual identities (see also Anderson 2005). Indeed, the awkwardness of watching female cheerleaders, often performing in skimpy and sexualized attire, cheering for female athletic teams, itself underscores the constructedness of gender. Although the dilemmas detailed in these studies are magnified among individuals navigating nontraditional spaces, they are only an exaggeration of the interactional and structural difficulties facing women and men who fail to perform gender according to cultural norms in everyday situations.

As these examples illustrate, doing gender reaffirms the social arrangements based on sex category as normal and natural and thus legitimates the prevailing social order. Differences between women and men created through these processes can be portrayed as fundamental and enduring, as essential. Doing gender is how social interaction sustains broader, macrolevel systems of gender hierarchy. This implies in turn that doing gender "wrong" may be the interactional foundation for social change in gender relations. Scholarly attention is only beginning to attend to the logic that if gender can be "done" in interaction, then it can also be "undone," and to explore the processes of undoing (Deutsch 2007; Hollander 2002; Lorber 2005; Risman 1998; West and Zimmerman 2009). It is important to note, however, that those who contest norms are often held accountable as individual actors; responsibility is attributed to the actors, rather than to the norms they contest. In the exceedingly individualistic U.S. society, persistent and coordinated efforts are necessary to pose effective challenges to social institutions.

The social constructionist approach emphasizes the social context of gendered behavior. Unlike traditional experimental social psychology, which isolates elements of social life in the supposedly neutral context of the laboratory, this perspective focuses on interactions among individuals in their specific social situations. Many aspects of the situation are influential: the expectations of those with whom one interacts, the differential opportunities for interaction, and the differential rewards and punishments for behavior accorded to women and men. Thus, the distinctive contribution of the social constructionist approach is its attention to the relationship between the person and the situation. "Gender is pervasive, but gender effects do not reside solely in either person or situation" (Spence et al. 1985:172). This, of course, is the mission of social psychology—to articulate the interface between individual and society.

We do not want to overstate the power of the social constructionist approach to gender, however. In its emphasis on individual agency, this approach minimizes the constraints of social structures and the effects of power inequities. Action is always situated somewhere. The particularities of actors' genders, class positions, races, and sexualities have direct material consequences for the range of actions they can envision, let alone perform. Although almost all actors have some degree of choice among potential behaviors, some people have a good deal more choice than others. The emphasis on agency comes at the cost of recognition of the reality of institutional and interpersonal constraints—that is, of social hierarchies. This brings us to the fourth perspective on gender, a structural account.

Structural Approaches

Gender is one basis for the systematic allocation of resources; in other words, gender is one form of social structure (Risman 2004). In previous sections of this chapter we have considered how gender operates as a microlevel structure, shaping interactional expectations and possibilities. Gender is also a basis for the macrolevel allocation of material resources and opportunities. Across societies, men continue to dominate women; as a group, they occupy more positions of power in government and business and score better on development indices for education, health, and literacy (Connell 2002; Epstein 2007; United Nations Development Fund for Women 2005). Women and men who seek to establish equitable divisions of labor in their intimate relationships must battle the structural arrangements of day care, parental leave policies, pay inequities and gender-segregated labor, as well as the gender-differentiated expectations of parents, employers, teachers, and children themselves (Schwartz 1994). At the same time, as detailed in the previous section, social structures are also continually negotiated and redefined through individual action and interaction (Howard 1994; Reskin 2000; Schwalbe et al. 2000). A structural approach to gender, then, examines the gendered distribution of resources in social institutions (from small groups, such as families, to large organizations, to society itself) and demonstrates how those resources shape gendered behaviors. Thus, theorizing gender as a social structure clarifies how gender operates:

> (1) At the individual level, for the development of gendered selves; (2) during interaction as men and women face different cultural expectations even when they fill identical structural positions; and (3) in institutional domains where explicit regulations regarding resource distribution and material goods are gender specific. (Risman 2004:433)

This structural approach has not been prevalent in social psychology; however, current feminist theorists are calling for scholars to theorize gender as a social structure (Risman 2004) or social institution (Martin 2004). As we argue in subsequent chapters, we believe that a comprehensive understanding of social behavior is impossible without serious analysis of the relationships between individuals and social structures. Social psychologists must consider the myriad ways in which the social organization of gender (and race, class, and sexuality) shapes both the microlevel interactional possibilities and the macrolevel material resources of women and men.

Returning to the principles of socialization, we might ask, for example, why it is that certain behaviors are rewarded when they are performed by boys and punished when they are performed by girls? Why are the sorts of behaviors girls are encouraged to perform valued less than the sorts of behaviors boys are encouraged to perform? Why there are many fewer female than male role models in prestigious, societally rewarded positions and many more female than male role models in less rewarded positions? Turning to the principles of the social constructionist approach to gender, we might ask whether all actors have the same degree of behavioral choice and control. Do all actors bring the same resources to their social interactions? What are the effects of what Kanter (1977) calls "tokenism"—interactional strategies whereby men in the numerical majority in institutions such as corporations ostracize and stigmatize the few women who are successful in entering these arenas? A structural approach emphasizes the profound effects of a pervasive system of male dominance, whereby men as a category have systematic advantages over women as a category. Note, too, that men have these advantages whether or not they consciously desire them; this is, of course, one aspect of a social structure.

Moreover, gender does not operate independent of other significant social structures. Newman's (1999) study of urban fast-food workers, for example, clearly outlines how gender, race, and social class simultaneously impact young people's life chances in completing high school, acquiring employment, and moving up job ladders. At the same time that men as a group have advantages over women as a group, whites—both women and men—have advantages over members of other racial categories; those who have substantial economic resources have considerable advantages over those who are poor. Because these systems are inextricably interconnected, the advantages that gender stratification accords to men accrue significantly more to some men (e.g., those who are white and/or wealthy) than to others. The intersections between these various structures make social hierarchy extremely complex: the dynamics of interactions between gay Latino men and poor white women, or between straight, wealthy black men and older lesbians, are not straightforward. Gender intersects with other social hierarchies, affecting social psychological phenomena from cognitive structures to the dynamics of social interaction, to macrolevel institutions and collective actions.

In summary, from a structural perspective, observed differences between women and men, whether in personality characteristics, interactional styles, educational levels, or income, are attributable to the differential access of women and men to material and social resources, rather than to deep-seated traits or biological factors. We suggest, as do other recent theorists (e.g., Lorber 2005; Martin 2004; Risman 2004), that the structural and social constructionist approaches are complementary. Everyday behavior is always enacted within the structural constraints and possibilities associated with actors' locations in significant social systems. Approaching gender as a structure makes the origins and perpetuation of gender explicit. Furthermore, it elevates gender to the level of the economy, politics, and other legitimate social phenomena long theorized and analyzed at the institutional or systems level (Martin 2004). We close this discussion of the various social psychological approaches to gender with the observation that a combination of social constructionist and structural perspectives seems to us to offer the most incisive lens for analyzing contemporary social life.

Conclusions

We have presented four theories of gender prominent in social psychological research. We have emphasized the construction of gender through social interaction and at the same time the importance of the location of human actors in particular social structures. We have been particularly critical of essentialist understandings of gender, whether these are based on assumptions about biological determinants of gender or on theories of socialization that treat gender-related characteristics as virtually unchangeable. We have suggested that essentialist approaches to gender, sexuality, race, socioeconomic position, or any other human attribute are not consistent with a wealth of empirical research. On the other hand, most cultures and societies have treated these categories and positions as if they were essential, innate, and stable. Accordingly, these systems have been the bases for the allocation of resources, both material and nonmaterial, across human history.

As the subsequent chapters make clear, there are consistent historical patterns in the treatment of gender, race, class, and sexuality in social psychological research. Research on gendered patterns of social behavior began to increase in the 1970s and has continued at a fairly consistent rate to the present. Many researchers began to attend to the hierarchical relationships between the sexes—to inequality and power, as well as to difference. These developments were not unrelated to the fact that more women have begun to earn doctorates and to conduct research in these areas. In recent years, women have earned one-third of sociology PhDs, and in 2007, for the first time ever, women represented a slight majority (50.5 percent) of American Sociological Association members (Spalter-Roth and Scelza 2008). Similarly, women earned two-thirds of the psychology PhDs awarded in 2004, and during 2005, women represented a majority (53 percent) of American Psychological Association members (Keita, Cameron, and Burrwell 2006).

In contrast, research on racialized patterns of social behavior was prominent in the 1970s but began to drop off during the 1980s and continues today primarily within research on attitudes, stereotypes, and immigration. The progress in incorporating more women into research has not been equaled in the study of race, at least not in research participation rates. Nearly 6 percent (5.8 percent) of American Psychological Association members, for example, identified themselves as racial and ethnic minorities in 2004 (American

Psychological Association, Office of Ethnic Minority Affairs 2008).[1] This figure represents a 17.8 percent increase since 1997 and is likely the result of a 1997 resolution aimed at recruiting and retaining people of color in the early stages of the academic pipeline. Nevertheless, during the two decades preceding that resolution, there was a marked decline in the proportion of published social psychological articles that include African Americans as research participants (Graham 1992). This pattern persists despite a marked increase in racial minorities in the profession.

Patterns of research on social class are similar to those of research on race, except that the drop during the 1980s is even more precipitous. Not only is social class rarely a focus of research, but the class position of research subjects is rarely assessed. Even in research that attempts to disentangle the effects of race and social class, only one-quarter of the relevant studies report the social class positions of the participants (Graham 1992). The importance of socioeconomic position for explaining social behavior has been "eclipsed" by gender and race, according to Smeser (1999), and thus class remains acknowledged only at the margins of social psychology (Reid 1993; Wexler 1983), rarely considered in experimental studies (for exceptions see Black and Gold 2008; Howard and Pike 1986), and even more rarely in book-length treatments (Argyle 1994 is one exception).

Considering these patterns together, the inescapable conclusion is that the real-world political vitality of particular social communities plays a central role in determining research agendas. Patterns of research that address gender mirror the sustained recent sociocultural awareness of gender. Patterns of research that address sexual orientation mirror the recent ascent to the national stage of this political community. Patterns of research that address race mirror the heights—and the depths—of the civil rights movement and its successors. As the 2008 presidential campaign and subsequent election of Barack Obama unfolded, social psychological dynamics were cited frequently, evidence of the critical role of sociohistorical context in shaping research agendas and in drawing public attention to this research.

Thus, we exhort the reader to evaluate what we report here as critically as the phenomena we critique. Throughout this chapter we have directed our comments and criticisms toward both the central theories and ideas of social psychology and the actual practices of the discipline of social psychology. We discuss these disciplinary practices because the lessons of social psychology apply as strongly to the discipline itself as to other arenas of social life. Social context shapes all social behavior, including the production of social psychological scholarship. We turn now to that scholarship.

The four approaches we have reviewed—essentialist, socialization, social constructionist, and structural—trace the evolution of social psychology's conceptualizations of gender over the last century. In general, this evolution has been productive: each advance has brought new insights into the sources and content of gender. In the remainder of this book, we examine specific areas of social psychology in greater depth. We begin by analyzing the three dominant theories in social psychology—social exchange, social cognition, and symbolic interactionism—and then illustrate these through applications to two interrelated topics—aggression and altruism. In each chapter, we analyze in detail how research in the area has dealt with gender and related social systems and how further attention to gender can illuminate our understanding of both social psychology and gender. In the next three chapters, we discuss theories that social psychologists have used to explain human social behavior, looking particularly at how each theory would explain the existence and persistence of gender. It will be evident to the reader that these three social psychological theories vary considerably in the extent to which they reflect the observation that gender is socially constructed. Some of these theories are stronger at showing how gender is constructed and accomplished through interaction, and others tend to emphasize that gender is the product of social structure. The fact that all three social psychological theories demonstrate that gender is a social product, however, is fully inconsistent with the logic of essentialist arguments.

Note

1. The American Sociological Association does not provide comparable statistics on members' self-reported race and ethnicity; however, recent reports do suggest there have been increases in membership across racial and ethnic groups (Spalter-Roth and Scelza 2008).

3

Social Exchange and Related Theories

O UR DAILY LIVES INVOLVE A CONSTANT stream of choices about how we will behave. We choose what we eat, what we wear, to whom (if anyone) we talk, what we do with our time. We may also make decisions about how we spend whatever money we have, what books we read or what films we see, and with whom we form or maintain intimate relationships. Why do we make the choices we do? Why do we often make the same choices day after day—to wear certain types of clothes, to talk with particular friends, or to buy particular products? In this chapter we discuss three theories—behaviorism, social learning, and social exchange—that share a common perspective on such questions. Each theory assumes that human behavior is driven by the pursuit of rewards, whether material (such as money, food, or physical pleasure) or symbolic (such as status, prestige, or love). Humans behave in ways that they expect will bring them such rewards, and avoid behaving in ways they expect will bring punishments—negative events such as pain, hunger, loneliness, or loss of status.

In this chapter we survey these three theories, focusing on their treatment of gender. We begin with brief reviews of behaviorism and social learning theory, both of which have been very influential in psychology. We conclude with a more extended discussion of social exchange theory; this is arguably the dominant social psychological perspective in sociology and is gaining currency throughout the social sciences. We combine these three theories in a single chapter because of their shared reliance on the assumption that human behavior is driven by rewards and punishments.

Behaviorism

Behaviorism was the dominant paradigm in social psychology for the first half of the twentieth century. Although it has in large part been superseded by more recent theories, we discuss it here because its principles form the basis for both social learning and social exchange theories. Behaviorism grew out of animal research. Scientists found that animal behavior could be changed by a process they called *reinforcement*—the association of a particular behavior with specific consequences, either positive (such as receiving food) or negative (such as experiencing electric shocks). Behavioral psychologists (e.g., Skinner 1938, 1974; Watson 1924) suggested that the same principles could explain human behavior as well.

The key to understanding behavior, according to these theorists, lies in the consequences that follow from the behavior. But how do people know what the consequences will be before they occur? By looking back at the consequences that have been associated with the action in the past. If we have found that a certain behavior has been associated with rewards in the past, we tend to repeat it; similarly, if we have found that a behavior has been associated with punishments, we avoid repeating it.

It is crucial to note that behaviorist theory focuses on *behavior*, not on thought or feeling. According to behaviorism, the environment affects behavior *directly*, without intervening processes such as thought or feeling. These thoughts and feelings may occur, but they are simply by-products of the effects of the environment on behavior (Skinner 1974) and do not cause behavior (Molm 2006; Skinner 1974). In contrast, most other social psychological theories assume that thought and emotion mediate between the environment and individual behavior.

Behaviorism's Treatment of Gender, Race, and Class

Behaviorism has paid almost no attention to social statuses such as gender, race, or class. The theory postulates that all creatures—animals and humans, males and females, whites and people of color, poor and rich, old and young—operate according to the same behavioral principles. Gender is therefore not considered relevant to behaviorist questions.

Is it even possible to integrate gender into a behaviorist model? If researchers were interested in including gender in their theories, we suggest the integration might take the following form. Behaviorists could expand on their insight that consequences are the real causes of behavior, using this principle to explore gender differences and similarities in behavior. Experiments could be devised to assess whether gendered patterns of behavior (such as nurturance or aggression) could be produced in a similar fashion in males and females by modifying patterns of reinforcement. For example, might men behave nurturingly and women aggressively if they were rewarded for these behaviors? Moving out of the laboratory, behaviorists could examine the environmental conditions that differentially affect men and women and theorize about how these might affect behavior. For example, men might behave aggressively because, over time, they have been rewarded for displaying aggressive behavior. Women, on the other hand, might not behave aggressively because they are consistently punished for such behavior. Thus, apparent sex differences in behavior could be explained by environmental consequences rather than individual or group characteristics.

In the previous chapter, we described four different ways of conceptualizing gender. Behaviorism's treatment of gender in some ways resembles both the socialization and the structural models of gender, because both emphasize the effects of the environment on individuals. The socialization perspective, however, relies far more on cognition than behaviorism does, and the structural perspective's conception of environment is far richer than behaviorism's. The social constructionist approach to gender is fundamentally incompatible with behaviorist theory because of the former's heavy reliance on cognition. The social constructionist approach argues that people behave in gendered ways because of their ideas about appropriate behavior and their perceptions of others' expectations; these factors are explicitly excluded from the behaviorist model. To the extent that behaviorism considers cognition, it sees cognition as a behavior resulting from external stimuli, rather than as a stimulus for other behavior. To include cognition as a cause of gendered behavior, we must look to the two other theories developed from behaviorism— social learning and social exchange. Although these theories do not focus on cognition as directly as other social psychological perspectives (e.g., social cognition and symbolic interactionism), they do recognize that cognition plays a mediating role in social behavior.

Social Learning Theory

Social learning theory retains the behaviorist emphasis on reward and punishment, but expands and extends these principles in several important respects. First, it emphasizes the role of other people as the agents of reinforcement. When rewards or punishments are administered by influential others, they are likely to be more effective. Social learning theory has been particularly important in the field of developmental psychology, which studies how children develop psychologically and learn the norms and values of their society.

Second, social learning theory differs from behaviorism in its focus on modeling and imitation. According to Bandura and his colleagues, children observe the behavior of real-life (e.g., parents, teachers, or other children) and symbolic (e.g., television or literary) models and then reproduce this behavior themselves (Bandura 1977; Bandura and Walters 1963). The reproduced behavior need not be reinforced directly in order to become part of the child's repertoire; observation of the consequences of the model's behavior may be sufficient (Bandura, Ross, and Ross 1963). Thus, children do not have to perform a behavior themselves in order to experience its consequences and learn from it. This is a significant departure from behaviorism, which suggests that learning of new behaviors occurs only through *successive approximation*—in other words, through trying out different versions of a behavior and being rewarded or punished for them.

Most importantly, social learning theory departs from behaviorism in its inclusion of cognitive processes as mediating factors between the environment and individual behavior.[1] While reward and punishment remain important concepts, social learning theory focuses on the ways in which individuals think about their social experiences and how those thoughts affect their subsequent behaviors. Social learning theory thus introduces the realm of the symbolic: to learn from experience, people must retain experiences in memory (as images or verbal representations), integrate them with other knowledge, generalize them into rules for behavior, and apply these rules to new situations. Although social learning theory acknowledges these cognitive processes, it does not explore them in detail. That task is left to social cognition, the theory to which we turn in the next chapter.

Social Learning Theory's Treatment of Gender

Unlike behaviorism, social learning theory has been applied extensively to understanding gender, particularly the development of gender differences in behavior. The idea here is quite simple: children observe the behavior of others, including other children, adults, and symbolic models such as television actors. Children imitate the behavior of people of both sexes; however, the consequences of this imitation often vary depending on the sex of the child. Boys are rewarded more for performing typically masculine behaviors, and girls for performing typically feminine behaviors. Because only rewarded behaviors tend to be repeated, children develop gendered repertoires of behavior (Bandura 1969; Bussey and Bandura 1984; Mischel 1966), either through direct reinforcement or through observation of consequences experienced by others. The influence of behaviorism on this model of learning should be clear.

The importance of both of these processes—imitation and reinforcement—is illustrated by Bandura's research on aggression, which we discuss in more detail in chapter 7. Bandura and his colleagues conducted a series of experiments (Bandura 1965, 1973; Bandura et al. 1963) that demonstrated that aggression can be learned from others. Children were shown films in which an adult hit and kicked an inflatable "Bobo doll." The children were then allowed to play with a similar doll. Those who had seen the aggressive behavior abused the doll in the same ways the adult had; children in a control condition, who had not seen the adult behaving aggressively, did not. The degree of reinforcement was also important: when the adult was rewarded for aggressive behavior, the children imitated the adult more. Overall, boys were more aggressive than girls; however, when the children were rewarded for aggressive behavior, the levels of aggression were equal. Both imitation and reinforcement are thus important in learning gendered behavior.

How does social learning theory map onto the four approaches to gender? Social learning theory is in fact the basis of the socialization approach to gender. Most social learning research focuses on the acquisition of gender-typed behaviors in childhood, implying that gender, once learned, becomes a relatively stable facet of one's personality. However, the theory does not address the question of why reinforcers are sex-typed, and it does not challenge the conception of gender as an individual characteristic. In contrast, social learning theory is fundamentally incompatible with the essentialist perspective, because it views gender as learned, not innate. With some modifications, social learning theory could be compatible with the social constructionist and structural perspectives on gender, because it focuses on contextual influences on behavior.

Why has the theory not moved in these directions? There are several probable reasons. First, social learning theory grew out of behaviorism and has inherited some of its assumptions. Although behaviorism does conceptualize behavior as driven by the environment, the behaviorist's idea of environmental influences is limited to the immediate context and the reinforcement contingencies it presents. This is a very different conception of context than the sociologist's notion of social structure. As a result, social learning theory tends to ignore significant structural patterns, such as the fact that the organization of social institutions such as families, schools, or religions reinforces males and females differently for the same behaviors. Second, social learning theory has historically focused on children, perhaps because the theory was first generated by developmental psychologists. The theory could, however, be equally applicable to adults—because, after all, adults are not immune to rewards and punishments. Applying the theory to adults would suggest that gendered behavior is constantly modeled and reinforced, even among adults—an idea that is much closer to the social constructionist approach to gender.

Social Exchange Theory

Like social learning theory, social exchange theory derives from behaviorism. We consider social exchange theory in greater depth than we have behaviorism or social learning, because it is quite influential in sociology and because the imagery of exchange theory (markets, transactions, and the like) resonates with hegemonic cultural ideas, making exchange processes salient in social interaction.

Like behaviorism and social learning theory, social exchange theory assumes that individuals pursue rewards and attempt to avoid punishments, and considers an individual's past history of rewards and punishments to be important for predicting future behavior. However, social exchange diverges from behaviorism and social learning theory in several crucial ways.

First, the focus of exchange theory is not individual behavior, but interaction. The exchange relationship—a series of transactions between two or more actors occurring over time (Emerson 1972a, 1972b; Thibaut and Kelley 1959)—is the unit of analysis. The major question addressed by exchange theory is not "Why does an individual behave in a certain way?" but instead "Under what circumstances does a certain interaction (or exchange) take place?" Exchange theory contends that interaction takes place when it is mutually rewarding to the parties involved.

Second, as the above paragraph suggests, the model for exchange theory's view of interaction is the economic transaction. For example, when we go to the store, we exchange money in return for food. Social exchange theory takes this economic model and applies it to other situations, such as choosing a job or a dating partner. In each of these situations, the actor exchanges her or his personal resources (work skills, status, attractiveness, conversational skills, and so on) for a desired benefit such as employment or a date with a desirable partner. Thus, the resources transferred in social exchanges need not be material; social approval, respect, and compliance are other valuable rewards (Blau 1964). However, as in market-based economic exchanges, actors in social exchanges are assumed to be seeking the best possible outcomes from interactions. When buying a loaf of bread, when accepting a job, or when choosing a dating partner, the actor considers whether the exchange in question is a "good deal" or whether he or she can find a better deal with a different exchange partner.

Like social learning theory, social exchange theory explicitly includes cognition in its model of interaction. When deciding on a course of action, actors are assumed to weigh the costs and benefits of the available options and choose rationally between them. Thus, consideration of alternatives and choice are the principal forms of cognition in this theory. Of course, actors do not always know the actual consequences of their choices. What matters is perception: people choose the alternative they believe will be best, based on their assessment of the costs and benefits of the alternatives combined with their estimates of the probability of receiving these outcomes.

This is a very different kind of cognition than in social learning theory. Social learning theory's model of cognition envisions actors looking back toward the past, evaluating the results of similar choices (by oneself or others). In contrast, exchange theory's actors look toward the future as well as the past: what advantages, they ask, will different situations bring, and what is the likelihood that these situations will come to pass (Macy 1993)? Although decision-making is clearly an important part of cognition, there is far more to thought than either social learning or exchange theory suggests. In social exchange, individuals are assumed to weigh the costs and benefits of particular outcomes. But we know from research on cognition (a topic we take up in greater depth in the next chapter) that other factors also influence decision-making: beliefs, attitudes, membership in and identification with certain groups (e.g., based on ethnicity, gender, or religion). The richness of cognitive processes has not yet been incorporated into exchange theory's model of behavior.

A third way that social exchange theory differs from social learning theory and behaviorism is that exchange theory brings social structure into the model of interaction. Unlike behaviorism and social learning theory, which limit their conceptualization of environmental factors to reinforcement (and, in the case of social learning, modeling by other actors), social exchange theory considers individuals in a broader social context. According to exchange theory, interaction occurs because of individuals' interdependence—in other words, because each person depends on others for valued resources, both material and emotional, and because access to resources depends on structural locations (see Cook and Rice 2003). In addition, choices may be affected by an actor's position in a larger social network. For example, other exchanges occurring within a social group may affect what is considered to be a "good deal": if a friend's new job pays $35,000 a year, you may expect to receive the same salary for a similar position. In turn, what is considered to be a good deal also varies by actors' structural locations; for example, a woman may consider $35,000 to be a better salary than does a man, given sex differences in pay. In addition, actors may join together to negotiate transactions with a more powerful party. For example, a group of workers may form a coalition to protest exploitive work conditions. (This, of course, is the principle behind labor unions.) Moreover, the position of an actor in a social network is also important: actors who are more central (i.e., who mediate a large number of other relationships) may have more power, as well as more alternatives available to them (Cook and Rice 2003; Molm 2006; Yamagishi, Gillmore, and Cook 1988). Thus, exchange theory uses the structure of social relationships to explain behavior: "Rather than try to explain the nature of a relationship as a result of qualities within the actors, this research explains the qualities of the actors by exploring the nature of the relationship" (Cook, O'Brien, and Kollock 1990:162).

Social Exchange and Power

One of the most useful aspects of social exchange theory is its attention to power as a central mechanism of social interaction. *Power* is defined as an actor's ability to achieve a favorable outcome at the expense of another and is a quality of a relationship, not an individual. One's power over another person depends on the value of one's resources to that other person, together with the availability of those resources from alternate sources. Thus, to return to the example used in the first chapter, if a professor possesses information that is very important to a student, and if there is no other source from which the student can obtain this information, then the professor holds a great deal of power over the student. However, the professor's power is due to the relationship with the student (and the underlying network of relationships among the student, the professor, and the university) rather than to the professor's personal qualities. In another relationship—for example, with a police officer who has stopped the professor for speeding—the professor's specialized knowledge will not be a valuable resource, and he will have little power over the police officer. The student, but not the police officer, is dependent upon the professor; thus power and dependence vary together in exchange relationships.

This insight leads to what Homans (1974) called the "principle of least interest": the person who is least dependent on a relationship has the greatest power in it, because that person can more easily abandon the relationship. The professor presumably has many students, so the good regard of any one student is not particularly compelling. The student, however, has only one professor for any given class, and so that professor's behavior is very important to her. Later in the play from which we borrow this example, however, we see the power dynamics shift: the student has developed access to other resources, and in fact gains partial control of the professor's access to tenure. This student's power over the professor thus increases dramatically. This change shows another strength of exchange theory: the acknowledgment that power is not a static quality of a person, but a dynamic, shifting property of a relationship.

Critiques of Social Exchange Theory

Exchange theory has been tremendously influential in many of the social sciences, including sociology, economics, and anthropology, as well as social psychology. Perhaps because of that influence, it has also been subject to extensive critiques. For example, despite its recognition of power, exchange theory has generally been applied only to *voluntary* interaction. Coercive interaction—when one party forces the other to act through the use or threat of violence—is often seen as outside the scope of the theory. Although exchange theory could easily be used to understand coercive situations—one actor simply has very few resources and alternatives relative to the other—it has rarely been used in this way. Perhaps this is because of the association of exchange with choice; conceptualizing coercive interaction as involving choice could be viewed as problematic. Some recent research has begun to include "punishment power" in studies of exchange (e.g., Molm 1988, 1989a, 1989b, 1990, 1997); however, this terrain remains largely underexplored by exchange researchers.

It is also curious that although the *theory* of social exchange is built around conceptions of power and social structure, very little of the *research* in this tradition explores power or stratification in any real-world sense. As we point out in the next section, exchange theory has rarely analyzed the way one's position in existing systems of social stratification—such as one's race, class, sex, age—affects one's resources, alternatives, and choices. (We discuss two exceptions in the second half of this chapter: research on power in long-term relationships and on equity and justice.) One reason for this inattention is clear: the experimental methodology used in much exchange research precludes investigation of these issues. Many exchange experiments (see Molm and Cook 1995) take the following form: participants sit in separate rooms and interact by typing messages over a computer network or by pushing buttons that illuminate lights on a panel in another room; they never see or hear each other. These arrangements have the advantage of reducing the effects of "extraneous" factors such as gender, race, or attractiveness. However, these situations also lack external validity; they are so unlike everyday interaction that the experimental results may not be generalizable to the real world. The factors that are "controlled" in the lab (gender, age, attractiveness, rewards, etc.) are central to social interaction and may influence the process of social exchange in unexamined ways. For example, people in different social groups may value different outcomes or have different perceptions about their alternatives in a given situation; these kinds of issues are rarely examined in exchange research.

Critics have also questioned the tasks frequently used in exchange research. For example, many studies involve pushing buttons to receive rewards, and many of these rewards are very small—a few cents or dollars. Money is used as the reward in these experiments because it is presumed to have relatively equal value for everyone. Class variation among subjects may make this assumption untrue, however. The small sums that are earned through participation may be important to a poorer participant, but incidental (and therefore less compelling) to a wealthier participant. Indeed, the entire question of the value of various resources to exchange participants remains unaddressed. Thus, although social exchange is *theoretically* sophisticated, its *implementation* in research is less so.

The limited focus of exchange research has also been subject to critique. The groups used in experimental research are usually composed of people who have never met and who are recruited specifically to serve as experimental volunteers. While some everyday interaction does take place with strangers, most people spend the majority of their time interacting with people they already know—family members, romantic partners, friends, coworkers, and so on—and with whom they have a long history of interaction and a great deal of prior knowledge. The theory of social exchange emphasizes the effect of this history on interaction. In fact, in Emerson's (1972a, 1972b) formulation, history *defines* the exchange relation, which is conceptualized as repeated interaction over time. In practice, however, history is often left out of exchange experiments, or is represented by a series of transactions that occur a few minutes or hours before the experiment begins. Thus, we know little about how real-world history affects exchange relations.

Finally, some feminists argue that exchange theory (and other theories rooted in neoclassical economics) is gender biased. England and Kilbourne (1990), for example, note that women and men tend to differ on the dimension of separation-connection. Because of their different life experiences, men tend to develop a "separative" self that emphasizes independence and autonomy, while women tend to develop a "connective" self that values empathy and caring. England and Kilbourne argue that social exchange–type theories are biased toward the separative model of self. For example, these theories often assume that actors are selfish and pursue only what will benefit themselves, and that rationality, rather than emotion or empathy, guides behavior. Hartsock (1985) concludes that exchange theory's basis in men's experience "both justifies and obscures relations of gender domination" (57). Others challenge these criticisms, arguing that they result from a misreading of exchange theory, and that in fact such theories can help to explain gender inequality by showing how women and men make choices within different sets of social constraints (Friedman and Diem 1993). While we agree with Friedman and Diem that exchange theory has the potential to address gender inequality, we must underscore the fact that such applications continue to be rare in practice.

Exchange Theory's Treatment of Gender

The exchange framework has been adopted by practitioners in a wide variety of disciplines, including social work, communications, and criminal justice, who have used the basic concepts of exchange theory to explain a broad range of social phenomena. Many of the topics to which these concepts have been applied are deeply gendered, such as the perception of and responses to sexual harassment (Jones and Remland 1992), the disclosure of intimate information in relationships (Byrd 2006, 2009; Cline and Musolf 1985), sexual practices among couples (Baumeister and Vohs 2004; Sprecher 1998), and even homicide (Rodriquez and Henderson 1995; Rodriguez and Smithey 1999). However, these applications are far removed from the mainstream of social exchange research in social psychology, often using the concepts of social exchange (rewards, costs, and alternatives) without integrating the full richness of the theory.

In contrast, most research by social exchange theorists barely mentions gender, let alone race or social class. These studies offer no insights into the origins of persistence of gender inequality, and provide no account for the similarities and differences in women's and men's experiences of social life. Many studies do include sex as an independent variable: most use equal numbers of male and female subjects, and a few report sex differences (or similarities) in behavior. As in many areas of social research, little work in the social exchange tradition has gone beyond the concept of sex differences to a more sophisticated conceptualization of gender.

Why has social exchange theory neglected gender? Again, the experimental paradigm that has become normative in social exchange research is partly responsible. When subjects never see or hear each other, the everyday social cues that constitute sex and gender—appearance, speech, and behavior patterns—are artificially removed from the situation, and their effects on exchange behavior go unanalyzed. Other social psychological perspectives have been much more successful in integrating gender, race, and class into the experimental paradigm.

Another reason for the neglect of gender in exchange research is that exchange theory, like behaviorism, assumes that everyone's behavior is based on the same exchange principles. Regardless of race, gender, or class, every individual is believed to be guided by rewards and punishments, power and dependence. Although structural position and its effects on the availability of resources is a central part of the theory outlined by Emerson (1972a, 1972b), in practice structure tends to be operationalized quite narrowly, as a set of relationships among a small number of individual actors. The connection to real-world social structures based on social class, race, or gender is rarely explored.

Two traditions of research in social exchange do pay more attention to gender than most: the exploration of power in long-term intimate relationships and research on perceptions of justice and equity. In the remainder of this chapter, we discuss these two research traditions and their evolving approach to gender.

Example 1: Power in Marriage and Oher Long-Term Relationships

The earliest explorations of marital dynamics (e.g., Parsons 1955) did not focus on power at all. Families were believed to be locations of intimacy and communalism, places in which individuals could escape the competition and impersonal attitudes that characterize the public sphere. Thus, intimate relationships were presumed to be immune from power processes, and exchanges were assumed to be equal, even if the partners contributed different resources.

Later work, however, argued that these assumptions were naive, and that in fact intimate relationships are no less likely than other relationships to be arenas for the exercise of power and control. The first researchers in this tradition focused on the exchange of money for other resources. Measuring power by such factors as influence over important decisions, researchers noted that husbands tended to have more power than wives, especially when wives were not employed outside the home (Blood and Wolfe 1960; Turk and Bell 1972). Theorists hypothesized that this power differential resulted from the traditional organization of families, in which men were responsible for earning money while women were responsible for maintaining the home and rearing children. Marriage was thus conceptualized as an exchange: Women traded household service for financial support; men traded money and status for a comfortable home life. Men had more power because they contributed more of the more valuable resource: money.

Subsequent research has refined the rather crude equation of money and power. England and Farkas (1986), for example, argue that money is a key determinant of power not simply because it is a more valuable resource but because it (along with other resources such as prestige and social status) is a more *transferable* resource—one that can be used in a variety of situations. If a man ends one marriage and begins another, his financial resources are equally useful in the new relationship. Thus, it is relatively easy (financially speaking) for a man to change relationships. In traditional heterosexual relationships, however, women typically contribute fewer transferable resources such as money and status. Instead, they contribute household labor, child care, and social labor, such as maintaining relationships with friends and families—resources that are relatively nontransferable. A homemaker's investments in learning what kinds of foods her husband likes, or in maintaining bonds with his family, are not easily transferred to a new husband; rather, she must start afresh in a new relationship. Thus, in this traditional situation, the wife has a much greater investment in the specific relationship than the husband does. According to the principle of least interest, then, the husband will have more power because he is less invested in the relationship.

This analysis represents an important advance in understanding marital power. Resources are indeed the key to power in relationships, they argue; however, the *type* of resources is also crucial. Money is not the only important resource in relationships, but its transferability makes it more powerful. Most importantly, England and Farkas note that men and women tend to have different types of resources (because of the traditional division of labor and because of the fact that men continue to earn more than women); thus marital power is fundamentally gendered.

Brines (1993, 1994; see also Brines and Joyner 1999; Litzler and Brines 2005) offers a very different exchange approach to power in marriage. Brines takes issue with the assumption that the principles of exchange are gender neutral—that is, that men and women behave similarly in interaction, that they end up with different outcomes only because they have unequal resources, and that if they had equal resources, their outcomes would be the same. Brines examines a subset of marital decision-making—how heterosexual couples divide responsibility for housework—and asks why women tend to do over 70 percent of the cleaning, cooking, laundry, and child care, even when they also work outside the home (Bergen 1991; Coltrane 2000; Kessler-Harris 2003; Shelton and John 1993; South and Spitze 1994). This difference has been found to occur across racial groups (Cunningham 2007; Hossain and Roopnarine 1993; Landry 2000) and classes (Tichenor 2005; Wright et al. 1992) in the United States, as well as cross-culturally (Fuwa 2004; Hook 2006; Knudson and Wærness 2008; Sanchez 1993).

Brines (1993, 1994) examines how the relative earnings of husband and wife affect the time they spend on housework. Her findings are fascinating. When the couple divides paid and unpaid work in traditional ways (i.e., the husband is the primary earner and his wife is dependent on him for financial support), housework is distributed according to the predictions of exchange theory: women do the majority of the housework, and men do very little. However, when the division of labor is nontraditional—when the woman is the primary breadwinner and the man is economically dependent on her— the man, on average, does *not* do the majority of the housework. In fact, these dependent men actually do less housework on average than many of their employed brothers—a finding that runs directly counter to exchange theory predictions (see also Bittman et al. 2003).

How to explain these counterintuitive findings? Brines (1993) interprets these patterns as evidence of a "symbolic exchange" that operates along with the economic exchange predicted by exchange theory. She argues that marriage is an institution through which women and men can display masculinity and femininity—in other words, they can "do gender" in a socially expected and rewarded way. Despite changes in women's workforce participation over the past several decades, "gender accountability among married men remains tied to fulfillment of the provider role, and for wives to one's ability to manage adroitly the custodial and emotional needs of family members" (331). In marriages in which the male earns more than the female, doing gender fits seamlessly with the exchange of resources: men exchange their financial support for women's housework services, and both are able to fulfill gender expectations at the same time. When women outearn men, however, the situation becomes more complicated. The traditional exchange of money for housework would suggest that the men in these marriages should do the majority of the housework and that the women should do very little. However, doing so would run counter to norms of masculinity and femininity, seriously jeopardizing their ability to do gender.

Brines suggests that many of these couples solve this dilemma by distributing housework along traditional lines. In this way, they are able to bolster the gender differences that threaten to be undermined by the blurring of traditional economic roles. Both members of the couple are able to maintain the illusion that they are adhering to gender norms, despite their very nontraditional financial arrangements. Exchange is thus not gender neutral, Brines concludes, because the gender of the participants—and indeed, the gendered social system in which they live—does affect the processes of social exchange.

Interestingly, Brines's work (1994) suggests that "doing gender" may be more compelling for men than for women, at least when dividing household labor. She found that women's housework decreased steadily as their financial support for their husbands increased. However, men's housework patterns were not linear: men did less housework when they were the main breadwinner and when they were dependent on their wives for support, but more housework when financial contributions were relatively equal. Thus, women's housework patterns conform better to a traditional exchange model. Why might this be so? Perhaps, Brines speculates, because masculinity is associated with higher status and power than femininity. As a result, crossing gender lines by failing to be the family's main breadwinner threatens to lower men's status significantly. In order to compensate for not meeting these cultural expectations, men shore up their threatened masculinity by avoiding "feminine" housework (see also Greenstein 2000; Pitt and Borland 2008). Although crossing gender lines is not nearly as threatening for women as for men (because of the different valuations of masculinity and femininity), women nonetheless continue to do the bulk of the housework in these situations in order to bolster their femininity. At the same time, these women may be acting in ways that bolster their husbands' masculinity. The adequacy of a partner's gender performance may be seen as reflecting on one's self, hence there may be an indirect incentive to support his or her gender performance. Thus, doing gender is so compelling that it leads husbands and wives to divide housework in extremely inequitable ways—directly counter to the predictions of exchange theory.

Brines's (1993, 1994) theory seems to work when applied to heterosexual married couples. But what about people in other types of living situations? South and Spitze investigated this question in their 1994 study of the relationship between housework and marital status. Their findings support Brines's contention that doing gender plays an important role in the allocation of housework. In both married and cohabiting heterosexual couples, women did considerably more housework than men. Moreover, women and men in both types of couples differed in the types of work they did: whereas women performed mostly "female-typed" tasks (cooking, dishwashing, housecleaning, clothes washing and ironing, and shopping), men performed mainly "male-typed" tasks (outdoor chores and car maintenance). More recently, Davis, Greenstein, and Marks (2007) found similar results in a cross-national analysis of 17,636 individuals from twenty-eight nations. Taken together, these studies indicate that in heterosexual couples housework is tightly linked to gender in quality as well as quantity. However, the genderedness of tasks is more extreme in married couples: married women do far more housework than cohabiting women, and married men do far fewer female-typed tasks than cohabiting men—despite the fact that the household configuration is the same for both types of couples.

Thus, being married seems to make the gendered dynamics of household labor even more extreme. The total amount of housework performed in married households is considerably higher than in cohabitors' households;

moreover, the allocation of work is more deeply gendered. One explanation for these differences is that marriage brings with it an established set of gendered roles and expectations for each partner. In cohabiting heterosexual relationships, roles are less predetermined, and many of these expectations are less rigid. Aspects of coupled life that are routinized in marriage are available for negotiation in unmarried cohabiting couples. Thus, gender is invoked by cohabiting with someone, regardless of sex, but it is invoked even more by the institution of marriage.

If we limit our examination to heterosexual couples, however, we have no way of knowing whether the sex differences we see are the result of sex per se, or the result of some other factor. For example, because men often have greater power than women in intimate relationships, it is impossible to tell whether the gendered division of housework is due to sex differences or to power differences. Examining same-sex couples allows us to disentangle these factors and look at gender and power independently. (Note that looking at gay and lesbian couples does not "control" or eliminate the effects of sex or gender in these relationships. However, it does eliminate the sex *differences* present in heterosexual couples.)

As we have seen, heterosexual couples use sex to assign household tasks. Because same-sex couples do not have this built-in difference, they must use other criteria to allocate housework. Kurdek's (1993, 2004, 2005) research comparing gay, lesbian, and heterosexual married couples has found that the three types of couples have very different patterns of housework allocation. As described above, heterosexual couples tend to follow a pattern of segregation: one partner does the bulk of the household labor, while the other does much less, and the tasks of the two partners do not overlap. In contrast, gay male couples tend to follow a pattern of balance: as with heterosexual married couples, each partner specializes in particular tasks, but unlike married couples, each partner is responsible for an equal number of those tasks. Lesbians seem to follow a pattern of equality: most tasks are equally shared between the partners, either by doing them together or by alternating responsibility for each task. Although such a division is not entirely equal, these couples are "more likely than members of heterosexual couples to negotiate a balance between achieving a fair distribution of household labor and accommodating the different interests, skills, and work schedules of particular partners" (Kurdek 2005:252). We should note that Carrington (1999) suggests that the findings from quantitative studies such as Kurdek's may better describe the ideals held by same-sex couples than their actual behavior. His direct observations uncover considerable diversity in the division of household chores within same-sex couples, where the actual balance is a function of economic affluence, outside work demands, and time flexibility.

The question of why gay men and lesbians follow such different patterns is intriguing. The answer may have something to do with the different tasks boys and girls learn to do in their parents' households. A number of studies have found that girls do more household chores than do boys, spending up to twice as much time doing housework during the teenage years (Timmer, Eccles, and O'Brien 1985). Moreover, these tasks are strongly gender stereotyped (Berk 1985). When two women begin living together, each brings experience and skill at a wide range of household tasks. When two men begin living together, neither has the same kind of skill at the range of household chores. Developing expertise in particular areas may be easier than increasing skill in all areas; thus specialization may be the more logical outcome. In addition, Blumstein and Schwartz (1983) suggest that lesbians may be especially sensitive to any hint of inequality in task allocation because they reject "a role that has been symbolic of women's low status" (149). Thus, lesbians may self-consciously avoid doing gender in the way that heterosexual couples do because of a heightened sensitivity to power and inequity in relationships (Sullivan 2004). Moore's (2008) study of black lesbian stepfamilies highlights a notable exception. The biological mothers in these families often give their partner control of finances in exchange for more control in issues related to childrearing. This trade-off allows these women to maintain a sense of self as good mothers. Gay men, on the other hand, may not be as sensitized to these issues. It is interesting to note, however, that income seems to affect the division of household labor in the same way in all three types of couples—in each case, the partner with the higher income does less housework (Howard, Blumstein, and Schwartz 1986; Voicu, Voicu, and Strapcova 2008)—suggesting that power shapes exchange in same-sex as well as in cross-sex couples.

As Carrington (1999) notes, financial resources often determine whether the allocation of housework within a relationship is even necessary. Those couples who have greater financial resources can simply pay someone else to do their housework for them, avoiding (or at least minimizing) the issue altogether. However, even this contingency is itself deeply influenced by gender. Because of the gendered distribution of jobs and wealth, those couples who are able to afford this option are likely to include one or two men. In other words, heterosexual and gay male couples are likely to have greater financial resources than lesbian couples. Moreover, regardless of the sexual orientation and sex of the employer(s), the person they hire to do their housework is likely to be a woman—and a person of color. Finally, if a heterosexual couple does pay someone else to do their housework, the hiring and supervision of that person is assumed to be the responsibility of the woman.

A striking example of this assumption is the failed political nominations of Zoe Baird, Kimba Wood, and Linda Chavez. Baird was President Bill

Clinton's first choice for attorney general of the United States in 1993; her nomination was withdrawn after it was disclosed that she had hired two undocumented workers from Peru as household help. Wood, Clinton's next choice, was forced to withdraw for similar reasons, even though her hiring of an undocumented worker from Trinidad to care for her children was not illegal at the time. In 2001, President George W. Bush's nominee for secretary of labor, Linda Chavez, stepped down when a neighbor revealed that Chavez had taken in an undocumented Guatemalan woman, given her money, and assisted her in leaving an abusive relationship. Although the woman did not formally work in the household and therefore no law was broken, the incident compromised Chavez's image. Would these concerns have been raised if the nominees had been men? Probably not. As Kathleen Brown, treasurer of the state of California, noted during the Clinton administration, "For every man who has ever been confirmed to a Cabinet position, there has never been the notion of disclosure of his housekeeping arrangement, much less how much time he spent with his child. It has never been on anyone's mind. It just doesn't come up for male nominees to think about their pattern of child care as a matter for disclosure on an FBI search" (Manegold 1993:A6). Brown's point continues to resonate. The distribution of housework, even when it is performed by an employee, continues to be deeply influenced by gender, class, and race.

The various approaches to marital power described above suggest both the limitations and possibilities of social exchange theory. The theory itself is usually interpreted as gender neutral: men and women are assumed to behave similarly in similar situations, and no mention is made of the fact that their situations are not usually similar. Some research, of course, does consider gender, but usually in the form of sex differences. When such differences are found, there is usually little attempt to explain why they occur; interpretation is left open, implying that biological and social causes are equally plausible. This is the approach taken by early social exchange theory explanations of marital power. Men and women were assumed to exchange household labor for financial support; the fact that men are almost always the ones to contribute the income and women are almost always the ones to do the housework was not questioned.

In contrast, England and Farkas's work does take gender seriously. Socialization and/or ongoing social structural constraints are understood to be sources of gender differences that influence the outcomes of exchange. Brines's work goes even further, incorporating symbolic exchange and gendered social expectations in her account of marital behavior. Some writers, however, have criticized Brines for not going far enough. Hartmann (1993), for example, while lauding Brines's attention to gender, questions her neglect of factors such as sexuality and coercion. She writes, "How does meeting sexual needs complicate the negotiations between women and men over housework? Nor does Brines's review mention domestic violence or wife-battering, rather widespread male behavior that must surely affect the domestic division of labor. Approximately half of women's emergency room admissions are thought to result from battering by men. Evidence suggests that battering often begins when women transgress gender norms" (384). Hartmann's critique suggests that exchange theorists must expand their idea of resources and pay more attention to power if they are to understand real-world behavior.

It is important to note, however, that Brines's study is not an orthodox use of social exchange theory. Brines is really borrowing ideas from another social psychological theory—symbolic interactionism, which we take up in more detail in chapter 5—to fill in the gaps that exchange theory does not address. Traditional exchange theory is more concerned with concrete resources (whether material, such as money, or immaterial, such as status) and the way individuals use these resources to achieve their goals, than with the broader symbolic meaning of those resources. As a result, social exchange theory cannot fully explain the distribution of housework in nontraditional heterosexual couples. We now turn to justice and equity as another example of a topic in social exchange that has grappled with the question of gender (and its intersection with race and social class).

Example 2: Justice, Equity, and Social Exchange

On the morning of August 29, 2005, Hurricane Katrina made landfall along the Gulf Coast near New Orleans. Raging winds and tidal surges from the category 3 hurricane overtook levees protecting the city. Entire sections of the city were flooded, with the brunt of the damage taking place in poor, predominantly black neighborhoods. Hundreds of people were killed and many more left homeless. For several weeks, the city was virtually paralyzed, as frantic rescue efforts continued and the nation struggled to deal with the emergency.

During those first few days, basic resources such as food and clean water were scarce. Numerous media accounts centered on the inadequacy of federal aid, while simultaneously questioning victims' own attempts to scavenge for supplies in the abandoned city (Fothergill and Peek forthcoming). In this situation—similar to what we saw following the 2007 tsunami in Thailand and the 2010 earthquake in Haiti—when food is scarce and everyone is hungry, how should food be distributed? What is a fair allocation of a limited resource? This question addresses notions of *justice*, or fairness, which is another major topic of study in social exchange. Issues of justice arise at all levels of social life, from the interpersonal (e.g., the allocation of food in a family, grades in a class, or salaries in an office) to the societal (e.g., the distribution of income or jobs among various groups in a nation, the use of affirmative action to counter past discrimination, or the use of the death penalty to punish the most heinous crimes). In each of these arenas, however, justice is an inherently subjective—and cognitive—concept: at issue are people's *perceptions* of fairness. There are many ways in which resources and punishments could be distributed, but not all of these are perceived to be fair. That is not to say that individuals' perceptions are idiosyncratic, however. Social norms strongly influence perceptions of justice. In general, people tend to feel that a situation is just when the actual distribution of rewards and punishments matches their expectations about what they deserve and what they are entitled to. These expectations vary depending on the situation, the individual actors involved, their social positions, and the social norms deemed relevant.

Distribution rule preferences   According to Eckhoff (1974), there are five "distribution rules" that are commonly used to allocate resources among individuals or groups. First, resources can be divided *equally* among individuals. For example, food and fresh water in the aftermath of a natural disaster such as Hurricane Katrina could be divided into equal portions, and one portion distributed to each person. Second, resources can be allocated to individuals on the basis of *need*, such that those who have the greatest need receive the most resources. Thus, after the hurricane, those people who were bigger, hungrier, injured, ill, or otherwise more in need of sustenance would get the most food. Third, an assessment can be made of the contributions each person has made to the group, and resources allocated relative to those contributions, according to the principle of *equity*. The person who has contributed the most—rescued the most hurricane survivors, or carried the most fresh water back to the group—would get the largest share of the food. Fourth, resources can be allocated according to *status*, such that those with higher status (in this case, perhaps men, economically privileged, or community leaders) receive a greater share of the scarce resources. Finally, fair procedures (such as drawing straws or participating in a contest) can be established such that each person has an *equal opportunity* to get the food, although the final outcomes may not in fact be equal.

Which of these rules will apply in a given situation? Most studies of this question involve experiments in which subjects are asked to allocate some reward (usually money) between themselves and another person based on their performance on some task. These experiments have found that a range of factors affect people's preferences for various distribution rules (Deutsch 1975; Mikula 1980). These experimental studies are reinforced by results of large-scale stratification surveys (e.g., Kluegel and Smith 1986) that investi-gate people's ideas about fairness and inequality.

First, characteristics of the relationship are important. When the relation-ship is one of friendship and intimacy, when there is a great deal of similarity between individuals, and/or when there is a high expectation of future in-teraction, people prefer to use the equality rule (Greenberg 1978; Leventhal, Karuza, and Fry 1980). Equality rules are also preferred when performance is attributed to luck or other external factors beyond an individual's control rather than to individual effort (Wittig, Marks, and Jones 1981), and when preferences have to be stated publicly (Major and Adams 1983). However, when the welfare of individuals is the primary goal or when individuals are dependent on the group for essential needs (as in a family), the need rule is preferred. Notice that in all of these situations, individuals are interdepen-dent—for friendship, support, or resources. In impersonal situations, in con-trast—when the parties do not know each other and do not expect to interact in the future or when preferences are private—individuals tend to base their preferences on their own self-interest. In addition, those who perform well prefer equity rules, whereas those who perform poorly prefer equality rules (Hegtvedt and Markovsky 1995).

Other kinds of contextual factors also affect distribution rule preferences. For example, a number of studies have found cultural differences in rule pref-erences. In particular, members of collectively oriented Asian cultures (e.g., China, Japan, or India) prefer equality or need-based rules; members of indi-vidually oriented Western cultures (e.g., Australia or the United States) prefer equity-based rules (Kashima et al. 1988; Leung and Bond 1984; Murphy-Berman et al. 1984). This preference extends across both interpersonal and macrolevel situations; for example, individuals in the United States also tend to believe that unequal distributions of economic wealth (i.e., distribu-tions believed to be based on equity) are fair because the economic system is perceived to allow individuals ample opportunity to improve their position through hard work (e.g., Kluegel and Smith 1986).

Not all U.S. citizens believe equally strongly in this "dominant ideology" of economic opportunity, however. An individual's position in various strati-fication hierarchies has also been found to affect preferences for particular distribution rules. In exchange experiments, people in advantaged or pow-erful positions are likely to perceive an unequal distribution as just, while those in disadvantaged positions are more likely to feel it is unjust (Cook and Hegtvedt 1986; Molm 2006; Stolte 1987). These experimental findings are echoed by studies of perceptions of fairness outside the laboratory. For example, people in lower social classes are less likely to perceive inequality to be fair (e.g., Robinson and Bell 1978) and more likely to prefer an economic distribution based on need than are people in upper classes (Form and Hanson 1985; Kluegel and Smith 1986). People in lower socioeconomic groups are also less likely to believe that people in general, and themselves in particular, have a fair opportunity to get ahead (Kluegel and Smith 1986). Race and gender have also been found to affect perceptions of inequality and fairness. Kluegel and Smith (1986) report that blacks are far more likely than whites to express doubts about the fairness of the American stratification system. Their study also found similar, although smaller, differences between women and men: in general, women believed the economic system to be less fair than did men. In addition, race, sex, and class interact to produce variation in belief among groups. Wealthier whites (and, to a lesser extent, wealthier blacks) expressed more faith in the economic system than did poorer whites and blacks. Black men perceived more opportunities for blacks and the poor than did black women.

Despite these differences, however, faith in the existing system of economic distribution is surprisingly high. In every social group, most respondents in this study did not question the dominant ideology that economic inequality is necessary and fair and that individuals are responsible for their economic position. Although they may question the fairness of the economic system for specific groups (e.g., people of color, women, or the poor) or for themselves as individuals, "most Americans believe that economic inequality is just in principle, and correspondingly, endorse individual and societal equity as just criteria for the distribution of income" (Kluegel and Smith 1986:141).

We must note, however, that much of this research on group differences in stratification beliefs has been conducted outside the mainstream of social psychology. In particular, sociologists have been much more actively interested in these questions than have psychologists. Within social psychology, most of the research on group differences has focused on sex differences, perhaps because researchers have fewer qualms about exposing power differences between men and women than between racial categories, and are more comfortable attributing these differences to "innate" qualities of women and men. Many studies (Kahn, Nelson, and Gaeddert 1980; Major and Deaux 1982) find gender differences in rule preferences:

> When asked to split rewards between themselves and a partner with performance inferior to theirs, men tend to allocate the rewards equitably (i.e., in proportion to inputs or performance) whereas women tend to allocate the rewards equally. When the partner's performance is superior to theirs, both men and women tend to divide rewards equitably, but women generally take less for themselves than men do. Even when the allocator's and partner's performances are equal . . . women tend to take less reward for themselves and give more to their partners than men do. (Major 1987:126)

In short, women seem to engage in "hyperpoliteness," always allocating less to themselves than do men.

How can these differences in allocation be explained? Kahn and Gaeddert (1985) conclude that there are at least four explanations. The first proposes that both men and women use the equity rule when allocating resources, but each sex (for unspecified reasons) considers different factors to be relevant when calculating investments. For example, men may consider skill to be more relevant, while women may consider participation or effort to be more relevant.

A second approach (e.g., Deaux 1976; Gager and Hohmann-Marriott 2006; Kahn et al. 1980; Sampson 1975) takes at face value the claim that women and men prefer different distribution rules and focuses instead on the causes for this difference. Males and females, according to this approach, have different desires, goals, and motivations (as a result of biology or socialization). For example, a great deal of research has suggested that men tend to be *agentic*—in other words, their motives center on achievement and success. Women, in contrast, tend to be more *communal*, having motives that focus on interpersonal relationships, intimacy, and attachment (Carlson 1971). These different motives lead to different allocation strategies: agentic goals are best met through equity, and communal goals through equality.

As we have noted throughout this book, however, an observation of gender differences does not mean that sex itself is the causal variable. A more sophisticated approach to gender takes a correlation between sex and other variables as something to be explained, rather than as an explanation in itself. For example, Watts, Messe, and Vallacher (1982) tried to disentangle the relationship between sex, motivation, and the distribution of resources. They found that agentic individuals, regardless of their sex, distributed rewards more competitively. In contrast, those who had a communal orientation distributed rewards more equally. The researchers concluded that although men and women tended to allocate rewards differently, the cause was not sex per se, but sex-related differences in agentic/communal motives.

A third perspective suggests that other researchers have overlooked an important confounding variable in allocation research: the sex of the stimulus person (i.e., the person with whom the subject is interacting in an experiment). Most allocation research has been based on same-sex dyads: men are asked to interact with other men and women with other women. This perspective suggests that the sex differences in allocation found in these experiments are due not to the sex of the subject but to the sex of the stimulus person (Hansen and O'Leary 1983). In other words, the differences observed between male and female allocators are due not to some internal difference between males and females but rather to social expectations about how people (of either sex) should interact with males and females. As Kahn and Gaeddert (1985) summarize this hypothesis, "Women and men do not necessarily have different conceptions of how to solve the distribution problem, but all people solve the problem differently when they interact with women than when they interact with men" (133).

Finally, the fourth perspective argues that power and status are the real confounding variables in studies of justice (Lips and Lawson 2009; Meeker and Weitzel-O'Neill 1977; Unger 1976, 1978). As noted earlier, those in advantaged positions in a stratification system tend to prefer distribution rules based on equity, whereas those in less advantaged positions tend to prefer equality or need-based rules. Because gender and power are correlated, we see a similar difference in preference for distribution rules. Thus, again, gender differences are not the result of sex per se but of the fact that men tend to be more powerful than women.

In summary, distribution rule preferences seem to vary depending on the characteristics and relationship of the persons involved, the goals of the distribution, and the social context. The observation of gender differences in these experiments has stimulated extensive research; however, exploring these differences further has demonstrated that exchanges are far from gender neutral. The same conclusion can be drawn from research on perceptions of fairness, to which we now turn.

The equity of exchange   Matching a given distribution rule does not ensure that a situation will be perceived as fair. As we noted above, many objectively equal situations are perceived as unfair, and many unequal situations are widely perceived to be just. In other cases, it is difficult to assess what factors should be considered in determining fairness. How are perceptions of fairness developed?

The distribution of housework is an example of a seemingly unfair exchange. As we discussed earlier, research on heterosexual couples consistently shows that women perform far more housework than men do, regardless of the amount of paid work either partner does outside the home. Is this situation fair? If we use a principle of equality to evaluate this situation, it is clearly not fair; housework is rarely distributed equally. Nor is housework distributed according to need or equal opportunity. If we examine traditional couples in which the man works for pay outside the home and the woman works inside the home, it can appear that housework is distributed according to a principle of equity: the person who contributes more economic support to the household is rewarded by being relieved of household chores. However, if we look at dual-earner couples, the principle of equity breaks down. Even when both partners work an equal number of hours outside the home, wives do the majority of the housework. And, as Brines found, when wives are the main breadwinner for the family, their husbands do even less housework than other married men. The distribution of housework, then, does not seem to follow any rule of just distribution.

However, as we noted above, justice is based on subjective perceptions of fairness rather than objective distributions of time or money. Thus, it is appropriate to ask whether women (or men) feel that this skewed distribution of labor is unfair. Interestingly, the answer to this question appears to be no. Although recent studies are beginning to report increased perceptions of unfairness (Coltrane 2000; Forry, Leslie, and Letiecq 2007), both women and men have generally reported that they are satisfied with the existing distribution of housework in their families, even though they recognize that it may be inequitable (Major 1993; Spitze 1988; Thompson 1991). A similar statement has held true for women's pay in the work world: although women consistently earn less than men for comparable jobs, many report very little sense of injustice (Buchanan 2008; Crosby 1982; Major 1987, 1989).

How can this be? How can a situation that appears unfair according to every rule of justice discussed above be considered fair by the people involved? The traditional explanation for this phenomenon attributes this sense of fairness to sex differences: men and women are simply different and want different things from their work and family relationships. In other words, women simply enjoy housework, or are more concerned with the communal good, or wish to maximize the interpersonal harmony of their relationships; men, in contrast, like housework less, are less competent at it, are more concerned with agentic goals, and wish to maximize material rewards.

Other scholars propose a different explanation, which looks outside the relationship (Buchanan 2008; Gager and Hohmann-Marritott 2006; Litzler and Brines 2005; Major 1987, 1993; Thompson 1991). Major (1993), for example, suggests that evaluations of fairness do not simply take into account the distribution of rewards within a particular relationship, but also include comparisons to other relationships and existing social norms, as well as an assessment of the fairness of the procedures used to allocate labor. Major (1987) proposes "that women and men use different comparative referents when they evaluate their existing outcomes or when they estimate what they deserve or are entitled to receive" (125). Specifically, they use different *social comparisons*: they compare their contribution to housework not with their spouses, but with others of the same sex. Thus,

> to the extent that wives compare their family work load with that of other women, rather than that of their husbands, or other men, they may feel that they are doing the amount of work that they should. Similarly, to the extent that wives compare their husbands' family work with the amount of work done by

other husbands, rather than with the amount of work done by themselves, they may feel that their husband is doing no less than he should. (Major 1993:148–49)

Normative comparisons also come into play when evaluating the household division of labor. According to this view, "awareness of what is a socially acceptable or appropriate distribution creates the expectation that this is the level or distribution one is entitled to" (Major 1993:50). Despite changes in gender expectations over the last several decades, research shows that both women and men still consider housework to be "women's work" (Coltrane 2000; Greenstein 1996; Thompson and Walker 1989; Tichenor 2005). Thus, women may feel that an unequal distribution of labor is fair because it accords with prevailing gender norms.

Third, *feasibility comparisons* play a role in perceptions of fairness. Exchange theorists argue that the availability of attractive alternatives is important when evaluating a situation. Wives, in particular, may evaluate unequal distributions of labor as fair relative to the possible alternatives—which may involve giving up paid employment (Spitze 1988), dealing with increased marital conflict (Thompson and Walker 1989), or even divorce (Litzler and Brines 2005).

Finally, self-comparisons, or comparisons of current outcomes with outcomes received in the past, are also relevant. Research shows that sex differences in housework exist even for boys and girls living in their parents' homes (South and Spitze 1994); thus women's greater contribution may be proportional to their contributions in other settings. Because women's housework level decreases when they are employed (although men's does not increase to compensate), women who work outside the home may feel that their contribution to housework is fair because they have done more in the past.

Major also believes that notions of fairness are affected by the perceived legitimacy of allocation procedures. For example, if women believe they had a "voice" in the decision-making process that led to the existing distribution or if they believe some goal other than fairness is served by the distribution (e.g., communal welfare, closeness, or caring), they may believe an objectively unjust distribution to be fair. Moreover, Wilkie, Ferree, and Ratcliff (1998) note that the meaning attributed to work inside and outside of the home is important (see also Ferree 1991; Ferree and Hall 2000). In households in which wives work outside the home, their income is frequently considered "supplementary," even if it is crucial to the family's economic survival. Men are still considered to have primary responsibility for breadwinning, regardless of the wife's income. These conceptions of responsibility may legitimize the uneven division of labor.

Thus, attempting to understand the gendered dynamics of housework exposes some of the weaknesses of social exchange theory. To explain differences in perceptions of just distributions of housework, scholars have been forced to go far afield from the tenets of exchange theory. Specifically, understanding perceptions of justice necessitates understanding how people think about what is fair. The types of cognition included in explanations for justice preferences go far beyond consideration and choice, the cognitive processes usually included in exchange theory models. The example of justice, like the example of the household division of labor, suggests that a synthesis of multiple theories may be more powerful than any single theory alone.

Conclusions

Although social exchange theory is based on principles assumed to be gender neutral, researchers have found that human behavior does not always conform to these principles. Gender frequently throws a wrench into the workings of the theory, and explaining sex differences in behavior may require bringing in other theories, such as social cognition and symbolic interactionism. We explore these theories further in the following chapters.

Social exchange theory could be combined with any of the perspectives on gender discussed in chapter 2. Women and men might behave differently because they are innately different, because they have been socialized differently, or because they find themselves in different structural positions. Indeed, social exchange theory is strongest in its conceptualization of social structure as a primary determinant of human behavior. Social exchange theory also could be compatible with social constructionist approaches to gender if it were combined with other theories that attend to the symbolic realm. Brines (1993, 1994), for example, integrates exchange theory with symbolic interactionism, arguing that men and women behave differently because they are negotiating not only economic resources but also gender expectations and performances.

A number of other theorists have seen the same potential for combining social exchange theory and symbolic interactionism. Triandis (1976), for example, questions exchange theory's neglect of the question of value. What do people find rewarding? How can we account for differences and similarities between people in their perceptions of rewards and costs? Triandis argues that in order to answer these questions, we must look beyond social exchange theory and explore the meaning of particular resources, a task for which symbolic interactionism is well suited, as we discuss further in chapter 5. Kollock and O'Brien (1992) note the ways in which social exchanges are themselves socially constructed: "Minds are private and reliable information is a costly commodity. For these reasons information asymmetries often exist between exchange partners" (89). As a result, exchange partners must constantly gather information about the resources of their exchange partners, and at the same time control the information they provide to others about their own resources. Stolte, Fine, and Cook (2001) add that power-disadvantaged individuals may collectively define an exchange situation as unsatisfactory and through joint action build coalitions against the power advantaged. Management of impressions and definitions of situations, however, are the realm of symbolic interactionism, not exchange theory. Thus, Kollock and O'Brien assert that a combination of these two theories is more powerful than social exchange theory alone.

With its emphasis on relationships, structure, interdependence, and power, social exchange theory has the potential to add a great deal to our understanding of gender. However, social exchange *research* has not yet explored this potential. Although some versions of the theory focus on power as a central determinant of social behavior, in practice, researchers have ignored the social statuses—such as gender, race, and class—that are central to power in the world outside the experimental laboratory. Indeed, Turner (1982) notes that Marx's theory of class conflict is "a variety of exchange theory" (231), yet social exchange theorists have rarely examined social class in any real-world sense.

Why is there such a disjuncture between social exchange theory and research? We have discussed one reason above: a dominant research paradigm that emphasizes tightly controlled research procedures and discrete, easily measurable variables. Although the theory focuses on relationships between people, the experimental procedures typically sanitize interaction to such an extent that the subjects may not ever see, hear, or talk to each other. As a result, the *process* of interaction—which might be described as the process of "doing exchange"—disappears. In addition, exchange researchers tend to focus on individual-level manifestations of supposedly multilevel processes and limit their analyses to dyadic or small-group interaction rather than examining social groups, organizations, and institutions. Further, we speculate that social exchange theory (like other contemporary scholarship) is influenced by its location within a capitalist market economy. The assumptions inherent in this kind of economic system tend to shift researchers' attention toward marketlike transactions between individuals and away from potential unfairness and inequality.

Finally, exchange theory performs best when analyzing the exchange of quantifiable factors, such as dollars of income or hours of housework. As we have seen, the theory proves more problematic when symbolic factors, such as the value of doing gender (or race or class) appropriately, are considered. This is not to imply that gender, race, and class are *only* symbolic markers. Each has very real material consequences, for both individuals and social groups. Nonetheless, while it is relatively easy to include rudimentary measures of gender, race, and class in exchange studies (by measuring the subject's sex, racial category, and dollars of income or occupation), capturing the full symbolic import of these categories is far more difficult. Factors such as gender identity or race-based prejudice do not fit easily into exchange theory equations, and thus the symbolic meanings of group membership are often neglected.

Social exchange theory does not address any of these social positions in great depth, but race has been particularly invisible. The most recent review of exchange theory and research (Cook and Rice 2003) includes no mention of race or ethnicity in the twenty-six-page chapter. This gap seems curious, particularly given exchange theory's focus on social structure and power. We suggest two explanations for the invisibility of race in social exchange theory.

First, exchange theory is especially ill-equipped to deal with race because of the theory's conceptualization of social actors. According to exchange theory, individuals come to the marketplace of interaction essentially as equals. They may have different amounts or types of resources or different structural positions, but they are otherwise interchangeable. The theory implies that these resources and positions are not permanently attached to individuals; they are malleable and transferable. The meanings of these resources, and other personal or group characteristics of individuals, are not central. This allows the exchange theorist to ignore the more insidious consequences of social positions. According to exchange theory, women and men, whites and people of color, people from the working class and people from the upper class, appear different only insofar as they hold different resources. This approach fits neatly with what Frankenberg has called "color evasion." She writes, "For many people in the United States . . . 'color-blindness'—a mode of thinking about race organized around an effort not to 'see,' or at any rate not to acknowledge, race differences—continues to be the 'polite' language of race" (142; see also Bonilla-Silva 2006). More than any other social psychological theory, the assumptions of exchange theory mirror this practice of color evasion; race becomes essentially invisible and unexamined.

Second, the neglect of race (and class) in social exchange research parallels their neglect throughout social psychology and academia more generally. As we noted in chapter 2, this pattern is due in part to the composition of the academy: although the proportion of women faculty and students has increased dramatically in recent years, the proportion of people of color and members of the poor and working classes working as professional academics and researchers remains shockingly low. Although Marxist academics have always believed social class to be central to understanding social life, their influence on other scholars has been relatively limited. Although many social science disciplines have devoted considerably more attention to race, class, and gender than in previous years, there is still dramatically more to be done.

As we have noted, social exchange theory has a number of significant problems, as well as a number of potential strengths. Nonetheless, it remains one of the most influential theories in social psychology and the social sciences more generally. On the basis of our discussion above, we suggest that the most fruitful direction for social exchange theory may involve integration with other social psychological theories. We now turn to one such theory: social cognition.

Note

1. In fact, Bandura (1986) has renamed his theory "social cognitive theory" to more precisely reflect its model of behavior.

4

Social Cognition

O N THE MORNING OF SEPTEMBER 11, 2001, nineteen members of al-Qaeda, an Islamist extremist organization guided by Osama bin Laden's call for violent attacks against the United States, boarded four American commercial passenger airplanes. The men hijacked each plane. Over the next two hours, the hijackers crashed two planes into the Twin Towers of the World Trade Center and another into the Pentagon. The fourth plane crashed in a field in rural Pennsylvania while passengers on board fought to take back the plane. These attacks produced over three thousand civilian deaths and over six thousand injuries.[1]

The September 11 attacks created a climate of intense distrust and suspicion of those from Arab and Islamic backgrounds. The U.S. government responded with the USA PATRIOT Act, which reduced civil liberties and formed the Department of Homeland Security with which to wage a "war on terror." Using racial profiling techniques permitted under this new policy, law enforcement officers removed dozens of "suspicious" individuals from planes and detained them. During the brief two months following the attacks, over five hundred incidents of violence in the United States directed toward people of Middle Eastern descent were reported to the American Arab Anti-Discrimination Committee. Although three years had passed since the terrorist attacks, fear and suspicion linger, as Rhonda Roumani (2004) describes in an autobiographical account:

A few weeks ago, I boarded a Virgin Atlantic flight from Los Angeles to London. Behind me sat an Egyptian man and his son. They spoke Arabic and were obviously somewhat devout—I heard Muslim phrases such as Insha'allah (God willing) echoing behind me.

I fly frequently—across the United States, across the Atlantic. Over the last few years, I have flown from New York to Los Angeles, from Los Angeles to London, from London to Beirut countless times. I have never worried or felt fear.

But this time was different. The man and his son had sparked suspicion in me. I found myself listening to their conversation. Something troubled me, but I wasn't sure what—so I decided to monitor them. I understand Arabic. If something was up, I would know.

Maybe it was the harrowing details of the September 11 Commission Report released before my departure. Reading transcripts of passengers' conversations with loved ones during the last minutes of the hijacked planes had made my stomach turn. On Sept. 11, 2001, I was a graduate student in New York City. I had seen the smoke billowing from the two towers that I had used as my compass in the city—and I saw them collapse.

Or maybe it was the security alerts issued in the days before I left Los Angeles—we're at a yellow alert, orange alert. No, wait—we're back at yellow. No, orange. Or the incessant talk of an "imminent attack."

Soon after take-off, the older man got up and took out a cell phone. My heart started beating faster. Strange behavior?

I paused, then turned around and spoke to them. "Cell phones aren't allowed in the middle of the flights," I told him in Arabic.

He was surprised. Maybe I was the one who was acting strange. After all, I had been watching them through the corner of my eye, listening to them over the whispers of passengers and announcements over the loud speaker.

"Yes, I know. We are not using them. Where are you from?"

"I am originally Syrian," I said.

He replied with a smile.

We spoke briefly. By then, I was calm, but troubled. I—an American Muslim, an Arab-American, a Syrian-American—had felt suspicious of my own people. Was I guilty of profiling—of accusing innocents of "Flying While Arab?"

Definition

This account illustrates many of the features of social cognition, the perspective we present in this chapter. In reacting to the man and his son, Roumani drew on cognitive schemas about race, ethnicity, and gender to form particular judgments—generalizations about broad social categories, evaluations of the men's character and behavior, inferences regarding their intentions, and assessments about the appropriateness of response (both hers and theirs). Cognitive schemas, cognitive judgments, and the processes through which we form those judgments: these are the components of social cognition. *Social cognition* is a theory of how we process information; the term refers both to the name of the theory and to the process itself. Individual reactions to historical events such as those in the situation above reflect the social significance of cognition in everyday life.

Traditionally, social cognition has emphasized psychological, intra-individual aspects of human thought. Psychologists Fiske and Taylor (1991) define social cognition as "the study of how people make sense of other people and themselves" (1). Social cognition describes the elements of thought and how those elements come into play as people process the rich array of social information they encounter daily. Years of research and theorizing have led to the development of an increasingly sophisticated cognitive model. Beginning in the 1950s, scholars characterized individuals as *consistency seekers*, who search for consistency between their thoughts and behaviors. In a classic study, Festinger and Carlsmith (1959), for example, paid individuals either $1 or $20 to complete a boring task and to tell another person that it was enjoyable and interesting. The results showed that respondents who were paid $1 were more likely than those paid $20 to report that they enjoyed the task, suggesting their greater need to reduce cognitive dissonance (i.e., to have consistency between their belief and behavior). By the 1970s, social psychologists began to utilize the metaphor of the *naive scientist* to describe the processes through which people gather information about the social world to reach decisions. This model suggests laypeople undertake many of the same steps that scientists use. The model of the *cognitive miser* highlighted the limitations of social cognition, arguing that individuals have a limited capacity to deal with the vast amount of information available to them. Thus, humans must rely on numerous cognitive shortcuts such as heuristics to guide decision-making in situations of uncertainty (Tversky and Kahneman 1982). More recent models from the 1990s emphasized other strategies that bear on cognitive processes. The *motivated tactician* model suggests that individuals have multiple strategies, including goals, emotions, evaluations, and needs, which shape how they process information and make decisions (Higgins 1997; Higgins and Molden 2003). Most recently, social psychologists characterize individuals as *activated actors*, who perceive and respond—often outside of their own awareness—to cues from the social environment. This line of research draws on new technology that allows researchers to assess how individuals respond to a condition within a fraction of a second, identifying attitudes that might otherwise remain unseen. Working in this tradition, Greenwald, Smith, and colleagues (2009) assessed voting preferences among registered voters a week before the 2008 presidential election. They found that voters' implicit racial attitudes—measured by rapid responses to combinations of focal words and objects on a computer screen—better predicted voting preference than other leading constructs. The *activated actor* incorporates assumptions from prior models and harnesses new technologies to provide a fuller, more sophisticated cognitive model than ever before. Social cognition research has thus begun to pay more attention to the social contexts in which people think (Howard and Renfrow 2003).

As we present the key principles of social cognition, we pay special attention to the *social* aspects of thought. We consider not only the elements and organization of human thought, but also how knowledge is created, shared, affirmed, and changed. We address both the major steps in processing information and how social forces shape these processes. We emphasize how individual cognitive processes shape social action. We weave into our discussion examples that illustrate the treatment of gender, in particular its intersections with race, class, and sexuality, in social cognition.

Working Assumptions of Social Cognition

In the previous chapter we noted that behaviorism does not attend to cognition; the effect of the environment on behavior is assumed to be unmediated by thought. In contrast, social cognition assumes that how we think about the world around us shapes how we feel and how we behave. One interpretation of the play *Oleanna*, for example, suggests that the student does not immediately perceive the professor's embrace as inappropriate; it is only after she thinks about it, and thinks about it within particular cognitive frameworks provided to her by her friends, that she decides she has been sexually harassed.

If behavior depends on human thought, our minds must be continually active. At times, thought is deliberate, perhaps the result of our goals or needs in the situation. At other times, however, thought may be automatic, the near instantaneous response to cues in our social environment. These automatic responses often occur outside of our awareness. In either case, our behavior is mediated by thought. Furthermore, human cognitive capacities are limited. We cannot possibly attend to or remember all the information to which we are exposed in the course of daily life. Were we to try, we would experience "cognitive overload." Anyone who has ever crammed for an exam or tried to coordinate too many professional and family commitments has experienced this state. Thus, a second assumption of social cognition is that we often streamline information to manage the demands of everyday interaction. As we shall see, the metaphor of the human being as cognitive miser underlies many of the principles of social cognition.

One of the ways we manage this need for cognitive efficiency is by categorizing information; dissimilar information is split into distinct categories and similar information is lumped together into mental clusters (Zerubavel 1996). We categorize information about people, objects, and situations before we store it in memory, retrieve it from memory, or use this information in forming judgments. Categories allow us to organize, store, and retrieve information efficiently. Without categorization, we would experience cognitive overload. There are, of course, costs to categorization. The very act of categorizing people means defining them in terms of a subset of their characteristics, whether this includes their accent, the fact that they have children, or their racial identities. To categorize is usually to reduce; potentially valuable information is lost in such summaries. Moreover, to categorize is also often to evaluate. Categorization is almost always accompanied by evaluations of some categories as better or worse than others, particularly when they refer to human groups. These evaluations may well reflect prevailing political values; they are not inherent to the process of categorization. Nonetheless, the two almost always go together. Because categorization may be cognitively unavoidable, exploring how the principles of categorization could be used to undermine systematic devaluation of certain groups may be more fruitful than trying to eliminate this process.

Thus, social cognition rests on three assumptions: first, that the influence of the social environment on human behavior is mediated by active or automatic thought; second, that the limits of human cognitive capacities lead us to behave as cognitive misers; and third, that this need for cognitive efficiency leads to a fundamental reliance on categorization. In the next section, we describe the basic building blocks of human thought, cognitive structures. These structures provide the bases for categorization.

The Organization of Thought

Early approaches to social cognition identified beliefs, attitudes, and values as the major elements of thought (Bem 1970). These constructs emphasize the content and evaluation of thought, rather than its organization. While research on attitudes continues, much contemporary social cognition research emphasizes instead the organization of thought in cognitive structures; social schemas are the primary form of cognitive structure. Gender has been an important theme in both approaches. We begin by discussing attitudes, emphasizing attitudes about significant social categories, and then turn to an extended discussion of social schemas.

Attitudes

Attitudes are evaluations of a specific object or concept. Social psychologists posit that attitudes conform to a principle of consistency: social actors are motivated to seek consistency among our attitudes, feelings, and behaviors (Festinger 1957). Attitudes, therefore, should shape human behavior. If a prospective air passenger has a strong negative attitude toward men of Middle Eastern descent, coupled with the belief that most Muslims are fundamental extremists, for example, we might assume that these attitudes would shape whether this passenger attends to presumably Muslim copassengers and alerts the flight crew of their ostensibly suspicious actions. Research results, however, have never fully supported the prediction of attitude-behavior consistency. In an early review of research in this area, Wicker (1969) reported that attitudes explained only 10 percent of the variability in behavior. Although social psychologists are considerably better able to predict behavior from attitudes today than they were in the 1960s (due primarily to more adequate measurement procedures), it is clear that knowledge of attitudes and other cognitions may be necessary, but not sufficient, to predict behavior (Maio et al. 2003). The immediacy of situations and factors such as the opinions of others also shape human behavior, as examples in the next section illustrate, sometimes overriding the effects of individual attitudes.

Social psychologists have developed measures of attitudes toward members of particular social categories. Attitudes toward both women and blacks began to receive attention in the 1970s, in response to the civil rights and women's movements. Measures such as the Attitudes Toward Women Scale, or ATW (Spence and Helmreich 1972, 1978), are among the most widely used of the thousands of social psychological scales. Attitudes toward women have been assessed in terms of the endorsement of gender-prescribed roles. Take, for example, an item from the ATW: "Women should be concerned with their duties of childbearing and house tending, rather than with desires for professional and business careers." More recently, Glick and Fiske's (1996) Ambivalent Sexism Inventory distinguishes between hostile (e.g., resentful attitudes such as "women seek to gain power by getting control over men") and benevolent (e.g., paternalistic attitudes such as "women should be cherished and protected by men") attitudes toward women. Across studies, women tend to have less traditional attitudes than men do on such scales; in recent years, however, the distance between men and women's scores appears to be shrinking (Carter, Corra, and Carter 2009).

Interestingly, attitudes toward blacks have focused not on role-based prescriptions of behavior, but rather on general evaluations. One prong of this research has focused on attitudes of members of various racial minority groups toward their own and other racial groups. For example, the literature on children's racial attitudes (Stephan and Rosenfield 1982) shows that both white and black children attribute positive traits (e.g., clean, nice, smart) more often to whites than they do to blacks; this pattern is stronger among white children than among black children, however, and blacks' tendency to follow this pattern declines with age. Bryson (1998) presented black and white college students with his Attitudes Towards Black Males Scale and found significant racial differences in attitudes regarding black men's intellectual abilities, sociability, and unfair treatment by the criminal justice system; blacks expressed more positive attitudes toward black men than did whites. More recently, Persson and Musher-Eizenman (2005) assessed undergraduate attitudes toward blacks and Arabs immediately following the September 11 attacks and again one year later. At both times, students expressed more hostility toward Arabs than toward blacks, and this pattern, at least in the short term, was correlated with self-reports of media exposure (e.g., Internet, television, newspapers, and radio). Those who expressed more hostility to Arabs also reported higher media exposure.

A second prong of work on racial attitudes addresses the changing nature of racism. Focusing on relations between blacks and whites, Sears (1988), for example, is one of many who have suggested that "symbolic racism" (antiblack sentiment and beliefs that blacks violate American values of self-reliance, work ethic, and discipline) is replacing "old-fashioned racism," or open bigotry. Symbolic racism is a set of attitudes distinct from ideological conservativism and antiegalitarianism, and it takes on both individual and institutional forms (Bonilla-Silva 2006; Tarman and Sears 2005). Research on attitudes toward blacks tends to be oriented to real-world social conflicts; research on attitudes toward women, in contrast, emphasizes accommodation to social roles. Note that both literatures focus on attitudes toward those in the less powerful position of a social category—women in a gender system, blacks in a racial system. Attitudes about men and about whites have received considerably less attention.

Social Schemas

Attitudes emphasize the content of thought and the evaluation of that content. *Cognitive schemas*, in contrast, emphasize the organization of social information. Schemas store and organize information about a particular object or concept. A schema for one's mother, for example, includes what one perceives as her typical attributes, ways of behaving, common emotions, interactional styles, and the relationships among these. Schemas are abstract. They serve as theories, as preconceptions that drive cognitive processes. The construction of social schemas is precisely what allows us to think as cognitive misers. Through schemas, people simplify reality, interpreting specific instances in light of a general category. We create schemas for other persons, for ourselves, for social groups, and for social situations.

Schemas are vital for processing information. Schemas influence what information we attend to and what information we do not "see" in social situations. Schemas shape the storage and retrieval of information from memory; we store new information in categories determined by our existing schemas, and we retrieve already stored information from schemas relevant to the situation. Cognitive schemas about the professor-student relationship, for example, may guide some viewers of *Oleanna* to almost not notice the short embrace in scene 1. To those who view professors primarily as mentors, this gesture appears to be a supportive hug. Viewers whose schemas about the professor-student relationship emphasize the potential abuse of power differences may perceive this gesture as a sexual advance. What each viewer perceives will dictate how she or he responds later in the play. As we combine new and existing information to make inferences, schemas guide what information we select and how we form judgments. Those who have a well-developed cognitive schema for terrorist, for example, are likely to engage in the type of racial profiling described by Roumani by attending to the language someone is speaking, references to *Allah*, and "suspicious" cell phone behavior; at the same time, such onlookers may overlook or even ignore information inconsistent with this impression (e.g., a loving father traveling with his son).

Thus, we rely heavily on preexisting schemas both when we encounter new information and when we interact in familiar situations. One consequence of this reliance is what Ellen Langer (1989) calls "mindlessness." When we process information through schemas, we pay less careful attention to the details of the situation. We behave in accord with what our schemas lead us to expect (Langer, Blank, and Chanowitz 1978). When someone replies to our absentminded "how are you?" with an honest "not so well," we may respond with an equally absentminded, and inappropriate, "good." The implications of this default inattention are not trivial. When we process information mindlessly, we are less likely to notice or retain disconfirming information, such as the "not so well" in this hypothetical encounter.

Recent developments in social psychology have further refined our understanding of these automatic cognitive processes. Numerous studies by Anthony Greenwald and colleagues (2002, 2009) suggest that interactional cues trigger unconscious or so-called implicit associations, which impact almost instantaneously how people perceive and process social information. Greenwald, Oakes, and Hoffman (2003), for example, asked research participants to perform a gun shooting simulation exercise where they would confront black and white police officers, criminals, and civilians. Some targets held guns; others held harmless objects. Results indicated that participants shot black targets more than white targets. Moreover, they treated any object held by black targets as if it was a gun, suggesting implicit associations between blacks and criminality. It is important to note that these associations are common not only among those who admit prejudiced attitudes, but also among those who believe themselves to be unprejudiced (Petty, Fazio, and Briñol 2009; Wittenbrink and Schwarz 2007). Similar implicit associations have also been found to exist regarding gender (Rudman and Kilianski 2000), sexual orientation (Banse, Seise, and Zerbes 2001; Geer and Robertson 2005), age (Hummert et al. 2002), and other characteristics.

It is important to note that social schemas are more likely to shape cognitive judgments when some degree of interpretation is required. When situational information is extremely clear, people usually rely on that information in forming their judgments. When the situation is ambiguous (probably the more typical pattern), schemas are one important basis upon which ambiguity is resolved (Baron, Albright and Malloy 1995).

Cognitive schemas thus contribute to the perpetuation of social expectations. When we process information in terms of preexisting schemas, we are likely to see and remember information that is consistent with those schemas. When we make judgments on the basis of schemas, we are likely to make judgments that confirm those schemas. Schematic information processing is a highly reproductive cognitive system. Through the influence of social schemas, we perpetuate both our individual and societal expectations about others. This is one consequence of the need for cognitive efficiency. If schemas did not reduce the dense array of social information into a more streamlined package, if schemas were not resilient and highly resistant to change, they would not serve the needs of the cognitive miser. As we elaborate below, these tendencies are the cognitive underpinnings of social stratification.

Self-schemas

The social cognitive perspective on gender and other social categories is reflected in two types of schemas: schemas about ourselves and schemas about social groups. *Self-schemas* include organized knowledge about the self. From the social cognitive perspective, self-schemas represent identity, our answers to the question: "Who am I?" (The term *identity* is used in various ways by different social psychologies; we revisit this term in chapter 5.) In contrast to social exchange theory, which lacks a theory of self and identity, social cognition has devoted a great deal of attention to elaborating the nature of self and identity. Self-schemas include the characteristics, preferences, goals, and behavior patterns we come to associate with ourselves.

Gender self-schemas Development of a self-schema based on gender means that gender is an element of one's self-concept. (Gender can also be the basis for a group schema; in this case one classifies other people, behaviors, and situations on the basis of polarized conceptions of masculinity and femininity. We return to this broader conception below.)

Developing measures of constructs such as personality, identity, attitude, or schema presents a formidable methodological challenge. Cognitions are inherently unobservable. Unlike behavior, thought cannot be seen. Therefore, it is necessary to look for indirect traces of these hypothesized constructs. The first test of gendered personality, the M-F Test developed by Terman and Miles (1936), demonstrates several of the problems that arise in measuring unobservable constructs. Virtually all of the items on this test are easily identifiable as more typical either of males or of females. For example, femininity points can be acquired by saying one is afraid of the dark or is careful about how one dresses. Masculinity points are earned by saying one is able to stand pain or was disobedient as a child. If respondents are well versed in the cultural stereotypes of Western culture, they know which responses are appropriate for their sex. Hence responses may reflect the pressures of social norms rather than respondents' underlying personalities. Moreover, the method of scoring represents masculinity and femininity as opposite ends of a single dimension. One can be either feminine or masculine, but never both or neither. Thus, the design of this instrument necessarily produces the appearance of significant personality differences between women and men.

The Bem Sex-Role Inventory (BSRI), one of the most important developments in measures of gender identity, challenged each of these assumptions. As we noted in chapter 2, the BSRI was developed by Sandra Bem (1974) to assess psychological androgyny, a self-concept that incorporates both masculinity and femininity. Responses can range from high to low on both dimensions, thus challenging the idea that gender is a single dimension. That individuals may have little of either femininity or masculinity marks the first recognition that not all people form self-schemas on the dimension of gender. In other words, for some people gender is a central part of who they are, and for others, it is less so. Although the concept of androgyny has been severely criticized, as we discussed in chapter 2, this was an important step in the conceptualization of gender identity.

Hazel Markus (Markus et al. 1982) was one of the first to conduct empirical studies explicitly addressing self-schemas about gender. Markus assessed the extent to which individuals develop self-schemas about their gender and how these schemas influence subsequent information processing. Markus used the BSRI to assess gender schemas, then used gender schemas to predict various consequences of cognitive processing. Such consequences include the ability to supply behavioral examples of one's gender self-schema—for example, instances of one's nurturance—as well as how well one remembers information consistent or inconsistent with one's gender self-schema.

The potential utility of the concept of gender schemas has only begun to be realized. In analyzing variations in the strength of people's gender self-schemas, we could begin to trace how gender is culturally constructed. In contemporary Western society, for example, it is virtually impossible to avoid the labeling of many experiences in terms of gender: the way people drive, the way we throw a ball, the way we talk, all are accountable in terms of gendered expectations. Identification of those environments that might promote or minimize the significance of gender as a central way of defining the self would be an extremely important contribution to a theory of gender. Researchers are moving in this direction. Crouter and colleagues (2007), for example, observe that the family context (including birth order, the sex of siblings, and parental traditionality) contributes to significant fluctuations in children's and adolescents' gender expectations.

We should acknowledge that such questions are being asked only at the frontier of social cognition. Reflecting the deeply essentialist legacy of modern conceptions of both gender and identity, gender self-schemas have been treated as if they are static and transcend situations. In reality, the salience of gender varies across situations as well as across individuals. Being charged with sexual harassment is likely to heighten the salience of gender for any man; in contrast, one's gender is likely not to be salient when one is stuck in a traffic jam. Self-schemas, of course, can shape what situations we put ourselves in; Bem and Lenney (1976) demonstrated that women and men with strong gender self-schemas actually avoid even minor activities that contradict those schemas (e.g., for women, oiling a squeaky hinge). The salience of gender schemas varies across the life span; research suggests that gender is less salient for all individuals when they are very young and very old. Moreover, the rigidity of gender schemas varies across the life span: research suggests there is an increase in the flexibility of gender self-perceptions as children move into adolescence, followed by an increase in rigidity as they move into adulthood (Signorella and Frieze 2008). Likely explanations for these patterns emphasize that the meaning of gender is closely related to the social significance of reproduction and work; one's reproductive and work potential are both less central during the early and later years of the typical life span.

Racial self-schemas   As we have noted above and in chapter 2, the social psychological literature has tended to treat gender as a neutral and functional difference. In contrast, this literature has theorized racial difference more often in terms of structural and interactional inequalities. Accordingly, there is no research on racial self-schemas that directly parallels the concept of gender self-schemas. Scales that measure attributes of self in terms of racial polarities, for example, do not exist. This is due in part to the assumption that gender is dichotomous, while there are multiple racial and ethnic groups. More important, a structural approach to racial identity points away from a sense of racial identity as essential and natural and toward a focus on contextual influences.

Some research explores situational variations in the salience of one's race and the extent to which race is encoded into one's sense of self. McGuire and colleagues (1978) reported that only 1 percent of the Anglo students at a predominantly Anglo high school spontaneously mentioned their race in describing themselves. In contrast, 17 percent of the blacks and 14 percent of the Latinos mentioned their racial or ethnic background. (Similarly, men are more likely to mention being male when they come from predominantly female families.) In other words, social contexts shape the salience of social identities. A number of studies attest to the influence of context on racial and ethnic identity (see also Grossman and Charmaraman 2009; Phinney 1990; Saperstein and Penner 2010; Shinnar 2008).

Some recent studies address the effects of sustained historical and material circumstances on the development of racial identities. Hurtado, Gurin, and Peng (1994) explore the development of identities among persons of Mexican origin living in the United States. Chicana/os (longer-term residents who are U.S. citizens) make more numerous social categorizations of themselves and others (e.g., in terms of skin color, family roles, citizenship, language fluency, occupation, and so forth) than do first-generation immigrants. Hurtado and colleagues attribute these patterns to the different structural and historical conditions of these groups. Chicana/os are more competent in English, are more dispersed geographically, and work in a wider range of occupations; in short, they are located in more variable social structures than are first-generation immigrants, who tend to have much more limited intergroup contact.

One of the most prominent research questions concerns racial patterns of self-esteem, or the valence of one's attitudes toward one's self. Although early studies assumed that identifying with a low-status group would result in low self-regard, most of the empirical research suggests that those who identify more strongly with their racial and ethnic minority groups have higher self-esteem (Crocker and Major 1989; Buckley and Carter 2005; also see Phinney 1990). Twenge and Crocker's (2002) recent meta-analysis, for example, concludes that African Americans self-report higher levels of self-esteem than whites, who self-report higher self-esteem than Latinos, Asian Americans, and Native Americans. Kimura's (2007) analysis of data from the National Survey of Black Americans may help to explain these effects. This study explores the intersection of racial identity, discrimination, and self-esteem and finds that having a strong racial identity insulates one's self-esteem in the face of average to above-average levels of discrimination. Furthermore, attributing such attacks to external sources of discrimination rather than to internal, stable aspects of the self protects one's sense of self and self-esteem (Major et al. 2002, 2003).

A growing body of research explores the intersection of gender with racial identities. Settles (2006), for example, used a mixed-methods approach to examine the "black woman" identity. The results indicate that the black woman identity is clearly more important to women of color than either "woman" or "black person" identities. Similarly, Bell (2002) examined the intersection of these identities across educational contexts (e.g., at a primarily white coeducational university, a primarily black coeducational university, and a black all-female university) and found that the social setting is instrumental in the construction of intersecting identities. In other words, the identity or combination of identities that separate one from the dominant group become more central to one's sense of self in that context. Studies suggest that women may be more actively involved than men in sustaining ethnic identities; women, that is, may be the carriers of ethnic traditions (see Phinney 1990). Furthermore, women tend to be more aware of their racial identity and internalize race-related experiences differently than men. While the literature on the intersection of gender and racial identities is growing, there continues to be considerably less research on social class identities. This is consistent with the lesser attention directed by social psychologists to social class than to gender or race that we note in various places throughout this book.

Schemas of Social Groups

Group schemas are a second type of social schema; these include organized information about social roles such as parent or teacher and stratification statuses such as gender, race, age, and class position. These are more often referred to as role schemas. Because "role" implies that these categories serve societal functions, however, we refer to them instead as group schemas. Stereotypes, probably the most widely recognized cognitive construct, are roughly equivalent to group schemas. The processes of categorization and differential evaluation are particularly important to the operation of group schemas and stereotypes.

Categorization   *Categorization* seems to be a pervasive human tendency, as we noted earlier in this chapter. In a series of studies by Henri Tajfel (1981), people consistently formed cognitive groupings on the basis of virtually any characteristic. Whether we think we differ from others in significant social characteristics such as race or class, or in meaningless capacities, such as our skill at estimating numbers of dots in an ambiguous visual field or in preferences for particular artists, we form ingroups and outgroups. What characteristics are most likely to become the basis of group categorization? The need for cognitive efficiency suggests that we categorize on the basis of readily available information. Gender, race, and age are usually visually evident, hence readily available, characteristics. Prevailing norms of dress, hair style, stance, and so forth contribute to the visual prominence of gender and race, and perhaps also age, class, or sexual orientation. The tweed jacket, jeans, and deck shoes of the professor in *Oleanna* convey a very particular, age-specific, class-specific type of masculinity, for example. Although cognitive efficiency is not the sole basis for gender, racial, age, or class differentiation, it is the cognitive underpinning of these bases of social stratification.

Categorization can produce cognitive errors. When people encode information on the basis of group characteristics, individual differences are lost. In several studies by Taylor and her colleagues (1978), people listened to a conversation among three black and three white speakers (or three women and three men). Respondents were likely to make mistakes in remembering which black speaker and which white speaker (or which woman and which man) said what, but they made very few errors in identifying the race (or sex) of the speaker. Other studies document similar results across categories of age, sexual orientation, and skin color (Maddox and Chase 2004; Maddox and Gray 2002). Group membership also has consistent effects on cognition, emotions, and behavior. People show marked preferences for members of their own ingroups and marked biases against members of outgroups in allocating money and other valued goods, in evaluating the abilities and characteristics of others, and in assumptions about what beliefs they might have in common (Owens 2003). Categorization even affects how we gather information: we are less likely to seek information about outgroup members and therefore tend to have much less complex conceptions of outgroups than of ingroups.

Gender group schemas   As we noted in chapter 2, the earliest research on gender group schemas focused on personality attributes, reporting that men are generally rated high on instrumental attributes such as objectivity or competitiveness, whereas women are rated high on expressive attributes such as tact and being aware of the feelings of others (Broverman et al. 1972). Other researchers continue to show widespread support for these patterns across a wide variety of populations. Traits are not the only component of gender group schemas. Carpenter and Trentham (2001) report that such schemas include occupational types (e.g., nurse), interpersonal roles (e.g., grandmother), and sexual styles (e.g., prostitute), in addition to personality traits (see also Deaux and Lewis 1984).

Beliefs about gender are also represented at different levels of specificity (Deaux 1995); people develop subtypes of both female and male group schemas. The number of recognizable subtypes is considerable; in one series of studies, Ashmore and Del Boca (1986) identified 120 male and 115 female types. The number we commonly use is much smaller. There appear to be at least three common subtypes of women: "The housewife (traditional woman), the professional woman (independent, ambitious, self-confident), and the Playboy bunny (sex object)" (Basow 1992:6). More recent studies show that some of these gender subtypes persist. Vonk and Ashmore (2003), for example, provided respondents with 114 male and 115 female labels and identified the structure of gender types to include young-old, masculine-feminine, and traditional-modern subtypes. In addition, Green, Ashmore, and Manzi (2005) have identified contemporary subtypes for both women (e.g., bitch and whore) and men (e.g., nerd and wimp) who transgress gender expectations. Gender subtypes recognize variation within the schema, yet at the same time reinforce the overall picture of gender as dichotomous. Indeed, one might argue that some schemas are so embedded in cultural beliefs that they cannot be challenged, thereby forcing the development of subtypes.

Subtypes are also developed through the intersections of gender with other significant social statuses, including race, ethnicity, social class, sexual orientation, and age (as we noted in chapter 2). Stangor and colleagues (1992), for example, report that people are more likely to categorize others in terms of their race and gender together, rather than race or gender alone. Geiger, Harwood, and Hummert (2006) recently explored the intersection of gender and sexuality, uncovering eight lesbian subtypes (e.g., the lipstick lesbian, career-oriented feminist, sexual deviant, angry butch, and so on) operating within the symbolic universe of college students. Similarly, Brewer, Dull, and Lui (1981) demonstrated that there are gender subtypes within the general category of age. Subjects identified at least three variations within the general category of elderly person, for example: grandmotherly type, senior citizen, and elder statesman. Brewer and colleagues found that age-gender subcategories better characterized how subjects conceived of these groups than did age categories alone. Moreover, when pictures were categorized into meaningful groups (all grandmothers, for example) as opposed to being mixed up, subjects attributed many more traits to each set of pictures. Brewer and colleagues (1987) also suggest that the purpose for categorization shapes the nature of such intersections: When desired intimacy of interaction was at issue, gender categorization was more prominent than ethnic categorizations; when perceived similarity to self was at issue, ethnic categorizations were more prominent than gender categorizations.

Racial group schemas Echoing research on gender, personality traits have been the most common indicator of the attributes of racial group schemas, from the earliest studies through contemporary research. For example, in

1933 Katz and Braly assessed white male Princeton students' conceptions of ten racial, ethnic, and national groups. The students were given a list of eighty-four traits and asked to indicate the five traits that were most typical of each group. (Note that this measurement technique forced respondents to endorse some characteristics for each group.) Some examples: Blacks were believed to be superstitious, lazy, happy-go-lucky, ignorant, and musical; Jews to be shrewd, mercenary, industrious, grasping, and intelligent; and Chinese to be superstitious, sly, conservative, tradition loving, and loyal to family ties. "Americans" were described as industrious, intelligent, materialistic, progressive, and aggressive; "white" was not used as a category.

These scales were administered to Princeton students again in 1951 and 1967, allowing a rare examination of historical changes in group schemas (Karlins, Coffman, and Walters 1969). Some aspects of these schemas changed a great deal: The proportion describing Jews as shrewd, for example, dropped from 79 percent in 1933 to 30 percent in 1967, after World War II. The proportion describing Americans as materialistic increased from 33 percent in 1933 to 67 percent in 1967. Other aspects of these group schemas changed barely at all: Chinese were described as equally tradition loving, blacks as equally happy-go-lucky, and Japanese as equally industrious. Overall, however, many researchers have interpreted these data as suggesting that racial stereotypes in the United States have faded over the years. Devine and Elliot (1995) contest this interpretation. Focusing on stereotypes about blacks, they used the same scales as Katz and Braly but added more contemporary terms (e.g., hostile, criminal, athletic, poor), provided clearer instructions, distinguished explicitly between stereotypes (defined as a "well-learned set of associations that link a set of characteristics with a group label") and personal beliefs ("propositions that are endorsed and accepted as true"), and assessed white undergraduate subjects' levels of prejudice. Devine and Elliott maintain that rejection of a stereotype does not eradicate it from people's cognitive schemas. Thus, it is possible to categorize on the basis of a stereotype, while at the same time denying its truth. They conclude that these students have a clear, consistent, highly negative group schema of blacks, but also an equally consistent and positive set of personal beliefs about blacks.

Another study focused on the intersection of race and gender stereotypes. Weitz and Gordon (1993) used a modified version of the Katz and Braly scales to assess white students' images of black women, compared to perceptions of "American women in general." The most frequent descriptors of American women in general were intelligent, materialistic, sensitive, attractive, and sophisticated; the most frequent descriptors of black women were loud, talkative, aggressive, intelligent, and straightforward. Further analyses suggested the presence of three subtypes among the black female stereotype: a "threatening" type (loud, dishonest, argumentative), a "good mother/wife/daughter" type (intelligent, family oriented, loyal to family), and a "welfare mother" type (too many children, fat, lazy). Drawing on focus groups, Settles, Pratt-Hyatt, and Buchanan (2008) find considerable similarity in how black and white women characterize black and white women. One exception, however, is that focus group members were more likely to identify "inner strength" as a characteristic among women of color than of white women, consistent with stereotypes of the "strong black woman" or "Superwoman" (Beauboeuf-Lafontant 2003; Thomas, Witherspoon, and Speight 2004). Numerous recent studies examine the cognitive organization of subtypes of black men, which include the "ghetto male" type and the "musician" type (rapper) (Devine and Baker 1991; Green and Manzi 2002). These data show that gender images do not hold across racial categories. Given that these studies were conducted relatively recently, when respondents were highly likely to have recognized that negative images of members of racial minority groups are not socially desirable, the negativity of these responses is striking. This supports Devine and Elliot's position that racial stereotypes have not died out. Furthermore, the thoughtfulness with which individuals have selected words to describe Barack Obama and his wife, Michelle, in public discourse simultaneously attests to the persistence of these stereotypes and to individuals' desire to avoid them (although they are not always successful).

Respondents in these studies are asked to evaluate a given group, not to compare racial groups to each other. (In contrast, conceptions of gender have routinely been assessed through comparisons, presumably because gender is conceived as dichotomous.) This is not to say that respondents do not use a comparative framework to analyze such responses. Indeed, some of the same behaviors might be viewed in very different ways by different perceivers. This possibility was supported explicitly in a study by Campbell (1967): what Americans saw in themselves as friendly and outgoing, the British saw as intrusive and forward (and see Stephan and Rosenfield 1982). Note that these measures ask respondents to adopt an "all or none" framework: they are asked to judge whether these attributes are or are not typical of the target group, not to assess the degree to which an attribute might be characteristic. Recent studies have made improvements in the measures of group schemas: in some studies respondents are now asked to indicate the percentage of the group that possesses each trait or the extent to which a given group is perceived to differ from other groups on a trait.

Beliefs about race, like beliefs about gender, are organized at varying levels of specificity. Devine and Baker (1991) show that "streetwise," "athlete," "welfare," and "businessman" are recognizable subtypes of the global category "black." It is important to note that this study is based on the responses of white students; assessment of the responses of blacks and of others who do not identify as white is necessary to establish the generality of these subtypes.

Social class group schemas   Social psychologists have asked different, and fewer, questions about class than about gender or race. Some have argued that social class is an "unspeakable" topic in the United States. As one instance, we cite a story shared with us by a colleague, concerning her research on the perceptions held by high school students of their race and class positions. New York City school officials told her she could not ask students questions about their income or finances. Why? Because this would "remind them of their poverty." This incident suggests that it is talk about class that is unacceptable; class variation itself obviously exists. This "unspeakability" inhibits the social psychological study of social class.

There are only a handful of studies that have assessed the content of group schemas about class position. Several older studies do assess perceived traits of combinations of race and class position, however; these show that class influences these schemas more than race (Bayton, McAlister, and Hamer 1956). Both blacks and whites describe members of upper-class groups, across racial categories, as intelligent, ambitious, industrious, and progressive. Lower-class groups were described as ignorant, lazy, loud, and dirty. In contrast, there were no traits that the sample as a whole attributed to blacks of both classes or to whites of both classes. Showing the force of history, a similar study twenty years later reported the same pattern for white respondents, but dramatically increased salience of race for black respondents (Smedley and Bayton 1978).

More recently, Weeks and Lupfer (2004) highlight the intersection of racial and social class categories. In two experiments, they find that perceivers tend to categorize lower-class black targets by race, whereas they categorize middle-class black targets by social class. Lott and Saxon (2002) compared subjects' perceptions of working- and middle-class Jewish, Latina, and white women across social contexts (e.g., appropriateness to serve as vice president of the Parent and Teacher Organization [PTO] or to be the girlfriend of an older brother). Their subjects viewed working-class women across racial categories as more crude and more irresponsible than comparable middle-class women. Furthermore, subjects viewed working-class mothers in the PTO context as less strident, less perfectionist, and less suitable to serve as vice president. These results point to the impact of social class in shaping attributions of social actors.

Several studies have attempted to manipulate perceptions of the social class background of actors in vignettes shown to research participants. To the extent that these portraits successfully shape perceptions of class positions, they are at least indirect indicators of schemas of social class. Howard and Pike (1986) varied the number of children in a household, type of car, type of church, and degree of community participation, as well as more obvious financial information such as having a savings account, income, receipt of social welfare payments, and occupation. Baron and colleagues (1995) varied the size of home, type of neighborhood, and quality of school playground and buildings. In each study, subjects did successfully perceive the intended social class of the actors (and social class did affect subsequent cognitive inferences).

Social cognitive research has addressed two topics related to social class: (a) descriptive studies of how people conceptualize the class structure and their locations in it, and (b) attributional studies of how people explain class positions. Kelley and Evans (1995) show that people's images of class are based on strong perceptions of equality and consensus among family, friends, and coworkers. These relationships foster consensual rather than conflictual views of class relations, and contribute to the fact that most U.S. citizens describe themselves as middle class (although fewer do so if working class is included as an option [Evans, Kelley, and Kolosi 1992]).

Turning to explanations for social class position, the majority of respondents in several large national surveys attribute people's economic situations to their own individual skills, abilities, and motivations (Evans et al. 1992). At the same time, most surveys show that people think the gap between the incomes of the rich and poor is too large. Reflecting the deep individualism of Western societies, people generally evaluate both their own and others' economic situations as legitimate and just (see related discussion of justice in chapter 3). In one of the few comparative studies of the effects of lower status positions in systems of class, race, gender, and age on political perceptions and judgments, Gurin, Miller, and Gurin (1980) show that identification with these statuses is crucial to generating discontent with prevailing power structures. In the language of social cognition, those who have self-schemas about these positions are more likely to process their social experiences in terms of these schemas and to question the lack of political power associated with being black, a woman, or elderly, for example. Class is a striking exception. Even those who identify closely with lower economic strata do not question the legitimacy of economic differentials (Kluegel and Smith 1986). The working-class respondents in Gurin and colleagues' (1980) survey accepted the legitimacy of poverty, attributing the disadvantages of some and the advantages of others to their personal characteristics.

We have observed that studies of personality traits associated with social class are less common than studies of attributes associated with gender and race. Studies of how people explain class position are much more common; explanations of the "achievement" of gender and race do not exist. The different questions asked about class on the one hand, and gender and race on the other hand, reflect the beliefs that class is an achieved status and gender and race statuses are ascribed at birth. Questions of how people "obtain" their gender or race seem nonsensical. As we suggest in our discussion of the social constructionist approach, however, both gender and race have achieved as well as ascribed elements, while class clearly has ascriptive elements.

Connections among group schemas   Researchers have only begun to explore the potential complexities of the intersections among these statuses. The human need for cognitive efficiency works against too much complexity; in some situations, therefore, we may privilege one system of categorization over another. Thus, we might respond to the play *Oleanna* primarily in terms of our schemas about gender. Other social situations may encourage the activation of multiple and simultaneous categorizations; situations such as Roumani's encounter on the airplane simultaneously activated categories for gender, race, and religion. Imagine how Roumani's response to her copassengers might have differed if only one of the father's positions was varied— mother rather than father, white rather than Middle Eastern, or Christian rather than Muslim.

Social psychologists are also exploring how people balance the tendency to rely on social categories with the situational need for information about particular individuals (Brewer 1988; Fiske and Neuberg 1990). Reliance on social categories does have priority in how we form impressions of others. Moreover, some researchers suggest that "meta-stereotypes," or our ideas about how members of other groups perceive us and how we expect they are likely to respond to us, also shape situated behavior (Vorauer et al. 2000, Vorauer, Main, and O'Connell 1998). Yet, as we noted above, there is a good deal of evidence that people often pay less than complete attention to their social environments. Social behavior is not always under conscious control, suggesting that cognitive schemas may have undue influence on our behavior. Conscious attempts to override these schemas can be successful. Devine (1989), for example, shows that most members of majority groups of a given culture are familiar with cultural stereotypes about minority groups and that these preconceptions can lead to prejudicial behavior toward members of these groups. When situational factors lead people to attend more directly to their own behavior, however, those who have less prejudicial attitudes are capable of inhibiting the stereotypes and behaving in ways consistent with their attitudes.

Most (although not all) of the studies discussed above have been conducted in the United States. Citizens of the United States appear to believe that equality of opportunity is a reality in this country. Taken together with the general tendency of Westerners to attribute events to people rather than to environmental circumstances (discussed below), the conviction that we all have equal opportunities leads to a pattern of causal reasoning that argues that if some people have not achieved social and economic advantages, this must be due to their own individual failings. Della Fave (1980) traces this pattern in his analysis of how cognitive processes of self-evaluation and attribution contribute to the legitimation of social stratification. Jost and Banaji (1994) take this analysis one step further. They focus on two aspects of stereotypes (schemas about social groups): one, that disadvantaged individuals and groups often endorse negative stereotypes about themselves; and two, that stereotypic beliefs are highly consensual. In order to make sense of these patterns, they maintain that stereotypes justify and thus contribute to the preservation of existing social inequalities (see McKown and Weinstein 2003; Sidanius and Pratto 1999). Hoffman and Hurst (1990) provide experimental support for this reasoning; they show that gender stereotypes can arise solely to rationalize the distribution of the sexes into social roles—in this case, "child raisers" as opposed to "city workers."

Event Schemas

Both self and group schemas refer to preconceptions about human actors. Another type of schema refers to information about situations, the social environments in which humans act. *Event schemas* include preconceptions about the kinds of actions likely to happen, the sequence in which these actions evolve, and the props necessary to perform these actions. These situations may vary from the particular, such as a class one is taking in a specific semester, to the general, such as going to a movie. The essential element is that the event be habitual, so that it is possible for the individual who experiences it regularly to form a schema. As we noted earlier, reliance on event schemas encourages a state of "mindlessness" in which we pay less careful attention to the details of the situation, attending instead only to those details consistent with our expectations.

Some event schemas are shared within a group or within a culture; gender, race, and other social positions are important bases for such schemas. In a sense, these schemas combine expectations about social groups with expectations about particular situations. Assumptions about what women and men do in the kitchen, for example, reflect both event schemas and gender schemas. When event schemas carry expectations about the sex of the actors involved, we may describe these situations as gendered. Gender was relevant to Roumani's encounter aboard the airplane in that situations of risk highlight men's greater perceived dangerousness and women's greater perceived vulnerability (Hollander 2001). Although some women participate in and encourage terrorism, the much more prevalent profile (both statistically and cognitively) is that of a male religious fanatic and aggressor. In contrast,

Western media depict Muslim women as submissive and "backward" victims (Esposito 1998; Read and Bartkowski 2000). The recent increase in the numbers of women initiating acts of terrorism poses challenges for gender schemas. Some media have reported explanations of these acts by focusing on the ostensible control of these often very young women by older men who have undue influence over them, often through sexual relationships (Zavis 2008). Thus, when an instance of terrorism (or potential terrorism as in this case) comes under scrutiny, gender, race, and event expectations intersect to shape how individuals make sense of the situation and how they make decisions about how to respond (or not respond).

Schemas of Cognitive Social Psychologists

Social schemas shape the research agendas of social psychologists, and thus have influenced the very research we have summarized in this chapter. We illustrate with just a single study, but invite the reader to consider other studies in this light. Langer and colleagues (1976) examined whether the salience of people who are physically different might explain why they are avoided. In the first part of this study, respondents viewed photographs of a "physically normal" woman, a pregnant woman, and a woman wearing an intricate leg brace that suggested she was disabled. Women viewers directed more visual attention to the more novel pictures, while men looked at the three pictures roughly similar amounts of time. Langer and colleagues speculated that "male subjects' desire to stare at an attractive normal female may have been as great as their desire to stare at novel stimuli" (455). In the second part of the study, male subjects viewed pictures of two other males, one of whom was "physically normal" while the other had a hunchback. When they were unobserved, male subjects directed more visual attention to the picture of the hunchbacked man than to the other man. The authors concluded that when there are no norms against doing so, people direct more attention to novel, salient stimuli.

This study illustrates several intriguing assumptions. First, the researchers treat pregnancy as a form of physical handicap (a label echoed in laws that treat pregnancy as a disability). They note that people may have some degree of fear and discomfort around pregnant women because of a desire to stare at these presumably novel stimuli. If one assumes that men might find a pregnant woman more unusual than would women, this assumption suggests a male viewpoint on pregnancy (that three of the four authors of this study are women, notwithstanding). Second, the account provided for the failure of men to conform to predictions in the first round of the study assumes their heterosexuality. Men (and not women) are assumed to have a "natural" desire to look at an "attractive normal female." The design of the second version indicates that men are assumed not to have such a desire to look at other men. Note also that this second round did not use female subjects, a design element that would have allowed the researchers to evaluate the generality of their explanation of the gender difference in the first round.

This study is more than three decades old. It may well be that if the same researchers were conducting a follow-up today, they might use different stimuli. We suggest, however, that those stimuli would likely continue to reflect prevailing contemporary assumptions about gender, sexuality, race, or other social systems. Our point is that social schemas influence researchers as strongly as they do others; some phenomena are so taken for granted that scientific substantiation is thought to be unnecessary.

Thinking: Processing Information

Thus far, we have outlined numerous cognitive structures that permit individuals to organize information they take in from the social world. We form cognitive categories on the basis of self-perceptions, perceptions of others, and membership in significant social groups. These categories direct the several systems of information processing: attention, memory, and social inference. We devote this section to a discussion of these three cognitive processes.

Attention

The first step in thinking is *attention.* As social perceivers, we may direct our attention toward the external social environment or inward into our memory. Attention, in either instance, varies in both direction and intensity. The direction of our attention is determined in large part by the salience of various features of a given situation—that is, the extent to which they stand out. Novelty, physical features such as brightness or mobility, violation of prior expectations, and social characteristics all shape what is salient. Thus, a sole woman in a group of men, a white person among people of color, or an older person in a group of teenagers, is likely to be salient. The schemas we hold for each of these systems of social categories also shape salience: violation of schema-based expectations increases salience and therefore heightens attention. Any characteristic or behavior that is unusual for a given person, for a person's social categories, or for a given situation, will be salient.

One of the reasons for the widespread attention to the discharge of Colonel Grethe Cammermeyer from the U.S. Army in 1992 when she disclosed that she is a lesbian, for example, is that homosexuality is inconsistent with cultural schemas for the military. Cammermeyer's sex also heightened the salience of the case; despite the consistent participation of women in the U.S. armed services, the schematic expectation is that military personnel, particularly high-ranking officers, are male. Similarly, one of the reasons for the dramatic intensity of *Oleanna* is the extreme disjuncture between the event schemas in the two parts of the play. The first scene appears to concern a faculty-student mentoring relationship. The last scene, which focuses on a violent confrontation between the professor and the student, entails an adversarial relationship between a harasser and a victim. The later violation of expectations generated at the outset of the play leads the viewer to pay attention.

The goals a perceiver brings to the situation also shape the salience of social objects within that situation. A student's goal to be seen as a good student by a favored professor may increase the salience of that professor's presence at social gatherings and thereby direct the student's attention toward that professor. Moreover, the dispersion of social objects across the visual field may impact their salience. Individuals seated directly across the seminar table from an instructor are particularly salient. Faculty expect students who choose seats directly in front of the professor to be leaders, but expect less of students who choose seats on the margins (Raghubir and Valenzuela 2006). Students often implicitly draw on such lay knowledge in selecting where to sit in the classroom.

Salience and attention also shape subsequent stages of information processing. McArthur and Solomon (1978) showed that actors who are more visually salient are assumed by observers to exert more control over social interactions. In this study, subjects watched a videotaped interaction between two women arguing about a bridge hand. One of the two women was verbally aggressive toward the other. In one version of this encounter the "victim" of this aggression wore a leg brace, making her particularly salient; in another version she did not wear the brace. Although the majority of blame was attributed to the aggressor, a portion of blame was also attributed to the victim. Of the latter, observers attributed more blame for this encounter to the woman wearing the brace than the woman without the brace—that is, to the more salient victim. This finding suggests that victims who are salient are more likely than nonsalient victims to be attributed some blame for the situations in which they are victimized. Lassiter and colleagues' (2002) recent study of videotaped confessions indicates that salience also shapes subjects' attributions about criminal offenders. Videotaped confessions that focus only on the offender—as opposed to those that show the offender and the interrogator—promote causal attributions focusing on the offender's underlying disposition rather than on situational factors present when the offense occurred (see also Lassiter et al. 2007).

Memory

Having attended to information, we then may encode it into *memory*. At a later point, we may retrieve that information for use in a current situation. Social schemas shape both the encoding of information into memory and retrieval from memory. As preexisting information structures, schemas provide the frameworks into which new information can be encoded. In most situations, information that fits easily into existing schemas is more likely to be remembered than information for which we do not already have relevant schemas. Similarly, since we retain information by organizing it into schemas, retrieval also necessarily relies on social schemas.

Our group memberships and their associated social schemas thus strongly affect memory. People recall more information about ingroup than outgroup members and are more likely to recall negative details about members of disliked outgroups. They also tend to recall how outgroups differ from ingroups, rather than how they are similar. These effects of categorization and social schemas on memory thus perpetuate our stereotypes and preconceptions.

Snyder and Uranowitz (1978) offer a remarkable demonstration of these processes. Subjects first read an extensive case history of a woman named Betty K. After reading this narrative, some subjects were told Betty was now a lesbian. Others were told she was now heterosexual. (The case history had included no information about sexual orientation.) All were later asked to remember a variety of details concerning, for example, her attitudes about women and men, her social patterns in high school, and her relationship with her parents. Those who believed that Betty was now a lesbian remembered the events of her life as consistent with stereotyped beliefs about lesbians (e.g., she never went out with men) to a greater extent than did those who believed she was now heterosexual. Interestingly, this pattern did not occur for a third group who were told only that Betty was a lesbian and were asked to guess at her background. It was only those who were given specific information about her past who reconstructed a life history for a lesbian that differed significantly from that reconstructed for a heterosexual woman. This subtle study reveals that stereotypes and preconceptions interact with memory; stereotypes shape selective, rather than unbiased, memory.

Another classic study demonstrates the active, constructive nature of human memory. Cohen (1981) created a short videotape that showed a man and woman having a birthday dinner. Subjects were told before viewing the tape that the woman was either a librarian or a waitress. They were later asked a series of questions about the tape; participants were much more likely to remember having seen schema-consistent details. Those who thought they were viewing a waitress remembered her drinking beer, owning a TV, having a hamburger and chocolate cake for dinner, and liking to bowl. Those who thought they were viewing a librarian remembered her wearing glasses, owning classical records, having roast beef and champagne for dinner, and having fresh flowers on the table. In some cases these details were not a part of the videotape. Participants constructed situational details that were not present but that were consistent with their prior expectations. In other words, preexisting social schemas shaped retrieval so completely that subjects "remembered" details on the basis of these schemas rather than the actual videotape. This is the essence of the social construction of memory.

It is worth considering precisely what schemas are at work here. Cohen (1981) presents these as occupational schemas—that is, preconceptions about characteristics of waitresses and librarians. However, both are highly gender-typed occupations and both are typed as female. Indeed, *waitress* is an explicitly gendered term (in contrast to the neutral *server*). The different details manipulated in the study also suggest that these occupations are distinguished by their class; waitresses are ranked lower in the class hierarchy than are librarians. Thus, these occupational schemas also rely on schemas about gender and social class. These studies illustrate precisely how we can seem to see gender differences that are not really present; our reliance on schemas about gender leads us to remember those details that are consistent with our expectations, and, importantly, not to notice, and not to encode in memory, details that are not consistent with our expectations.

Social Inference

In the next stage of cognitive processing, we draw on memory, immediate situations, or both, to make a variety of types of judgments, from predictions to decisions to causal attributions. Guided by the need for cognitive efficiency, we often use cognitive shortcuts or *heuristics* in making inferences. Social schemas are no less influential in the formation of such social inferences than in attention or memory. In judging what groups people belong to, we often rely on preexisting group schemas—witness the hapless academic who mistakenly assumes the new assistant professor sitting in the department office is the secretary. (And witness the reader's possible assumption that the secretary is a woman and the academic is a man!)

Estimates of probability rely on the cognitive availability of information—instances or associations that easily come to mind influence perceived probabilities. This *availability heuristic* underlies significant social patterns: high status people exaggerate the size of upper classes, envisioning a relatively egalitarian society, for example, whereas low status people exaggerate the size of the lower classes, envisioning an elitist society (Evans et al. 1992). In making decisions or evaluating past events we may engage in cognitive simulations, imagining what might have been or what might come to pass, on the basis of cognitive schemas. Such simulations can affect other inferences; for example, Howard (1984a) reports that both women and men held female victims more accountable than male victims for being assaulted when they were hitchhiking. Presumably cognitive simulations of what might happen when one is hitchhiking lead subjects to assess higher probabilities of assault to women than to men, and in turn to attribute more blame to women who hitchhike.

Some of the most compelling examples of the effects of schemas on social inferences illustrate how group schemas affect *attribution*, the process through which we explain events. One study conducted in India examined the effects of intensely held group schemas, the beliefs held by Hindus about themselves and about Muslims, who are for Hindus a hated outgroup (Taylor and Jaggi 1974). Hindu subjects were asked to describe the traits characteristic of Hindus and of Muslims. Then they were asked to read a set of paragraphs, each of which described either a Hindu or a Muslim performing a behavior that was either clearly good or clearly bad. These Hindu subjects attributed the good behavior of Hindus to internal factors such as their own abilities or strong morals, and the bad behavior of Hindus to external factors such as the influence of other people. In contrast, they attributed the good behavior of Muslims to external factors and the bad behavior of Muslims to internal factors. Thus, on the basis of their preconceptions about these groups, they showed attributional patterns of ingroup favoritism and defensiveness and outgroup derogation.

The effects of group schemas on cognitive judgments are not always so straightforward. Howard (1984a) explored how attitudes toward women and men shape both attributions and evaluations. Subjects watched a videotaped interview between a police detective and a male or female victim of a rape or a robbery. Both women and men attributed more blame to female than to male victims and, interestingly, both female and male subjects attributed more blame to the character of female victims and to the behaviors of male victims. Women were blamed for stable, internal, uncontrollable characteristics—for example, their "trusting nature." Men were blamed for unstable, more controllable behaviors—for example, "not fighting back." These patterns are consistent with gender schemas that characterize women as passive and lacking control, and men as active, powerful, and exerting control. Evaluations of these victims were also gendered. Some patterns were consistent with gender schemas; female victims, for example, were rated as more foolish than males. Male victims, on the other hand, were rated as less forceful than female victims, directly contradicting masculine stereotypes (Howard 1984b). Victimization may be so deeply "female" an experience that a man who is victimized is literally "feminized" in subjects' cognitive evaluations. This gendered situation is another example of the connection between group and event schemas.

As is evident from this discussion, social inferences are not always "rational." When we rely on these cognitive heuristics to form inferences, we use only a subset of the relevant information. The attribution process is also vulnerable to a host of social and cognitive factors that lead us to emphasize some types of information at the expense of others. The "fundamental" attribution error, for example, is a tendency to attribute blame more to people than to situations (a tendency limited to Western societies [Miller 1984]). This bias is exacerbated when observers make attributions about the behavior of others and muted when people make attributions about their own behavior (the "actor-observer bias").

These biases, produced by both cognitive and motivational processes, underlie significant societal patterns. As we have noted above, members of groups with more social advantages generally attribute the disadvantaged positions of others to their personal inadequacies (Gurin et al. 1980), as self-interest would predict. These and other studies (Coleman, Rainwater, and McClelland 1978; Johnson, Dowd, and Ridgeway 2006; Kerbo 1976) have shown that members of lower economic classes often legitimize not only the social positions of those with more economic advantages, but also their own social positions. Attribution biases contribute to these perceptions. The fundamental attribution error encourages members of subordinate social positions to accept responsibility for their own disadvantages, and the actor-observer bias encourages members of advantaged social groups to view their own advantages as situational, and others' disadvantages as self-produced (Gurin et al. 1980).

Constructing Gender: Behavior and Cognition

Recent work in social cognition has stressed the behavioral confirmation of cognitive expectancies, a process whereby we essentially elicit from others the behavior we expect from them. This research falls at the intersection of social cognition and symbolic interaction, the theory we take up in the next chapter. The prolific research of Mark Snyder offers many examples of behavioral confirmation. In one study, for example, pairs of previously unacquainted college women and men became acquainted in phone conversations (Snyder, Tanke, and Berscheid 1977). The men were given photographs ostensibly of the women they would be talking to. In reality, these pictures were either of a "very attractive" or a "very unattractive" woman, not of the person with whom they would be talking. The conversational styles of these men were clearly guided by the expectations they formed on the basis of the pictures: Those who expected an attractive partner were warm, friendly, humorous, and animated. Those who expected an unattractive partner were distant and reserved. The women with whom they spoke responded to these conversational styles as one might expect: Those treated warmly responded warmly, those treated coldly responded coldly. Expectations based on gender schemas shaped these men's behavior so that their conversational partners confirmed the men's schemas. Snyder's research on behavioral confirmation illustrates powerfully how cognitive expectancies guide the construction of social systems such as gender. (See Snyder 1984 for other examples.)

This study also provides another example of how cognitive schemas shape the research of social psychologists themselves. Note the gendered expectations embedded in the design of this study: men are assigned the position of initiators of conversation, and it is men whose opinions of women are sought. Would the same effects have been obtained if women had been asked to initiate conversations with men whose pictures they had been given? Anderson and Bem (1981) replicated this study but reversed the sexes; they found that women also led men to confirm beliefs about their personalities but add the important caveat that it is highly gender-typed individuals who are most likely to initiate this behavioral confirmation process.

Conclusions: Social Cognition on Gender

In contrast to social exchange theory, social cognition offers an explicit account of the microlevel aspects of systems through which gender, and gender inequity, are created, sustained, and changed. Gender has been treated as an important category in social cognition, from early research on attitudes about gender through more recent research on gender schemas and gender identity. The effect of gender on cognitive processes has been addressed in research on attention, memory, and social inference.

The social cognitive account of gender draws from both the socialization and the social constructionist approaches. Some of the earlier research, particularly that on personality and androgyny, adopts a relatively static conception of gender as a set of characteristics acquired early in life that remains relatively stable throughout the life span. Later work emphasizes the informational basis of the social dynamics of gender, race, and other social systems. The social cognitive emphasis has been on the stability of such systems, due primarily to the human need for cognitive efficiency. Our reliance on preexisting cognitive expectations tends to perpetuate those expectations. For example, recent research on behavioral confirmation processes shows how cognitions shape behavior so as to reproduce our cognitive expectations. This approach also addresses how expectations can change, as we discuss in chapter 5; those toward whom behavior is directed may explicitly counteract the expectations, and those who hold certain expectations can explicitly try to elicit contradictory behavior. These recent syntheses of cognitive approaches with models of social interaction bring us closer to a social constructionist model of gender and other social systems.

As one example, research has treated memory as one of the most individualistic and cognitive of the cognitive processes. What could be more cognitive, after all, than human memory? Wegner (1986) challenges this conception of memory. Today many people store information in places such as file cabinets, computers, cell phones, and personal digital assistants (PDAs). More significant, we also allocate to other people responsibility for memory of particular categories of information. Is there a U.S. household, for example, that does not look to some members to know what food (if any) is in the refrigerator, to another to know what tax-deductible expenses the household has incurred over the year (if relevant), and to others to know how to reach family friends? Wegner's point is that even memory is a social process (see also Olick and Robbins 1998). In that the reader can make educated guesses about who is likely held responsible for remembering particular categories of information, we can speculate that gender shapes social memory and social memory shapes gender.

Despite the fact that the study of social cognition is increasingly social, what is often absent in the social cognitive analysis of gender and sexuality, and to some extent race and class as well, is explicit recognition of the power associated with membership in particular social categories. Social cognition has been relatively silent about power; categories are often treated as neutral. Difference is a fundamental principle of social cognition, but inequity has received a good deal less attention. Consider prevailing models of social identity (Owens 2003; Tajfel 1982). Social identity theory holds that members of ingroups tend to process information so as to bolster their own self-esteem through derogating members of outgroups and ennobling members of their own ingroups. In a society in which ingroups and outgroups do not have equal power, however, are these processes likely to hold for all groups? Argyle (1994) observes that outgroups are not always rejected; minority and lower status groups may believe that high status outgroups are superior. That significant proportions of lower status groups report that they accept the class system as just and legitimate and believe that middle-class people are superior in intelligence and leadership are striking reminders that social cognitive processes are not neutral but are shaped by the structural positions of individuals.

Accordingly, scholars have begun to critique measures of cognitive constructs that fail to consider existing relations of power (Hollander and

Howard 2000). In one such critique, Howard (1988) reconsiders Hendrick and colleagues' (1985) conclusion that gender differences in sexual attitudes reflect women's greater sexual conservatism. Hendrick and colleagues report, for example, that women are likely to disagree, and men to agree, that "I do not need to be committed to a person to have sex with him/her." Women are more likely than men to disagree that "sex is more fun with someone you don't love" and "it is all right to pressure someone into having sex." Howard argues that failure to consider the societal context in which sexual attitudes are formed invalidates Hendrick and colleagues' attribution of these patterns to women's greater sexual conservatism. Power differences, not sexual conservativism, underlie these gender differences in attitudes toward sexual behaviors.

Social cognition historically has paid much less attention to behavior than to cognition. Although the rationale for the importance of cognition is that ultimately it affects behavior, both theory and research have underemphasized the cognitive contribution to behavior. Contemporary research has been increasingly likely to place cognition in interactive situations. We anticipate and hope that the future of social psychology will see increasing interchange between social cognition and the theory to which we now turn—symbolic interaction.

Note

1. The number of injuries continues to rise, as rescue and recovery workers have begun to experience health problems because of their exposure to dust and other hazards at Ground Zero.

5

Symbolic Interactionism

R EADERS OF LOUISA MAY ALCOTT'S CLASSIC *Little Women* may remember a series of episodes centering around a lost glove. The four March sisters (Meg, Jo, Beth, and Amy) go on a picnic outing with their neighbor Laurie and his tutor, John Brooke. When they return, Meg realizes that she has lost a pair of gloves. Later, one of the pair is returned to her via the "office," a mailbox in the hedge between the neighboring properties:

> "Miss Meg March, one letter and a glove," continued Beth, delivering the articles to her sister, who sat near her mother, stitching wristbands.
> "Why, I left a pair over there, and here is only one," said Meg, looking at the grey cotton glove.
> "Didn't you drop the other one in the garden?"
> "No, I'm sure I didn't; for there was only one in the office."
> "I hate to have odd gloves! Never mind, the other may be found. My letter is only a translation of the German song I wanted; I think Mr. Brooke did it, for this isn't Laurie's writing." (Alcott 1924:161)

The disappearance of Meg's glove is odd, but none of the sisters takes much notice. Some time later, however, Jo and her friend Laurie (a young man whom she calls "Teddy") make a playful agreement to exchange secrets. Jo confides that one of her stories has been accepted for publication in a local newspaper; then she demands that Laurie reciprocate by sharing his secret:

"Where's *your* secret? Play fair, Teddy, or I'll never believe you again," [Jo] said.

"I may get into a scrape for telling; but I didn't promise not to, so I will, for I never feel easy in my mind till I've told you any plummy bit of news I get. I know where Meg's glove is."

"Is that all?" said Jo, looking disappointed, as Laurie nodded and twinkled, with a face full of mysterious intelligence.

"It's quite enough for the present, as you'll agree when I tell you where it is."

"Tell, then."

Laurie bent, and whispered three words in Jo's ear, which produced a comical change. She stood and stared at him for a minute, looking both surprised and displeased, then walked on, saying sharply, "How do you know?"

"Saw it."

"Where?"

"Pocket."

"All this time?"

"Yes, isn't that romantic?"

"No, it's horrid."

"Don't you like it?"

"Of course I don't. It's ridiculous; it won't be allowed. My patience! What would Meg say?" (Alcott 1924:202–3)

Laurie's disclosure worries Jo, and she eventually confides in her mother:

That evening, while Meg was writing to her father, to report the traveler's safe arrival, Jo slipped upstairs into Beth's room, and, finding her mother in her usual place, stood a minute twisting her fingers in her hair, with a worried gesture and an undecided look.

"What is it, deary?" asked Mrs. March, holding out her hand, with a face which invited confidence.

"I want to tell you something, mother."

"About Meg?"

"How quickly you guessed! Yes, it's about her, and though it's a little thing, it fidgets me. . . . Last summer Meg left a pair of gloves over at the Laurences' and only one was returned. We forgot all about it, til Teddy told me that Mr. Brooke had it. He kept it in his waistcoat pocket, and once it fell out, and Teddy joked him about it, and Mr. Brooke owned that he liked Meg, but didn't dare say so, she was so young and he so poor. Now isn't it a *dreadful* state of things?"

"Do you think Meg cares for him?" asked Mrs. March with an anxious look.

"Mercy me! I don't know anything about love and such nonsense!" cried Jo, with a funny mixture of interest and contempt. "In novels, the girls show it by starting and blushing, fainting away, growing thin, and acting like fools. Now Meg does not do anything of the sort: she eats and drinks and sleeps like a sensible creature; she looks straight in my face when I talk about that man, and only blushes a little bit when Teddy jokes about lovers. I forbid him to do it, but he doesn't mind me as he ought. . . . I knew there was mischief brewing; I felt it;

and now it's worse than I imagined. I just wish I could marry Meg myself, and keep her safe in the family."

This odd arrangement made Mrs. March smile; but she said gravely, "Jo, I confide in you, and don't wish you to say anything to Meg yet. When John comes back, and I see them together, I can judge better of her feelings toward him."

"She'll see his in those handsome eyes that she talks about, and then it will be all up with her. She's got such a soft heart, it will melt like butter in the sun if any one looks sentimentally at her. She read the short reports he sent more than she did your letters, and pinched me when I spoke of it, and likes brown eyes, and doesn't think John an ugly name, and she'll go off and fall in love, and there's an end of peace and fun, and cosey times together. I see it all! They'll go lovering around the house, and we shall have to dodge; Meg will be absorbed, and no good to me any more; Brooke will scratch up a fortune somehow, carry her off, and make a hole in the family; and I shall break my heart, and everything will be abominably uncomfortable. Oh, dear me! Why weren't we all boys, then there wouldn't be any bother."

Jo leaned her chin on her knees, in a disconsolate attitude, and shook her fist at the reprehensible John. (Alcott 1924:262–66)

This excerpt illustrates the basic argument of symbolic interaction: people attach symbolic meaning to objects, behaviors, and other people, and develop and transmit these meanings through interaction. Symbolic interactionism is used in many types of theory and research, ranging from macrolevel topics such as collective behavior, organizations, and social problems to traditional microlevel social psychological topics such as interpersonal interaction. Symbolic interactionists use a variety of methods, including introspection, fieldwork, interviews, participant observation, experiments, surveys, and the analysis of texts and other media. The breadth of symbolic interactionism makes a concise review difficult. In this chapter, we do not attempt to cover all of symbolic interactionism; rather, we focus on the aspects most relevant to our analysis of gender. These diverse aspects are unified by their reliance on a few key concepts and premises. We begin by discussing these foundational tools.

The Tools of Symbolic Interactionism

The most basic concept in symbolic interactionism is the *symbol.* Symbols are abstract meanings attached to objects, people, and behaviors. For example, some people wear religious symbols as necklaces: Christians often wear tiny crosses, Jews wear Stars of David, and so on. These pieces of jewelry are not simply geometric shapes cast in gold or silver; they carry complex meanings about religion, faith, and personal identity. Similarly, Meg's glove takes on symbolic meaning in the example above. Mr. Brooke keeps it in his waistcoat pocket because it symbolizes Meg and his affection for her. To him, the glove is not simply a few pieces of grey cotton sewn together; rather it takes on more extensive symbolic meaning because it belongs to a woman he admires. Thus, the first premise of symbolic interaction is that people behave toward symbols not on the basis of the concrete properties of the object, but on the meanings that these objects have for them.

Note, however, that the glove carries a very different set of meanings for Jo. To her, the glove comes to symbolize the prospect of Meg's being taken away from the family—which would be, in her eyes, "a dreadful state of affairs." Thus, a symbol can have different meanings for different people, and these meanings can also change over time. At first, Meg's glove is little more than a protective covering for the hand; over time, however, it comes to have much more symbolic meaning for Jo, her mother, and Mr. Brooke.

How do meanings become associated with objects? A second premise of symbolic interactionism is that meaning develops through *interaction*. The transformation in the meaning of the glove for Jo occurs through her conversation with Laurie. She passes this new symbol on to her mother in their subsequent conversation. Meaning-making is thus a creative activity that occurs through language, which is itself a symbolic system. Without language, humans would not have the capacity to create symbols and communicate them to others.

Some symbolic meanings are unique to particular individuals or groups. For example, a song or story may take on a particular symbolic meaning for a couple, or a specific item of clothing may develop into a good luck charm for an individual. More often, however, the development of meaning relies on a symbolic system shared by many people in a culture. Meg's glove symbolizes romance to both Jo and Mr. Brooke not simply because they independently attach romantic meaning to an object. Rather, both Jo and Brooke (as well as we readers) share a symbolic universe in which ideas about "romance" include the sentimentalization of objects belonging to the beloved. These meanings are conveyed through interaction, and especially through language. Jo learns about love by reading books: she knows that "in novels, the girls show it by starting and blushing, fainting away, growing thin, and acting like fools." All of these behaviors symbolize "love," and Jo compares Meg's behavior to these symbolic actions to determine whether she is in love with John Brooke. Thus, meaning is not constructed anew in every interaction; in many cases, individuals draw on a shared system of cultural meaning and adapt it to a new situation.

Note, however, that these symbolic meanings are gendered. In the quote above, Jo describes what she believes to be the signs of love in women: blushing, fainting, and so on. John Brooke has shown none of these signs, yet Jo is certain he is in love with Meg. For men, love is symbolized in different ways. Brooke romanticizes Meg's glove, but is otherwise stoic about his feelings until Laurie teases him. Once he is able to "scratch up a fortune somehow," however, he will be able to "carry Meg off." Meg, in contrast, is unlikely to scratch up her own fortune and carry him off; her task is to wait. Thus, gender (and other social positions, as we discuss in more detail below) is a crucial part of these cultural systems of meaning, transmitted and performed through the basic tools of symbolic interaction: symbols, meaning, and interaction.

Who Are We? Self and Identity

The most basic requisite for symbolic interaction is the existence of social selves who come together to share information, emotions, goods—the full range of human activities. The images people have of themselves and of others shape how they present themselves. In turn, how they present themselves allows others to infer what actors privately think of themselves and of others. Without an explicit definition of self, we cannot interact successfully with others. In this section we discuss how symbolic interactionists conceive of self and identity and how selves and identities are both constructed in and played out through interaction with others.

William James (1890/1991) was the first modern social psychologist to attempt to define self. He wrote, "In its widest possible sense . . . a man's Self is the sum total of all that he can call his" (279). People recognize that their attributes, possessions, and friends are associated with them and that others (as well as they themselves) categorize and evaluate them on the basis of these things. James, and George Herbert Mead (1934) after him, divided components of self into the "I," the self-as-knower, and the "Me," the self-as-known. The *I* is the experiencing, active being. The *me* is a person's perception of herself or himself as an object. *Self-awareness,* or reflexivity, is the uniquely human capacity to be both subject and object to one's self, literally to be able to think (as a subject) about one's self (as an object). *Self* is all the consequences of this self- and other-awareness—our convictions, values, motives, and experiential history, carried in the spatial and temporal boundaries of our physical bodies.

Identity typically refers to the more public aspects of self. Identities locate a person in social space by virtue of the relationships and memberships that these identities imply. Thus, we hold identities based on our memberships in social groups (both voluntary and ascribed) and on the character traits we enact in interaction and that others attribute to us. For Jo, a primary identity is sister. Her worry about the glove is based on her recognition that Meg may be considering another identity—lover, or perhaps wife. The salience of particular identities, unlike selves, is sensitive to situational context. When John Brooke is visiting with Meg, his primary identity is potential suitor. When he is working with Laurie, his identity is tutor.

Although many theorists present the idea of the self as though it were a universal concept, on closer analysis their definition may not be so generic. The full sentence in James's quote reads, "A man's Self is the sum total of all that he can call his, not only his body and his psychic powers, but his clothes and his house, his wife and his children, his ancestors and his friends, his reputation and works, his lands and horses, and yacht and bank account" (279). This statement suggests that to have a self is to be a man. It is also to be a man with substantial means. It is also probably to be white. Although no contemporary social psychologist would be caught dead using James's precise words, *Oleanna*'s John suggests a similar definition as he rants to Carol about his tenure decision:

> When the possibility of tenure opened, I was covetous of it. I desired it, I was not pure of longing for security. What was the price of this security? To obtain tenure. Which tenure the committee is in the process of granting me. And on the basis of which I contracted to purchase a house. Now . . . you may not know what this means. To me it is important. A home. A Good Home. To raise my family . . . the home I'd picked out for my wife and son. (Mamet 1992:43–45)

William James would recognize John's self.

The genesis of self lies in children's perceptions and feelings about how others treat them. An idea of the self develops, based on three elements: our imagination of how we appear to others, our imagination of how others judge us, and our emotional reactions to those presumed judgments—that is, our feelings about ourselves. The self-concept thus arises through taking the role of particular others, seeing one's self as others do. Over time, children develop a sense of the *generalized other*, a composite viewpoint from the perspective of society as perceived by the individual. In *Oleanna*, John's description of his intellectual self-development reveals the emotional intensity of this process—and the lifetime consequences: "If the young child is told he cannot understand. Then he takes it as a *description* of himself. What am I? I am *that which can not understand*. . . . They said I was incompetent. . . . And when I'm tested, the feelings of my youth about the very subject of learning come up. And I . . . become, I feel 'unworthy,' and 'unprepared'" (Mamet 1992:16–17). Through interactions with others, John developed a lasting sense of himself as unable to learn.

Approaches to conceptualizing self and identity vary in their emphasis on the structure of identity on the one hand, and the processes and interactions through which identity is constructed, on the other. (Note that this dual relationship between structure and process is very similar to social cognition, as discussed in the previous chapter.) The structural approach developed out of early quantitative surveys using the venerable Twenty Statements Test (Kuhn and McPartland 1954)—which asks participants to provide twenty answers to the question "Who am I?"—as a method for assessing identities.[1] Role-identities, the characters and the roles an individual develops as an occupant of particular social positions, explicitly link social structures to persons. Jo's identities as sister, daughter, and friend (especially to Laurie) are not only personal identities—although they are that as well—but also social positions accompanied by culturally specific duties and expectations. Jo's later relationship to Professor Bhaer, a man who lives in the boarding house where she is a governess, is a clear example of the identity-structure connection. At first, Jo has no readily available identity to help define her relationship to the professor. Is he a housemate? An editor? A lover? Until the two acknowledge and enact their attraction to each other through a role relationship, there is no firm identity that connects them. Thus, the full profile of an individual's role-identities is explicitly connected to and mirrors the multifaceted nature of society.

According to Stryker (1980), these role-identities are organized hierarchically, varying on the basis of their salience to the self and the degree to which we are committed to them. Identities are based in part on connections to other people. Our commitment to particular identities is based on the number of ties to other people and the emotional strength of the ties associated with those identities. The greater one's commitment to an identity, the greater the salience of that identity. The greater the salience of the identity, the greater its influence on behavioral choices (see Stryker and Vryan 2003). Particular identities are more salient in some situations than in others. The student identity of Carol, the student in *Oleanna*, is likely excruciatingly salient to her throughout much of the play. The professional identity of John, the professor, is probably less salient in act 1, but grows increasingly more salient to him as the play progresses. In act 1, John can take this identity for granted; in later acts, this identity is threatened. Summed over situations and time, those identities to which we are most committed shape behavioral continuities and personal resistance to change—that is, a sense of self.

Other approaches to conceptualizing self and identity emphasize the processes through which identity is constructed in naturally occurring social situations. Because individual actors enter particular situations with their own agendas, negotiation about who each actor will be is a fundamental aspect of defining those situations. McCall and Simmons (1978) present a detailed model of those cognitive and expressive processes through which actors attempt both to perform their desired identities (cognitively devising or improvising their own roles and then performing them) and encourage the other to perform the identities they want the other to perform (cognitively assessing the role the other is projecting and then *altercasting*, behaviorally trying to encourage the other into the role the actor wants them to play). Through these cognitive and expressive negotiations, particular identities are agreed upon (or not), and situations are defined consensually enough to allow interaction to proceed.

The following excerpt from *Little Women*, in which Laurie proposes marriage to Jo, is a poignant example of the interactional approach. Jo has anticipated his proposal and done all she could to prevent it:

> Something in his resolute tone made Jo look up quickly to find him looking down at her with an expression that assured her the dreaded moment had come, and made her put out her hand with an imploring: "No, Teddy, please don't!"
>
> "I will, and you must hear me. It's no use, Jo: we've got to have it out, and the sooner the better for both of us," he answered, getting flushed and excited all at once.
>
> "Say what you like then; I'll listen," said Jo, with a desperate sort of patience.
>
> "I've loved you ever since I've known you, Jo; couldn't help it, you've been so good to me. I've tried to show it, but you wouldn't let me; now I'm going to make you hear, and give me an answer, for I *can't* go on so any longer."
>
> "I wanted to save you this! I thought you'd understand—" began Jo, finding it a great deal harder than she expected.
>
> "I know you did; but girls are so queer you never know what they mean. They say 'No' when they mean 'Yes,' and drive a man out of his wits just for the fun of it," returned Laurie, entrenching himself behind an undeniable fact.
>
> "*I* don't. I never wanted to make you care for me so, and I went away to keep you from it if I could."
>
> "I thought so; it was like you, but it was no use. I only loved you all the more, and I worked hard to please you, and I gave up billiards and everything you didn't like, and waited and never complained, for I hoped you'd love me, though I'm not half good enough—"
>
> "Yes, you are; you're a great deal too good for me, and I'm grateful to you, and so proud and fond of you, I don't see why I can't love you as you want me to. I've tried, but I can't change the feeling, and it would be a lie to say I do when I don't."
>
> "Really, truly, Jo?" He stopped short, and caught both her hands as he put his question with a look that she did not soon forget.
>
> "Really, truly, dear." (Alcott 1924:402–3)

Laurie's first words allow Jo to impute his role as suitor; her response clearly casts him as friend rather than lover. Laurie has rehearsed this conversation many times before acting; he has already devised the role he wants to play and manages his self-presentation so as to make Jo listen. Nonetheless, Laurie cannot successfully altercast Jo as his future wife; ultimately her definition of the situation prevails.

Identity construction is thus an intentional, strategic process, often entailing considerable negotiation. From this perspective, identities are social constructions created through interaction, with significant social and material consequences. The self is not the focus of this approach; rather, multiple identities provide the basis and motivation for interaction.

Gendered Selves and Identities

Gender is consistently one of the most frequent responses provided on the Twenty Statements Test. As we noted in chapter 1, gender identity refers to the socially defined self-meanings one has as a female or male. Despite their basis in a presumed physiological dichotomy, these meanings are variable; they are constructed differently by those in different structural positions, particularly of race and of class. Even within individual actors, they vary depending on the time and situation. For example, one's gender identity might be quite different in childhood than in adulthood or old age.

Like all identities, gender identities are defined in part by our positions in social structures and institutions. In a study of the meanings of divorce, for example, Arendell (1992, 1995) suggests that the family is the primary social group that conveys and reinforces the meanings of gender. She demonstrates that masculine identities shape for some men the creation of paradoxical goals in marriage: they seek relationships in which they can be the dominant spouse (Arendell 1992), while at the same time they want relationships in which they are equal copartners, sharing a high degree of intimacy and reciprocity. The improbability of simultaneously having both types of marriage is largely obscured by their gendered assumptions. In fact, the contradictions between these two sets of goals ultimately led to the divorces of many of the men in Arendell's study.

These masculine identities also generate a "masculinist discourse of divorce, constructed and anchored in interaction and reinforced by the stratified social order, [making] available a set of practices and dispositions that prescribed and reaffirmed these men's gendered identities" (Arendell 1992:173). Among these practices are these men's reliance on a "rhetoric of rights" due to one as a man or as a father; their attempts to reassert a self as autonomous, independent, and controlling; their attributions of problems in the marriage to fundamental differences between women and men (rather than to relationship-specific problems); and their distancing themselves from the relationship by defining their postdivorce families as "me" and "them" (the ex-wife and children). These cognitive and interactional practices both express and reaffirm these men's masculine identities, while at the same time reaffirming a traditional conception of the family.

Gender identity is also shaped by an individual's position in other social hierarchies. Membership in racial, ethnic, and class-based groups interacts with gender to produce a wide range of gendered identities. For example, Karp (1986) studied a group of upper-middle-class professionals who had been poor or working class as children. He found that individuals' original class positions shaped their responses to their present status as professionals. Those who had been upwardly mobile had difficulty "creating and sustaining a 'coherent self' that integrates older and newer social identities" and continued to "harbor feelings of uncertainty, inauthenticity, marginality, and dis-ease" (20) because of their working-class origins, despite their current success. These women and men continued to feel like "strangers in an alien culture"—a very different conception of self than that of other upper-middle-class people who had not experienced such a class shift. Even within this group, however, gender was salient: "Working-class women of this generation no doubt felt the double discrimination of their class and gender. While the boys could believe in the American dream of advancement through their own work efforts, the girls typically did not see career as an avenue for mobility" (33). Thus, a person's self is influenced simultaneously by many social positions—including ethnicity, class, race, and gender.

Presenting Selves in Interaction

Our selves and identities serve as resources, as tools for interaction. We present particular aspects of ourselves in interaction so as to achieve the outcomes we desire. A key idea in social cognition is that our cognitive preconceptions of ourselves and others shape how we behave; this insight is also vital for understanding symbolic interactions. Our preconceptions of ourselves shape who we present ourselves to be; our preconceptions of others shape how we behave toward them. In the section that follows we discuss the presentation of self, or impression management, emphasizing the actor's own goals. In the next section we discuss the interactional consequences of our preconceptions of others, emphasizing the process of behavioral confirmation. Both impression management and behavioral confirmation have considerable potential for contributing to an account of gender hierarchy and stratification, as we elaborate below.

Impression Management

Impression management, sometimes referred to as *dramaturgy*, is the inter-actional presentation of self. Although some people are uncomfortable with this metaphor, our interactions with others do often resemble a theatrical performance. We behave differently (i.e., play different roles) with different people (or audiences). We dress differently (using different costumes and props) for different situations. We say some things directly to the people they concern; other comments we may say only behind their backs. In short, we present particular selves to particular others for particular reasons. Laurie's cessation of billiards, for example, is directly intended to win Jo's affection. Jo's everyday behavior with Laurie, in contrast, is directly intended to dis-suade him from wanting to marry her. Impression management has also been observed in a multitude of laboratory experiments. In a study of alcohol consumption among college students, for example, Suls and Green (2003) found that male students were less likely than female peers to explicitly ex-press concern over excessive drinking, in order to avoid the embarrassment of transgressing gender expectations. This set of experiments suggests that male students who initially hold similar personal sentiments toward drinking as do their female peers may over time learn to cope with excessive alcohol consumption out of the fear of being ostracized by and the desire to fit in with male peers. Thus, their drinking behavior and attitudes toward drinking are intentional and goal oriented, and designed to manage the selves they present to others in particular, gendered ways.

One cannot discuss the concept of impression management without refer-ring to the work of Erving Goffman (1959, 1961). Goffman maintained that like actors on a stage, individuals in social situations manipulate the impres-sions they give off to manage others' perceptions of them. Whether the social situation is a classroom, a date, or a workplace, individuals modify their ap-pearance and behavior in an attempt to control others' impressions of them (see also Tedeschi 1981).

Consider U.S. presidential politics: one of the primary challenges a candi-date faces is convincing a skeptical American public that she or he is capable of fulfilling the highly gendered role of commander in chief. The gendered nature of the presidency stems from the historical workings of both material and symbolic culture. For example, Kimmel (2006) suggests the American Revolution was triggered by the economic reality of taxation without rep-resentation, but metaphorically it also represents a rebellious, independent son's (i.e., America) battle against an overbearing, aristocratic father (Great Britain). The revolution contributed to the fashioning of a particular form of American manhood, which is embodied in the presidency and his (as of yet) richly choreographed election. As Duerst-Lahti (2006) says of the election process,

> Masculinity has been embedded through the traditions that dominate the presidency, but inside those traditions lie more implicit assumptions that make presidential elections masculine spaces: The test of executive toughness, a preference for military heroes, the sports and war metaphors of debates, and more. Implicit in the gendering of presidential election space is the common belief that the election picks a single leader and commander in chief of "the greatest nation on earth." (2006:22)

Accordingly, being a capable commander in chief in the eyes of an American public often requires readily identifiable displays of toughness and heroism. Gender performances lacking in these qualities raise questions about an individual's suitability to hold office. The defeat of sitting president Martin Van Buren by William Henry Harrison, a hero of the Battle of Tippecanoe, is a telling example. Van Buren, who was often compared to daintily dressed women with "fair, delicate, small and richly jeweled" hands and with flamboyant European tastes, was outmatched by Harrison, whose humility and strength were symbolized by masculine imagery, including the log cabin and hard cider jug (Tucker 1836, quoted in Widmer 2005:89; see also Kimmel 2006). More recently, Ronald Reagan and George W. Bush cultivated images of themselves as rugged American men by donning cowboy hats. Many of the messages candidates offered during the 2008 presidential election underscored themes of toughness and ability to lead a nation at war. John McCain's campaign, for example, used the slogan "Country First" to remind the public of his heroism as a prisoner of war. Demonstrating toughness and masculinity is even more challenging for women candidates. Hillary Rodham Clinton, the leading female candidate, provided perhaps the most explicit message in a television advertisement showing nighttime images from a quiet neighborhood accompanied by the following narration:

> It's 3 a.m. and your children are safe and asleep. But there's a phone in the White House, and it's ringing. Something's happening in the world. Your vote will decide who answers that call—whether it's someone who already knows the world's leaders, who knows the military, someone tested and ready to lead in a dangerous world. It's 3 a.m. and your children are safe and asleep. Who do you want answering the phone?

A final scene showing Clinton reaching for the telephone offered an answer.

It is no surprise then that scholarly attention to the presidency often centers on impression management (Sigelman 2001; Tetlock 1981; Verser and

Wicks 2006). Hall's (2005) work on impression management among past presidents distinguishes two interwoven processes of power: "the gathering of intelligence, the maintenance of secrecy, the planning and rehearsing of performance" and "the use of symbols, verbal and nonverbal, in various settings and forms to maintain or strengthen the position of the actor" (366). U.S. presidents, Hall argues, regularly utilize both processes in order to manipulate public opinion.

Take the 2008 presidential primary, in which a reporter's keen observation of a missing symbol sparked intense controversy. A close examination of this incident provides insight into the central features of political impression management:

> "You don't have the American flag pin on. Is that a fashion statement?" the reporter asked, at the end of a brief interview with Obama on Wednesday. "Those have been on politicians since Sept. 12, 2001."
>
> The standard political reply to that question might well have been, "My patriotism speaks for itself."
>
> But Obama didn't say that.
>
> Instead the Illinois senator answered the question at length, explaining that he no longer wears such a pin, at least in part, because of the Iraq War.
>
> "You know, the truth is that right after 9/11, I had a pin," Obama said. "Shortly after 9/11, particularly because as we're talking about the Iraq War, that became a substitute for I think true patriotism, which is speaking out on issues that are of importance to our national security, I decided I won't wear that pin on my chest.
>
> "Instead," he said, "I'm going to try to tell the American people what I believe will make this country great, and hopefully that will be a testimony to my patriotism."
>
> In Iowa, some Obama supporters applauded the candidate's fashion statement. Said Carrie Haurum of Waterloo: "He doesn't need to wear that flag on his lapel. He wears it in his heart." (Wright and Miller 2007)

Whether the missing pin reflects Obama's intention to distance himself from the Bush administration and other Democratic candidates vying for their party's nomination, social commentary on empty displays of American patriotism, or whether it was an unintentional oversight, we may never know. Nevertheless, Obama seized the opportunity to present himself in dramatic fashion.

Yet not everyone accepted Obama's performance, and his identity claims as a calm, thoughtful leader met fervent resistance. Pundits, for example, highlighted Obama's lack of military experience and his connections to an "elitist," academic community. They read his actions as indicators of his antimilitary sentiments, and further as a slight toward American armed service people stationed in "harm's way." Conservative television host and author Sean Hannity countered Obama's claims with, "Why do *we* wear pins? Because *our* country is under attack!" Here Hannity attempts to dramatize his own patriotism and cast Obama as un-American. The back and forth exchanges that ensued reconstructed Obama's biography, characterizing him as a dangerous black man with links to "domestic terrorists" and black liberation theology. Other commentators read the situation as a sophomoric misstep, testament to Obama's lack of experience. Laura Ingraham, a former Reagan speechwriter and conservative commentator, replied, "It just shows you he's not ready for the big time." Taken together, the responses to Obama's self-presentation made his gender, race, and even social class positions salient in the public consciousness, and in subtle fashion, they allowed critics to alter-cast Obama as *other*.

After roughly six months, Obama's lapel pin reappeared. Obama told reporters that he would continue wearing a flag pin because at a recent event a veteran gave one to him and spoke of its importance.

> "I've never been opposed to flag pins," Obama shrugged when asked about it, adding that he stopped wearing a pin when he disagreed with how the Bush Administration equated a flag pin with patriotism and the war in Iraq.
>
> He also said that the controversy is a "phony issue" and a "commentary on our politics" and how it deflects from real issues that affect voters' lives. (Chozick 2008)

Clearly, reporters and members of the public suspected that Obama's change of heart came as a response to the negative reactions he received from those who were not satisfied with the impression he made earlier, suggesting that audiences often are aware of social actors' attempts to shape their impressions. Nonetheless, Obama used the opportunity to realign his image not only as an American patriot and supporter of American troops, but also as a suitable commander in chief committed to protecting the United States from threats abroad. As further evidence of his patriotism, the Obama campaign shortly thereafter released their own line of flag pins, illustrating how identities are continually (re)constructed through interaction. All of the actors involved in this social drama—reporters, Obama, political pundits, even the public—managed the impressions they gave off in order to achieve their own goals. The refashioning of Obama's self-presentation—although spread over several months—demonstrates the turn-taking often required for successful identity negotiations.

As this example illustrates, impression management need not be a lone project; other people may aid or hinder one's attempts to manage an audience's impressions. Goffman (1963) identifies two significant groups that contribute to such teamwork. The *wise* are those others who possess personal information about an individual's identity. Gillespie's (2005) work on the "public wife" describes one such example. As she notes,

> To see a wife holding a Bible at an oath-taking or an official's wife and children "on display as living passports validating the humanity" of the public man (Edmondson and Cohen 1976:87) reassures onlookers of the man's sexual normality, and thus his morality. As a culture we have so romanticized the myth of the All-American Happy Political Family that the short-hand symbol for it, the public wife, thus appears for some parts of the general public to be a kind of moral and cultural absolute. (385)

The public wife's performance, her presence or even her absence at an event, communicates to the public information about the type of person her husband "really" is. Maintaining one's political impression often becomes a joint venture between the individual and the wise. Furthermore, as Gustav-Wrathall (1998) documents, public figures who remain unmarried—for whatever reason—often face unique challenges in presenting information about their gendered and sexual selves (and about who they are not).

The *own*, on the other hand, are those others who share the identity in common with the individual. Candidates often ask political allies to act as surrogates to both make and reject claims in the public arena, with the goal of insulating themselves from the appearance of negative campaigning. For example, John McCain used running mate Sarah Palin to remind the public of his history as a political "maverick" and war hero. Moreover, Palin's attacks on Obama's character allowed McCain to appear more positive.

Like a theater, social situations often have a "back stage," an area separate from the "front stage" performance visible to the audience. The behavior of actors in this back stage region may be very different than their front stage demeanor. In a theater's back stage, actors put on makeup and are coached on their lines, stagehands construct and move scenery, and directors plan how to create the dramatic effects they desire. Before each major political speech or debate, it is likely that a back stage observer would find political strategists conducting opinion polls, speech writers working through endless revisions, stylists searching for the most presidential look, the candidate rehearsing her or his opening comments, and all parties complaining to their friends and families about the duration and circus atmosphere of the campaign—all behaviors they would never perform in the public eye. Once the candidate emerges in front of an audience, however, all efforts are directed at maintaining the reality of the front stage and its separation from the back stage (Sigelman 2001).

Note, however, that *back stage* and *front stage* are relative terms: they are defined in relation to the specific role being played and the particular audience present at a given moment. Relative to a public wife's role as First Lady, for example, a state dinner or reception in the Rose Garden is a front stage area, while her private residence in the White House is a back stage area. In her role as mother of her children, however, her home is the front stage.

The metaphor of dramaturgy translates easily to the political arena. Goffman argued, however, that *every* social situation is a dramaturgical performance—more subtle than politics, perhaps, but nonetheless an active juggling of identities. Job applicants, for example, generally choose their clothes carefully, arrange their appearance neatly, and behave in ways that they hope will make them good candidates for the job. They may talk about their past successes at work, wax optimistic about their career goals, and neglect to disclose their past drug use or work conflicts. These same applicants may present a very different self with their friends, their families, their intimate partners, or their teachers.

This is not to say that self-presentations are dishonest. Some people feel that the concept of impression management implies an inauthenticity to human interaction. While some impression management might include intentional deception through cover stories (Roschelle and Kaufman 2004), concealment (Thorne and Anderson 2006), or passing (Renfrow 2004), we emphasize here that self-presentation is simply a fact of social life. Our intentions may at times be to deceive, but more frequently they are benign: to help new acquaintances quickly develop a picture of our "real selves," to have our talents recognized by a new boss, or to convey our sympathy to a bereaved friend. Most self-presentations are sincere attempts to show others who we "really are" in order to facilitate social interaction. Selves, after all, are not quickly and easily knowable. As Kollock and O'Brien (1994) note, "Minds are private, which is to say that our thoughts, desires, beliefs, and character cannot be directly perceived and evaluated. We are not a race of mind readers, and so we must depend on signs and symbols as substitutes for an underlying reality" (128). Indeed, much impression management occurs below the level of awareness and is simply an immediate, seamless adjustment to changing social situations. Because norms and goals vary across situations, we present different aspects of ourselves in different circumstances. Each of these identities, however, may be authentic.

The Consequences of Impression Management

Presentations of self provide information that is necessary for interaction: "Information about the individual helps to define the situation, enabling others to know in advance what he [sic] will expect of them and what they may expect of him" (Goffman 1959:1). Actors engaged in this dynamic process of mutual impression management, Goffman says, develop a *working consensus*, an agreement about what sort of situation they are in and what sort of roles or identities they are playing. This public agreement need not correspond to the actors' private beliefs. But it is the publicly agreed upon definition of the situation that guides subsequent interaction. Once this agreement has been reached, it acquires a certain moral force. Actors can then expect to be treated in accord with this working definition, and in turn have an obligation to behave in accord with this agreement.

These interactional negotiations often end up reproducing familiar cultural patterns. To present certain identities and positions, we must draw on symbolic representations of those identities. Laurie, in *Little Women*, has to conduct himself like the cultural image of a suitor; a politician running for president must align her or his self-presentation with the cultural image of commander in chief. As is often the case with symbols, there may be a good deal of slippage between a symbolic representation and our underlying emotions, identities, and experiences. Laurie's feelings about Jo, his best friend, may not fit perfectly the role of lover. Nonetheless, he—and we—must use familiar symbols in order to communicate. Over time, the reliance of members of a culture on a limited set of symbols may narrow the underlying range of emotions, identities, and realities; in other words, this process may affirm stereotypic understandings of positions such as husbands, wives, professors, students, or athletes. Blumstein (1991) has argued that the process of identity negotiation with our romantic partners can actually lead to changes in our sense of self: the wife who used to do her car repairs before she married may discover she is mechanically inept after years of her husband's telling her she should stay away from the car. Stets and colleagues conclude that a lower status spouse's sense of self tends to conform to the views of a higher status partner (Cast, Stets, and Burke 1999). Moreover, the failure of a spouse to verify her or his partner's identity may lead this partner to exert more control in the relationship, sometimes leading to aggression (Stets and Burke 2005). More generally, through the performance of particular identities in our habitual interactions with those with whom we share everyday interactions, our identities eventually ossify into our "true selves." As *Oleanna's* John states eloquently, "You have to look at what you are, and what you feel, and how you act. And, finally, you have to look at how you act. And say: If that's what I *did*, that must be how I think of myself" (Mamet 1992:22).

Behavioral Confirmation

Impression management concerns how we present ourselves and the extent to which these self-presentations achieve our interactional goals.

Self-presentations are shaped not only by our conceptions of selves, however, but also by our conceptions of others. As we noted briefly in chapter 4, one of the more fascinating phenomena in human interaction is that we often confirm these preconceptions about other people through our very own behavior, a process known as *behavioral confirmation*. The best known example of this "Pygmalion effect" is the musical *My Fair Lady*, based on the play *Pygmalion* by George Bernard Shaw (which was itself based on a Greek myth). In this story, the elite Henry Higgins transforms a poor Cockney woman into an elegant and poised society lady; his treatment of her elicits the woman he wants her to be. The social psychological analog is a study by Rosenthal and Jacobson (1968). Teachers in an elementary school were given "information" about their students at the beginning of the school year. They were told that some of these students were potential late bloomers who would excel with the proper support and motivation. In reality, the students were randomly assigned to these labels. By the year's end, however, the students identified as late bloomers were performing as teachers had been told to expect. Why? The teachers behaved differently toward these students, providing them with careful feedback, teaching them more difficult material, and giving them more opportunities for responding in class. The teachers' expectations became a self-fulfilling prophecy: because of their behaviors, the students who received additional attention did in fact perform more strongly.

This study of behavioral confirmation and the hundreds that have followed attest to the ubiquity of this general pattern: initially false definitions of a situation can evoke behaviors that subsequently make the false belief true. Consistent with our emphasis on the structural circumstances within which interaction occurs, it is also true that such expectations are more likely to lead to a self-fulfilling prophecy if the expectation is held by a higher status person—and we might speculate, if the expectations are held about a lower status person. Higher status individuals have more power with which to enforce their own preconceptions; lower status individuals have less power with which to combat false expectations held by others (Stets and Burke 2005). Indeed, there is some evidence that men are more likely than women to induce others to provide behavioral confirmation for their own beliefs, while women are more likely than men to provide behavioral confirmation for the beliefs of others (Snyder 1984).

The implications of this process are profound. Consider physical appearance. A commonplace expectation in (at least) Western societies is that physically attractive people possess more socially appealing personalities than do those who are viewed as unattractive. In the study by Snyder, Tanke, and Berscheid (1977) mentioned in chapter 4, male college students interacted very differently over the phone with female college students they believed to be attractive; their behaviors, in turn, elicited interactional responses from the women that confirmed the men's assumptions about the personality characteristics of attractive and unattractive women. Thus, although there is no inherent link between conventional good looks and personality, the expectation that physically attractive people will also be more socially attractive became a self-fulfilling prophecy.

It is not a great leap to move from characteristics such as attractiveness to status markers such as gender, race, or sexuality; evidence of behavioral confirmation is strong for all of these social positions. Gender stereotypes and expectations frequently serve as the basis for behavioral confirmation. In a study by Skrypnek and Snyder (1982), pairs of students negotiated a division of labor for gender-stereotypic tasks. The students were not able to see each other. One member of each pair was led to believe that the other person was either male or female. Through the process of negotiation, the target of this belief ended up choosing tasks consistent with the expectations of their interaction partner. Both women and men ended up choosing male-typed tasks if their partner thought they were a man; both women and men ended up choosing female-typed tasks if their partner thought they were a woman. Gendered behaviors, in other words, are in part the product of other people's beliefs about gender; this is the social construction of gender.

This process of gender construction begins as early as the moment of birth. Rubin, Provenzano, and Luria (1974) found that new parents perceived their male and female infants very differently, even though independent observers saw no differences between the baby boys and girls. For example, parents described daughters as softer, prettier, more delicate, and smaller than sons. A more recent study (Karraker, Vogel, and Lake 1995) found that parents continue to perceive their newborns in stereotyped ways, although to a lesser degree than in the 1970s. These gendered perceptions likely affect parents' behavior toward and expectations of their children; indeed, there is a great deal of evidence that parents treat girls quite differently than they do boys (Beal 1994). In general, "mothers seem to be more emotionally warm and responsive with girls, and more encouraging of independence with boys. Fathers often spend more time with their sons and engage in more physical play with sons than daughters" (Karraker et al. 1995:688; see also Hastings et al. 2007). Similarly, Frederickson and Harrison's (2005) analysis of girls in athletics concludes that internalized gender expectations promote self-objectification—the application of a third-party gaze to one's own body—among young women and girls, thereby inhibiting an efficacious sense of self and athletic performance. Thus, social expectations function in very real ways as self-fulfilling prophecies, eliciting gender-stereotypical behaviors from children and young people in everyday life.

Racial stereotypes also create self-fulfilling prophecies. Word, Zanna, and Cooper (1974) considered the behavior of white interviewers toward both white and black job applicants. When interviewing black applicants, interviewers maintained a "nonimmediate" interview style, one with greater physical distance, less eye contact and less perceptual availability, made more speech errors (stutters, repetitions, incomplete sentences), and conducted shorter interviews. When they interviewed white applicants, interviewers used an "immediate" interview style, made fewer speech errors, and conducted longer interviews. In a follow-up, interviewers were trained to work with either an immediate or nonimmediate interview style and then used this style with both white and black applicants. Applicants subjected to the nonimmediate style performed less adequately and were more nervous than those exposed to the immediate style, regardless of their race. Performance differences between white and black job applicants thus reflected the interviewers' behaviors, not the applicants' qualifications.

The studies described above address gender, on the one hand, and race, on the other. Few consider the possibility that gender and race may work together in creating cognitive preconceptions and ultimately confirming those preconceptions. Given the considerable research that attests to stereotypic conceptions about interactional patterns of women and men, we can assume that had Word and colleagues varied the sex, as well as the race, of the job applicants, the effects might have been even more extreme. Note, too, that the sex of the interviewer is not even mentioned, nor is the race of the interviewer varied. All of these possibilities complicate the process of behavioral confirmation.

These examples illustrate how beliefs lead us to test and ultimately to create reality through altering the behavior of others. Interestingly, this process does not require actual behavioral confirmation by the target; it can also occur through reconstructive memory. In the study by Snyder and Uranowitz (1978) described in chapter 4, subjects were presented with information about the current sexual orientation of a woman about whom they had already been given a good deal of background information. As a result, these subjects reconstructed her biography to be consistent with their preconceptions of lesbian or heterosexual partnerships. Behavioral confirmation can even occur simply through people's awareness of expectations others hold for them. Steele and Aronson (1995) describe the possible effects of stereotype threat, which they define as "being at risk of confirming . . . a negative stereotype about one's group" (797). They demonstrate that the knowledge that others hold a negative stereotype about the intellectual ability of African Americans may interfere with test performance of African American students. As a result, they may perform less competently than they otherwise would, thereby confirming the original stereotype. Recent studies of stereotype threat document effects across an extensive list of social categories including race (Steele and Aronson 1995; Stone et al. 1999), gender (Koenig and Eagly 2005; Spencer, Steele, and Quinn 1999), age (Chasteen et al. 2005), social class (Croizet and Clare 1998), and (dis)ability (Quinn, Kahng, and Crocker 2004). Taken together, such studies suggest that cognitive and interactional strategies combine to create a powerfully reproductive system whereby preconceptions and stereotypes about ourselves and others are enacted and maintained.

Status Expectations

The idea of behavioral confirmation has also been central to another social psychological approach: expectation states theory (Berger, Conner, and Fişek 1974; Correll and Ridgeway 2003). Expectation states theory is much narrower in scope than the three theories around which we have organized this book, limiting its focus to "behavioral indicators of power and prestige" (Ridgeway and Walker 1995:288) such as participation in group discussions or influence over others. Although not generally identified as a symbolic interactionist perspective—indeed, its laboratory-based experimental methods and rigorous use of quantitative methods to model interaction are antithetical to much symbolic interactionist work (and more closely resemble social exchange)—we include it in this chapter because it shares several important assumptions with symbolic interactionism. These include a focus on the perceptions of actors, an assumption that these perceptions are socially constructed, and an emphasis on the social context of interaction. In addition, expectation states theory has addressed gender (see Ridgeway and Bourg 2004; Ridgeway and Smith-Lovin 1999), race (Cohen 1982; Goar and Sell 2005), and their intersection with other positions (Childers 2000; Renfrow 2005; Webster and Driskell 1983; Webster, Hysom, and Fullmer 1998) considerably more explicitly than any of the other theories we have considered so far.

Expectation states theory limits its empirical focus to small, task-oriented groups. Examples of this kind of group include a jury trying to ascertain the guilt or innocence of a defendant, a workgroup trying to solve a problem, or a family discussing how to allocate household chores. In these kinds of groups, members evaluate their own and each other's potential contributions to the group task in order to figure out how to reach the group's goal most effectively. Because group members generally share similar cultural beliefs, they tend to reach similar conclusions about each other's likely competence. These shared *performance expectations* are often self-fulfilling, resulting in a "power and prestige order" that favors those for whom the group has high performance expectations. This process works in two interlocking ways. First, individuals who have high expectations for themselves tend to contribute more to the group discussion, defend their opinions if challenged, and speak and act assertively. At the same time, others in the group, because they share these expectations, tend to allow the high-status members more opportunities to participate and evaluate their contributions more highly. Thus, these individuals appear to be more competent and more influential relative to the rest of the group, regardless of their actual competence at the task at hand. A similar process occurs for actors who are expected to perform poorly: they expect less of themselves, defer more to others, are provided with fewer opportunities to participate, and if they do participate, their contributions are evaluated less favorably.

Where do these performance expectations come from? According to the theory, expectations are based on *status characteristics,* attributes that are culturally associated with greater esteem and value (Berger et al. 1977). These can be *specific* characteristics, such as skills relevant to the particular task at hand, or *diffuse* characteristics that transcend particular situations, such as gender, race, education, and age. Expectation states theory argues that status characteristics are associated not only with greater social esteem, but also with "implicit expectations for competence." For example, people in this society tend to accord greater status to men than to women: "Observers consider men to be more skillful and competent than women, even when there is no objective gender difference in performance" (Carli 1991:94). When a group includes both men and women, actors of both sexes tend to expect men to contribute more to the group's goal than women, even if gender is not relevant to the task at hand (Pugh and Wahrman 1983; Wagner, Ford, and Ford 1986). These expectations become self-fulfilling prophecies. Because of others' higher expectations of them, men tend to contribute more to group discussion, behave more assertively, and emerge as task leaders in group interactions (Eagly and Karau 1991; Rashotte and Webster 2005; Wood and Karten 1986). Moreover, evaluation of members' participation is based on a double standard: men's performances are evaluated more favorably than women's, even if they are objectively identical (Foschi 1989, 1991, 2000). Thus, this theory provides an explanation for how societal beliefs and values (such as the differential valuation of women and men) are reproduced in small group, face-to-face interaction (Ridgeway 2009).

What is the relative influence of specific versus diffuse status characteristics? When information is available, specific status characteristics (such as specialized skills) can overcome the effects of diffuse characteristics (such as race, gender, or sexual orientation). Thus, if a mixed-sex group is attempting to solve a mathematics problem and one of the women in the group reveals that she is a mathematician, the high performance expectations stemming from her skills will likely overwhelm the low expectations stemming from her sex. It is important to note, however, that specific information is not always readily available: "Gender, like a few other statuses in our society (e.g., age and race), can be quickly discerned. When you see or hear a person, usually one of the first things you recognize is the person's sex." If sex is salient, "gender becomes the basis for your initial performance expectations for yourself and the other. Information on other factors such as specific abilities . . . is usually not as quickly available as it is on gender and therefore is less likely to shape initial expectations. As a result, interaction proceeds on performance expectations based on gender" (Ridgeway 1993:183–84). This theory thus helps to explain the pervasive influence of beliefs about gender on social life.

Resisting Expectations

We do not mean to imply that behavioral confirmation is seamless; this process can be curtailed. Perceivers can compensate for expectations they hold about others. If one has reason to expect that a person with whom one will interact is hostile, one might treat that person particularly warmly. In so doing, one is attempting to produce behavior that contradicts expectations. Even though this strategy tends to be successful in eliciting the desired behavior, however, it does not always overturn the original expectation. In addition, the targets of expectations may actively try to dispel perceivers' false expectations in an attempt to assert and confirm their own self-definitions. (This implies, of course, that they are aware of others' expectations.) These strategies may be dramatically more successful when enacted by a higher status person than by a lower status person. Ridgeway (1993) reports that in expectation states experiments, women who challenge low performance expectations by contributing assertively to group discussions can experience a "backlash" reaction because their behavior is perceived as illegitimate (Butler and Geis 1990; Carli 1990; Ridgeway 1982; Ridgeway and Bourg 2004). The success of such strategies depends on how certain each party is of their own expectations, the intensity of these expectations, and on the social structural power of the actors. At the beginning of act 2 of *Oleanna*, for example, John has discovered that Carol has filed a complaint of sexual harassment against him and makes a speech that is clearly intended to convince her that he is genuinely concerned with the welfare of his students, that he is not, as he puts it, a bogeyman. His failure to convince her is eloquent testimony to the dramatic shift in each actor's power.

Interactional Repairs

Despite our best attempts at skillful self-presentations, interaction does not always proceed smoothly. Upon occasion, the identity we present is undermined.

For example, we may present ourselves as knowledgeable about a particular subject, but then find ourselves unable to answer our teacher's (or our students'!) questions. At other times, the working consensus about the definition of the situation breaks down. For example, a patient or doctor may become physically aroused during a medical exam, destroying the consensus that the examination of the patient's body is a medical, rather than sexual, procedure (Emerson 1970).

In many cases, the audience may help to repair these kinds of interactional breakdowns by pretending not to notice the problem or by facilitating the actor's recovery from the gaffe. This kind of teamwork is another example of the way that people work together to maintain the "reality" of the front stage (Goffman 1959). In other cases, the actor herself will undertake to repair the interactional breach. Often this repair is effected by offering an *account*, a statement explaining why the breach occurred. Accounts are closely related to impression management, because they are a means of controlling others' perceptions.

There are two types of accounts: *justifications*, which acknowledge that a behavior occurred but deny that it was problematic, and *excuses*, which acknowledge that a behavior was problematic but deny responsibility for it (Scott and Lyman 1968). In *Oleanna*, the professor admits to having touched the student, but justifies that touch by denying any sexual intent—rather, he says, he was attempting to comfort an obviously distraught student. In contrast, the professor might have admitted that the touch was sexual but attempted to excuse his behavior by explaining that he believed his advances to be welcome.

Note that justifications and excuses are both verbal repairs. Interaction relies not simply on behavior but fundamentally on language. Through language, identities, self-concepts, and impressions are constructed, justified, maintained, and altered.

Repairs and Social Structure

Once offered, accounts are not always honored. Whether an account is judged acceptable depends on the behavior in question, the situation, and the actors involved. One's family might excuse tardiness that an employer would find unacceptable. A man might be excused for forgetting to attend a business meeting, but not the birth of his child. Moreover, not everyone can call an individual to account: a professor might hold a student accountable for classroom performance, but another student could not. Thus, interactional repairs are not always available or effective.

The acceptability of accounts is closely correlated with structural differences, social position, and power. For example, gender affects the legitimacy of accounts. "Overwhelming desire" might be accepted as an excuse for a man's sexual improprieties, because cultural beliefs about masculinity include the idea that men are driven by their sexual impulses. The same excuse might not work as well for a woman, because women's responsibility in performing traditional femininity is to control their own and others' sexuality (Fox 1977). Situations may exist in which unexpected behavior is more likely to be accepted by others. Smith, Powers, and Suarez (2005) recently observed subjects' reactions to hypothetical politicians' errant behavior. Their findings suggest that—although women are less likely to accept politicians' accounts than are men, regardless of the politician's sex—individuals are most forgiving of acts inconsistent with gender stereotypes (e.g., a male engaging in a sexual affair with a superior or a female engaging in a sexual affair with a subordinate). Furthermore, they observed that individuals tend to be swayed by justifications more than by excuses.

Other social positions also affect whether one's accounts of questionable behavior will be honored or even heard. Gallant (1992) describes the accounts given by seventeenth- and eighteenth-century slave owners for the escape of their slaves, and notes that "history hears the planter but not the slave" (390). Slaves, because of their race and social position, were not entitled to give accounts; their understanding of situations, indeed their very selves, were not believed by white slave owners to be important or valuable. Individuals in stigmatized positions often find that their accounts are dishonored or disbelieved (Goffman 1963). Rosenhan's classic study (1973) demonstrates this fact forcefully. Eight mentally healthy research confederates managed to gain entry to mental hospitals as patients by claiming to hear voices. After entering the hospital, each patient behaved normally—yet in no case was the deception detected. Because these patients had been labeled insane, their subsequent behavior was interpreted as consistent with that label and their attempts to present themselves as sane were dishonored. The pseudopatients remained locked in the hospitals for an average of nineteen days; the longest stay was fifty-two days.

The election of Barack Obama to the U.S. presidency provides a fascinating example of how an individual's multiple social positions can interact and how this process shapes interactional repairs. Obama, the son of a white American woman and a black Kenyan man, attended Columbia University and later Harvard Law School before serving several terms in the Illinois Senate and later the United States Senate. Well educated, charismatic, and able to mobilize significant social networks developed through his early professional years, Obama gained national exposure with his keynote address at the 2004 Democratic National Convention, where he presented his unique autobiography as an example of what it means to be an American. Throughout Obama's campaign his attempts to shape others' impressions were challenged by opponents who brought to light his past affiliations with Bill Ayers, a participant in several domestic bombings during the 1970s, and the Reverend Jeremiah Wright, a liberation theologist known for drawing attention (sometimes confrontationally) to inequalities embedded in American society. However, Obama mastered the ability to discuss race in a polarized context, leaving commentators and the public simultaneously uncertain of whether he is "too black" or "not black enough." Because of the combination of his characteristics—his elite education, accumulated social capital, lofty oratory, and hip public persona—he was able to repair his image. Despite considerable resistance to his candidacy, Obama cultivated a mass of followers and won the presidency.

Contrast this with the 1972 candidacy of Shirley Chisholm, the daughter of immigrants and the first African American woman to run for the Democratic nomination. She shared striking similarities with Obama in regard to background (e.g., both lived abroad as children, attended Columbia University, were junior legislators) and campaign strategy (e.g., opposed a war, ran as candidates of change, concentrated on the youth vote). Her campaign was dogged by attacks—both in the media and physically—because of her endorsement by the Black Panthers. Others criticized Chisholm's "twofer" status, as both black and female. Even the National Black Political Convention and the Black Caucus failed to endorse her candidacy in large part because she was a woman. Yet, with little odds of winning and despite fierce opposition, Chisholm kept her focus on something larger than her own political goals:

> I ran for the Presidency, despite hopeless odds, to demonstrate the sheer will and refusal to accept the status quo. The next time a woman runs, or a black, or a Jew or anyone from a group that the country is "not ready" to elect to its highest office, I believe that he or she will be taken seriously from the start. . . . I ran because somebody had to do it first. (Chisholm 1973)

The 2008 election also illustrates how the meaning of social positions can change over time. The slave owners' accounts described in Gallant's study likely received different reactions before and after the Civil War. It would have been impossible for Barack Obama to acquire the public support and funding necessary to conduct a national campaign prior to the civil rights movement and the trail blazed by Shirley Chisholm. And the professor's abuse of power described in *Oleanna* would have aroused much less fury just thirty years ago—because the concept of sexual harassment had not yet been publicly constructed. Similarly, accounts may vary in acceptability across different cultures. For example, accusations of infidelity might justify a man's killing his wife in some cultures, but not in the United States. Thus, accounts, like symbols, are dynamic and situationally variable.

Self-Presentation and Social Structure

Social structures, then, play a crucial role in face-to-face interaction, a fact that much symbolic interactionist work (and much social psychological research more generally) does not adequately acknowledge. Erving Goffman's work stands in sharp contrast to this general trend. Goffman was deeply interested in social structure and its effects on interaction. Presentations of self, Goffman argued, are closely tied to individuals' positions in social structures:

> It is plain that if an individual is to give and receive what is considered his [sic] ritual due in social situations, then he must—whether by intent or in effect—style himself so that others present can immediately know the social (and sometimes the personal) identity of he who is to be dealt with; and in turn he must be able to acquire this information about those he thus informs. Some displays seem to be specialized for this identificatory, early-warning function: in the case of gender, hair style, clothing, and tone of voice. (Goffman 1976:2)

Presentations of self are thus manifestations of social structure in face-to-face interaction: they alert others to one's social positions even before interaction begins.

Goffman (1976, 1977) was particularly interested in the ways in which actors manage their presentations of gendered selves in social situations. Many people believe that "masculine" and "feminine" behaviors are simply automatic expressions of males' and females' underlying natures—a belief Goffman termed the "doctrine of natural expression." (Note the similarity between the doctrine of natural expression and essentialism, discussed in chapter 1.) However, Goffman (1976) claims that "expression in the main is not instinctive but socially learned and socially patterned. . . . And this is so even though individuals come to employ expressions in what is sensed to be a spontaneous and unselfconscious way, that is, uncalculated, unfaked, natural" (7). Gender displays, then, are not so much representations of underlying difference between males and females as they are indications of actors' cultural competence—in other words, their ability to perform the culturally prescribed roles believed appropriate for males and females. This contention, of course, is fundamental to the social constructionist perspective discussed in chapter 2. In addition, these displays signal to others that the actor is claiming a particular kind of self with a set of associated traits, abilities, privileges, and feelings. Through these displays, actors position themselves in the social hierarchy.

Like other aspects of self-presentation, gender is actively manipulated in the service of particular goals. Take, for example, the gendered self-presentation of Hillary Rodham Clinton during the 2008 Democratic presidential primary. Earlier in this chapter, we described how the Clinton campaign strategically used media advertisements to portray Hillary as strong and ready to lead. She and other female leaders—such as Secretary of State Condoleezza Rice and Speaker of the House Nancy Pelosi—who wish to succeed in a traditionally male sphere must become what Connell (2009) calls "honorary men" who are "tougher than the toughest" (75). Although such performances helped others see Clinton as an effective politician, her demeanor often led the public and commentators alike to perceive her as unfeminine and unlikable (Thomas 1999), and Clinton was urged to soften her presentation of self (Stansell 2008). On several occasions she did exactly this. Consider a pivotal moment during the Democratic primary. After placing third in the Iowa caucus and heading into the New Hampshire primary, Clinton allowed the public to see her more feminine side as she fought back tears during emotional interviews. Some onlookers were pleasantly surprised by this rare glimpse into the personality of a public figure; others framed it as just another highly choreographed performance. (Presumably, both masculine and feminine traits cannot coexist within the same person without raising questions of authenticity.) For Clinton, it seemed, there was no way to "do gender" appropriately and win.

Perhaps the most fascinating aspect of political self-presentation is that everyone (the media, public, and other politicians) presumably knows that a candidate's self-presentation is deliberate, strategic, and probably not entirely true to her or his own character and beliefs—yet these efforts appear to be taken at face value by most observers. Thus, although on some level we know that impressions are strategically managed, our faith in the "doctrine of natural expression"—the belief that the impressions people give off offer insight into their character—remains strong. (This case is another example of the fundamental attribution error, discussed in chapter 4: we tend to attribute others' behavior to their character, rather than to situational influences.)

Impression management may go beyond the superficial level of appearances. Hochschild (1983) describes the ways in which flight attendants and other service workers are instructed to manage not only their behavior but also their feelings. She calls this process "emotional work," which she defines as "the management of feeling to create a publicly observable facial and bodily display" (7). Part of the flight attendant's job is to provide a convincing appearance of enthusiastic, willing service for the passengers' comfort; attendants must suppress other emotions such as anger and resentment at treatment from inconsiderate passengers. Hochschild notes that these expec-

tations for emotion work are not gender neutral. Women are disproportionately located in service jobs requiring emotional labor. But even when women
and men occupy the same position, as in the case of flight attendants, women
are expected to care emotionally for the passengers more than are their male
counterparts.

Goffman's (1976, 1977) description of impression management challenges
the belief that gender displays reveal individuals' essential natures. In contrast, he argues that these displays are the interactional expression of social hierarchy. Goffman notes that people who are socially subordinate—including
women and "subordinate males" (those men who, by virtue of their youth,
social class, sexual orientation, or other social positions, have less power than
other men)—rarely challenge their place in the social structure. In fact, these
people often defer to others. The explanation, Goffman argues, is pragmatic:
by demonstrating that they acknowledge their subordination, they signal to
those with more power that a direct display of dominance is unnecessary.
(Note the parallels to exchange theory: the person with less power is exchanging his or her deference for the more powerful person's forbearance.) In most
cases, these self-subordinating presentations are subtle, but

> however trivial some of these little gains and losses may appear to be, by summing
> them all up across all the social situations in which they occur, one can see that
> their total effect is enormous. The expression of subordination and domination
> through this swarm of situational means is more than a mere tracing or symbol
> or ritualistic affirmation of the social hierarchy. These expressions considerably
> constitute the hierarchy; they are the shadow *and* the substance. (Goffman 1976:6)

Thus, these displays both express and reinforce power and stratification.

Resistance and Negotiation

In some situations, individuals may present themselves in accord with gender
expectations, as we have discussed. In other situations, however, individuals
may resist these traditional expectations, manipulating their self-presentation
to avoid association with some stereotype. A good example of this process is
women's self-protective behavior in public spaces. According to the research
of Carol Brooks Gardner (1990), women know that being female suggests to
others that they are vulnerable to attack, and they strategically alter their self-
presentation in order to reduce their risk of becoming targets of street crime:

> As aspiring criminals will have to depend on judgments of appearance to select
> prospective victims, so those who seek to escape victimization must depend on
> assessment of strangers' appearance and manipulation of their own in order to

avoid crime. One way to cope with crime in public therefore will be to develop an array of behavioral strategies that are also appearance dependent; alternatively, people will curtail others' visual access in order to prevent being judged a suitable target. (314)

Women may avoid certain parts of town or stay home after dark. They may dress "tough," walk with a confidence they do not feel, or choose their company (another woman, a man, a cell phone, or a dog) with an eye to safety. They may even feign the company of a male protector by leaving male belongings visible in their car or home or adding a man's name to their mailbox or answering machine message. These findings "remind us that public places are arenas for the enactment and display of power and privilege"—and that one basis of power is gender (Gardner 1989:55).

Men's self-presentations may also be affected by their knowledge of women's concerns. Staples (1994), for example, describes the way in which his appearance as a large African American man affects the women with whom he shares public space:

My first victim was a woman—white, well dressed, probably in her early twenties. I came upon her late one evening on a deserted street in Hyde Park, a relatively affluent neighborhood in an otherwise mean, impoverished section of Chicago. As I swung onto the avenue behind her, there seemed to be a discreet, uninflammatory distance between us. Not so. She cast back a worried glance. To her, the youngish black man—a broad six feet two inches with a beard and billowing hair, both hands shoved into the pockets of a bulky military jacket— seemed menacingly close. After a few more quick glimpses, she picked up her pace and was soon running in earnest. Within seconds she disappeared into a cross street. (156)

Staples goes on to describe the strategies he has developed to present himself as unthreatening, including walking slowly, keeping a comfortable distance away from others, and speaking hyperpolitely to police officers. Finally,

On late-evening constitutionals, I employ what has proved to be an excellent tension-reducing measure: I whistle melodies from Beethoven and Vivaldi and the more popular classical composers. Even steely New Yorkers hunching forward toward nighttime destinations seem to relax, and occasionally they even join in the tune. Virtually everybody seems to sense that a mugger wouldn't be warbling bright, sunny selections from Vivaldi's *Four Seasons*. It is my equivalent of the cowbell that hikers wear when they know they are in bear country. (158)

Staples's self-presentation resists the stereotypical association of black men with danger and threat. Thus, individuals attempt to present themselves in a manner that will help them to achieve their interactional goals.

Snow and Anderson (1987, 1993) found that street people in Austin, Texas, similarly resisted negative class-based stereotypes. The homeless people they studied tended to construct positive personal identities through three distinct forms of "identity talk." First, some individuals distanced themselves from the roles, people, and institutions associated with homelessness: "I'm not like the other guys who hang out at the 'Sally' [Salvation Army] . . . you can't really learn about street people from studying me, because I'm different" (Snow and Anderson 1987:1349). Alternately, some people embraced these roles, people, and ideologies: "It would have to be a bigger purpose than just money to get me off the streets, like a religious mission." "I'm a bum and I know who my friends are" (Snow and Anderson 1987:1356–57). Finally, some people engaged in fictive storytelling, embellishing past accomplishments and fantasizing about future possibilities. Snow and Anderson also note that these forms of identity talk can be gendered. Homeless men's fictive stories, for example, "were generally organized around four themes: self-employment, money, material possessions, and the opposite sex." The content of these fantasies demonstrates that gender expectations condition even those who have become separated from other normative social institutions:

> That these four factors function as springboards for fanciful identities constructed by homeless men in particular is hardly surprising, given that success as an adult male in America is defined in large part in terms of job, money, possessions, and women. This thematic connection also suggests that, while homeless males tend to stand very much outside the normative order in their way of life, some of them are, nonetheless, very much of that order in their dreams and fantasies. (1361)

Duneier's (2000) observations of unhoused men living and selling printed material on the sidewalks of New York City's Greenwich Village offer other insights into the intersection of gender and the stigma of life on the streets. While Duneier's primary focus is identifying the highly organized and sustainable systems—both material and social—that underpin life and commerce in a seemingly chaotic locale, his observations of low status men (i.e., poor, black, and lacking conventional housing and employment) in conversation with female passersby also illuminate the methods through which they exert control over women of all statuses. Whether the women they encounter are black or white, poor or rich, unemployed or employed, the men are able to break the norms governing openings and closings in polite conversation—what Duneier and Molotch (1999) term "interactional vandalism"—to entangle these women in a web of undesired, flirtatious conversation. Consequently, their ability to "get over" on others is not limited to getting good prices from customers; "getting over" on others carries over into everyday talk with the women they encounter. Although these men find themselves in lower status positions across social categories, it is their position as men that enables them to dominate women in conversation and bolster their sense of self as men. Taken together, these studies indicate that identities are not simply assigned; they are negotiated and can be resisted by those in stigmatized positions.

On occasion, resistance may entail playing into others' stereotypes. Ramos (1979) describes an interaction between an elementary school principal and the father of a Mexican American student accused of breaking a window, whom Ramos calls Mr. Perez. Although he knew Mr. Perez to be interactionally competent and articulate in English, Ramos observed quite a different presentation of self in Perez's interaction with the principal:

> As I watched Mr. Perez talk with the principal, it occurred to me that he appeared to be both nervous and stupid. He spoke with broken English, and acted as though he did not understand the situation very well. . . . He conformed to the typification of a Mexican American who speaks little English, and who can only deal with people in informal situations. (141–42)

When Ramos later asked Mr. Perez "why he had presented himself in such a demeaning way," Mr. Perez answered:

> Oh, I was pulling a *movida* [strategy]. You know, I came on like the dumb Mexican, all lost and confused. You know how that guy thinks of us most of the time. Besides, had I come on straight, he might have held me responsible for the window Freddy broke. I am not about to pay for a window my boy broke by accident. They ought to provide a bigger play area so that kids don't break a window every time they throw a ball. (142)

Thus, in some situations, strategies for resistance may actually involve using others' preconceptions for one's own ends (Morris 2005; Renfrow 2004).

It is important to recognize, however, that resistance is not always successful. The term *negotiation* implies that the interacting parties have equal opportunity to control the social identities presented; they come to the bargaining table with equal resources and together develop a joint definition of the situation. This image of fair negotiation is not always accurate, especially in the case of stigmatized groups. Those people with more resources and more power can exert more control over interaction and the negotiation of identities. Despite homeless individuals' attempts to present themselves favorably, they are deeply stigmatized by the rest of the population. Despite Staples's (1994) attempt to present himself as nonthreatening, he may be harassed by police officers who perceive all black men as dangerous. And, despite a woman's attempts to avoid conversation with poor men on the sidewalk, she may be verbally harassed and entangled in a web of undesired conversation. Some people, in short, have more control over negotiation than others. Social structural factors condition social interaction.

Conclusions

The symbolic interactionist approach to self and identity has clear connections to both social cognition and social exchange. Cognition is central to symbolic interaction: it is through thought that meanings come to be attached to symbols, and it is through thought that we are able to interpret these symbols. In addition, the negotiation of identities requires a set of cognitive processes. An actor must review her identities and select those she deems appropriate for a situation; at the same time she must review the identities she wants to impute to the other person. Put in the terms of social cognition, the actor must scan her self-schemas; on the basis of a cognitive appraisal of the situation, certain identities will be more salient than others. At the same time, she must scan the possible selves others might perform and coordinate her behavior strategically with these selves. Like all cognitive processes, this need not be—and perhaps most often is not—conscious. On the other hand, particular structural circumstances may make this everyday negotiation acutely conscious. Dorothy Allison (1994) offers searing examples of this selective screening. Writing of her negotiation of the interactive challenges of being poor, she avows,

> My people were not remarkable. We were ordinary, but even so we were mythical. We were the *they* everyone talks about—the ungrateful poor. I grew up trying to run away from the fate that destroyed so many of the people I loved, and having learned the habit of hiding, I found I had also learned to hide from myself. I did not know who I was, only that I did not want to be *they*, the ones who are destroyed or dismissed to make the "real" people, the important people, feel safer. . . . The habit of hiding was deeply set in me. . . . If I told the truth about my life, my family, my sexual desire, my history, I would move over into that unknown territory, the land of they, would never have the chance to name my own life, to understand it or claim it. (13–14)

Symbolic interaction is also linked to social exchange. Both theories take the interaction, rather than the individual, as their unit of analysis. However, the two theories offer quite different pictures of social interaction. While empirical work in social exchange has focused mainly on the exchange of resources between actors, symbolic interaction focuses on the *meaning* of these

resources, as well as on the exchange of cognitive and behavioral manifestations of identities, adding a far more complex and subtle level of analysis.
Moreover, exchange theory considers the resources possessed by each actor,
and actors' positions in the social structure, to be the keys to understanding
behavior. Thus, actors are essentially interchangeable: the implication is that
in the same structural position, every individual will behave similarly. Symbolic interactionism, in contrast, focuses much more on the selves of actors.
The individual's self-concept, identities, and subjective interpretations of
meaning guide behavior.

As a result, symbolic interactionism is able to explain the subtleties of interaction neglected by exchange theory. On the other hand, exchange theory's
conceptions of social structure, inequality, and power are better developed
than those of symbolic interactionism. In fact, the most frequent critique of
symbolic interactionism is its failure to adequately address social structure
and power. For example, Stryker and Statham (1985) write:

> Symbolic interactionism's strength is its ability to conceptualize social actors
> who can construct their lines of action individually and cooperatively and who
> can also alter the social structural conditions within which they act. Its weak-
> ness is its inadequate conceptualization and analyses of the social structural
> constraints—ranging from minimal to virtually total—within which social ac-
> tion is constructed and its inability to deal with stability in individual and social
> behavior. (313)

Although symbolic interactionism helps to illuminate how beliefs and
expectations about other people are maintained and perpetuated, it does not
always address the question of where these expectations originate, and why.
What do they accomplish, and for whom? When they are resisted, who resists
and who enforces them? To answer these questions, we must look beyond the
interactional level and address more macrolevel issues of power, social structure, and inequality. Although we have discussed a number of studies that do
integrate social positions and structures into their analyses, these studies do
not constitute the mainstream of symbolic interactionist research. Identity
work, meaning construction, and self-presentation are important, but so are
material resources and structural positions. Without an understanding of factors such as stratification and power, the picture is incomplete.

This is acutely evident in the interactions between John and Carol in *Oleanna*. In act 1, John has virtually all the power to set up the interaction, to
decide who can speak and what they can say, to decide when the interaction
starts and when it is over, and, most importantly, to decide literally who each
person will be. The interactional model McCall and Simmons outline may not
even apply to Carol: she may not be able to devise identities for herself and

for John, so great is his power over her. In other words, substantial imbalances of power may short-circuit the negotiation of identities. Actors import into these interactions the full force of those structural positions they occupy. Although both social exchange and symbolic interaction offer analytic insight, neither alone can explain such an interaction.

Finally, both symbolic interactionism and social exchange theory assume that self-interest motivates human action: people act in ways that they believe will result in desirable outcomes for themselves. These two theories conceptualize self-interest in radically different ways, however. Because exchange theory conceptualizes the self narrowly as a possessor of resources and social position, self-interest can only entail the maximization of those resources. Symbolic interactionism's richer idea of self, however, results in a much broader conceptualization of self-interest. Individuals are believed to be motivated by many desires, including the admiration and well-being of significant others and the maintenance of valued identities, as well as the maximization of one's own resources. Thus, self-interest may involve sacrificing resources to meet other goals.

Recent developments in social cognitive understandings of selves and identities also suggest future questions for symbolic interactionism. There is increasing interest in how an individual's various structural positions and social roles are integrated to form a social self. How do being female, black, a grandmother, and having a professional job combine into a coherent identity? Self-schemas have been assumed to be organized as a relatively harmonious set of many distinct identities, some more salient than others. What happens to the definition of self-schemas if we think of these identities as not so separable, but as always interconnected in complex and often contradictory ways, and experienced simultaneously (Fenstermaker and West 2002; West and Fenstermaker 1995)? *Oleanna's* John is an arrogant college professor who grew up thinking he was stupid; *Little Women's* Jo is a woman who wants a career and does not want to marry but is also eager to have children. Barack Obama is a man who rose from community organizer to commander in chief. He appears to be a devoted husband and a loving father to his children, yet he lives in a culture that often vilifies men of color. Nevertheless, Obama, who was awarded the Nobel Peace Prize, has come to symbolize the movement to unite people across racial and cultural divisions. Because we are always selecting and performing various identities in complex, situated combinations, playing off of other actors doing the same things in the same situations, our models both of selves and of interactions must be considerably more complex.

How does symbolic interactionism correspond to the four approaches to gender we described in chapter 2? Because of its theoretical allegiance to the social construction of self and identity, symbolic interaction is incompatible with essentialist approaches to gender. Because of its commitment to the ongoing, active nature of this construction, it is also somewhat incompatible with the socialization perspective, which tends to view gender as instilled in childhood and relatively static thereafter. It should be clear that symbolic interactionism is closely related to the social constructionist approach to gender; indeed, it is from this tradition that the social constructionist approach developed. As we have suggested throughout this chapter, symbolic interaction is also compatible with a structural approach to gender, although many practitioners of symbolic interactionism tend to deemphasize or even ignore the effects of social structure. While it is true that symbolic interactionists at the margins of the discipline (as well as many nonsocial psychologists who use symbolic interactionist ideas in their work) do attend to these issues, their research often goes unread by mainstream social psychologists. Thus, this work, although important and illuminating, often does not affect the bulk of social psychological research.

We have now completed our overview of the three main theories of social psychology: social exchange, social cognition, and symbolic interactionism. Many social psychology textbooks and courses, however, are organized not by theory but by topic. We believe that the theoretical grounding presented in the preceding chapters can also illuminate the traditional topical areas of social psychology. To illustrate, we now turn to two of the most intriguing topics in social psychology: aggression and altruism.

Note

1. Respondents are asked to provide twenty short-phrase answers to the question "Who am I?" The most common categories of responses to this question are personality characteristics, social structural positions, and personal evaluations.

6

Altruism and Aggression

Gendered Dynamics of Helping and Harming Others

U P TO THIS POINT, OUR JOURNEY through social psychology has been organized by the major theoretical perspectives in this field. We have explored the ways in which social exchange, social cognition, and symbolic interactionism explain the relationships among individuals and the societies in which they live and the ways in which each perspective incorporates, facilitates, or impedes a gendered analysis of these relationships. At this point, we shift orientation from theory to thematic topic.

A glance at the table of contents of virtually any social psychology text reveals a list of only loosely connected topics. Our choice to organize this volume around key social psychological theories reflects our conviction that ideas provide a preferable organizational framework. As the reader has discovered, however, in our analyses of these theories we have also discussed the details of socialization, stereotyping, attribution, impression management, the development and negotiation of selves and identities, and other central social psychological topics. In this chapter, we focus in considerably greater detail on two popular areas of social psychological research: altruism and aggression. We shift focus here to illustrate how using gender (and other dimensions of societal inequalities) as an analytic lens allows us to make connections across specific topics.

Altruism and aggression each earn a full chapter in almost all social psychology texts. Typically, these chapters are located sequentially, in recognition that there is an intuitive link between helping and harming others. Altruism and aggression are assumed to be opposite behaviors. As is often true with opposites, however, their dynamics are more similar than they might at first appear. In this chapter we consider the substance of the connections between them, drawing on a series of examples to show that gender and other systems of hierarchy form a good deal of this substance. We analyze explanations for altruism and aggression offered by the major social psychological theories. We then review the key questions that have organized research in each field, illustrating with empirical research and critiquing assumptions made about gender, race, sexuality, and class positions. We also discuss some of the implications of researchers' methodological preferences, and finally, turn to thematic issues that crosscut these two fields. We begin with definitions, since neither altruism nor aggression is as easily defined as it might at first appear.

Definitions

John: I'll make you a deal. You stay here. We'll start the whole course over. I'm going to say it was not you, it was I who was not paying attention. We'll start the whole course over. Your grade is an "A." Your final grade is an "A."

Carol: But the class is only half over . . .

John: Your grade for the whole term is an "A." If you will come back and meet with me. A few more times. Your grade's an "A." Forget about the paper. You didn't like it, you didn't like writing it. It's not important. What's important is that I awake your interest, if I can, and that I answer your questions. Let's start over.

Carol: Over. With what?

John: Say this is the beginning.

Carol: Of what?

John: Of the class.

Carol: But we can't start over.

John: I say we can. I say we can.

Carol: But I don't believe it.

John: Yes, I know that. But it's true. What is The Class but you and me?

Carol: There are rules.

John: Well. We'll break them.

Carol: How can we?

John: We won't tell anybody.

Carol: Is that all right?

John: I say that it's fine.

Carol: Why would you do this for me?

John: I like you.

Carol: Um . . .

John: There's no one here but you and me.

Carol: All right. I did not understand. When you referred . . .

John: All right, yes?

Carol: When you referred to hazing.

John: Hazing.

Carol: You write, in your book. About the comparative . . . the comparative . . .

John: Are you checking your notes?

Carol: Yes. (Mamet 1992:26–27)

Altruism

This passage is the central "action" of Mamet's play *Oleanna*. In this scene John offers to help Carol do better in his class, a direct response to her plea that she does not understand. What do we mean by the term *help*? *Helping behavior* refers simply to any act that provides assistance to another person. The motives or intentions of the helper are irrelevant. The consequences of the behavior define helping. Note that consequences can be both material (e.g., grades or medical aid) and psychological (e.g., feeling supported).

If John were so busy that taking this time with Carol would cost him dearly in some other realm, we might label his behavior altruistic. *Altruism* refers to action performed voluntarily to help someone when the actor has no expectation of receiving a reward; some people define acts as altruistic only if the actor also incurs costs. Here, the intentions and motives of the helper are crucial. Although most acts of altruism are also acts of helping, this is not always the case. An act intended to be helpful, even at great cost to the helper, does not always have helpful consequences. Intervening in a fight, for example, can sometimes accelerate the conflict. Also, actions intended to be helpful are not always perceived as such. Consider the dynamics of chivalry: How does it feel to have someone offer to walk you home at night or to carry your groceries? One might feel flattered, relieved, humiliated, or annoyed.

Prosocial behavior is another related concept. This term refers to acts that are in accord with or support the norms of a given community or culture. Fighting in war generally is considered prosocial behavior, in that such service is consistent with the predominant values and norms of a society. This is an even broader category than helping, since some prosocial behaviors are not helpful to their immediate targets, even though they may advance the interests of the relevant society.

Thus, in order to understand the general domain of positive actions, one must take into account the intentions and motives of the actor(s), the consequences of the action, and the perceptions and reactions of the person(s) being helped. We emphasize in the remainder of this chapter that the social contexts within which such actions occur are also important. Social behaviors are not benign; they reflect prevailing relationships of power. Helping and harming behaviors are no exception, as the following discussion demonstrates.

Aggression

Let us return to the extended example from *Oleanna*. John's offer appears to be altruistic: he will spend extra time to help Carol understand the class material. As we find out in act 2, however, Carol does not interpret this offer as altruism. Rather, she perceives it, and John's consoling hug, as an aggressive attempt at sexual harassment. As the play continues, the physical aggression becomes clearer, culminating in a scene in which John physically assaults Carol. The focus of the play shifts from altruism to aggression.

Defining aggression appears simple. *Aggression*, most people would agree, is any behavior that hurts someone else: hitting someone, shooting someone, stabbing someone, and so on. But what if the harm is unintentional? A driver might hit a pedestrian crossing the street, causing severe injury, but is this accidental injury really aggression? On the other hand, what if a person tries to shoot someone, but misses? Most people would define this act as aggressive, even though it does not result in harm. Although intent is more difficult to assess than harm (since, as we noted in chapter 5, minds are private), it is clearly an important component of aggression.

Motivation is also important. If a homeowner shoots and kills an armed robber who breaks into his or her house, is that shooting aggressive? When soldiers kill others during a war, are those deaths the result of aggression? (And if so, whose aggression—the soldiers' or their government's?) War and self-defense are two circumstances in which most people consider violence to be legitimate; indeed, they are often considered prosocial behavior. Discipline is another such situation. Many people approve of using a moderate degree of physical punishment to control children, and the death penalty is accepted by some people as punishment for the most heinous crimes. These normative uses of aggression are culturally defined as *prosocial*, in contrast with criminal violence, collectively defined as *antisocial*.

It is important to note that what is defined as prosocial and as antisocial reflects the systems of power that prevail in a given society. Thus, political changes can also lead to changes in definitions of aggression. Until the last few decades, for example, many states had laws that allowed husbands to beat their wives or force their wives to have sex against their will. Most states have now redefined these behaviors as wife battering and marital rape. There are also cross-cultural differences in what is defined as antisocial aggression, as illustrated in American anthropologist Paul Winther's (2007) account of the killing (murder?) of Neni Bai, a mentally and physically disabled Indian girl. After she became pregnant with the child of a lower-caste man, Neni's father cut her throat and dumped her body in a well. In some cultures, it is permissible for male family members to kill a woman whose sexual or social virtue has become tarnished. Such an action would be defined as murder in the United States and severely punished.

Whose viewpoint is considered when defining aggression? Most people would define rape as an aggressive act, but definitions of a sexual encounter can be contested. If a woman says she was raped, but the man says they engaged in consensual sex, how does one decide whether his behavior was in fact aggressive? If the woman did consent to intercourse, but did so not out of desire but rather emotional coercion, fear, or threats of injury or death, was it aggression? And what about the status of words? Some people believe that words, as well as actions, can be violent: if a man regularly threatens to kill his wife, but never actually does so, are his words aggressive? These examples make clear the importance of interpretation and meaning—and power—in defining aggression and violence. As we noted in our discussion of symbolic interaction in chapter 5, the same behavior can carry different meanings in different contexts. In one situation, shooting someone might be considered aggressive; in another, it might be considered patriotic or heroic.

Social psychologists often distinguish three types of aggression. In *instrumental aggression*, actors know their actions will hurt others but use aggression strategically to achieve a specific outcome, such as discipline, obedience, or material gain. *Expressive aggression*, in contrast, results from emotions such as anger and is intended simply to harm another. In *indirect aggression*, actors use manipulative methods, such as gossiping, exchanging friends, trying to win others to one's side, excluding from groups, and so on (Björkqvist 1994:182) to harm others. These forms of aggression are not always separable: consider, for example, parents who strike their children out of anger but with an ultimate goal of control or discipline. Breines and Gordon (1983) also note that violence can be expressive on an individual level but instrumental on a collective level: A given incident of wife battering, for example, can express individual anger, but large-scale patterns of battering can be "an important ingredient in the continued subordination of women; even to women not directly victimized, these attacks teach lessons" (515).

Helping versus Harming

Helping is positive behavior, with consequences that presumably benefit another person, whereas aggression is negative behavior meant to hurt another person. In one sense, helping behavior is often reactive; we notice that someone else needs help, and we react by providing it. Aggression, in contrast, is more often proactive; actors generally initiate aggression. Furthermore, although both behaviors involve an interaction between two actors, the relationship between the actors is fundamentally different. The person providing help and the person receiving help are often treated as participants in a relationship. Indeed, the receipt of help creates indebtedness, which is itself the basis of a relationship. As we discussed in chapter 3, the norm of reciprocity suggests that the provision and receipt of help are a basis for social relationships. For example, a Thanksgiving Day news story in the *Seattle Times* reported the formation of an enduring relationship based on the rescue of a man stranded in river floods by two men who happened to be driving by. The potential victim was so grateful that he had made one of his rescuers a regular part of his family holiday gatherings (Routman 1995:A1). Thus, helping often generates reciprocal relationships.

In contrast, aggression is generally not the basis for formation of a relationship. Whereas helping brings people together, aggression separates them. The parallel to a norm of reciprocity is a norm of retaliation, but in practice people do not always retaliate against aggression, whereas they usually do reciprocate helping. What keeps targets of aggression from retaliating? The structural power of the aggressor and of the person against whom aggression is directed determine whether retaliation is possible. If the aggressor has significantly more power, retaliation is unlikely. Helping behavior thus often generates a relationship, whereas aggression does not.

Social Psychological Explanations of Altruism and Aggression

The social psychological theories that we have reviewed in earlier chapters present very different approaches to social behavior. Each of these theories has been used to explain both altruistic and aggressive behavior. In the next section of this chapter, we discuss the explanations each theory provides for altruism and aggression, paying close attention to the relationships between these behaviors and gender.

Essentialist/Biological Perspectives

Altruism

In chapter 2, we noted that social psychological patterns of gendered behavior have been attributed to biological differences between the sexes. Although most social psychologists reject this essentialist perspective as an outdated theory of gender, biological factors continue to be the basis for one theory of altruism and helping behavior. Drawing on evolutionary principles, some scholars observe that numerous species of insects, rodents, and mammals structure most of their activities around collective interests and survival (Dugatkin 1999). The basic logic is that altruism toward one's own offspring (whether in humans or other animals) contributes to the maintenance of one's gene pool. Furthermore, one's genes have a significantly greater chance of being passed on if one's group is cooperative (Kenrick, Ackerman, and Ledlow 2003). This literature implies that people should be most altruistic toward those who are most closely linked genetically to themselves, they should be more altruistic toward healthy than unhealthy offspring, and mothers should be more altruistic toward offspring than are fathers, based on the numbers of offspring each sex can produce in a lifetime.

This perspective has specific implications for patterns of helping behavior by gender. Social scientists have hypothesized that, due to their different reproductive processes, women and men differ in their sensitivity to distress and emotional cues. Indeed, women are more likely than men to intervene at low levels of harm to others, women have more intense responses to others' expressions of emotion than do men, and girls report more distress than do boys (Piliavin and Charng 1990). Whether these patterns require a genetic explanation is debatable, however. Women may report more distress and intervene at different levels of harm than do men due to gender-based patterns of socialization, cognitive schemas and behavioral expectations, or interactional demands. Piliavin and Unger's (1985) review of empirical research suggests no gender-related differences in physiological arousal or in impulsive responses to emergency situations. Thus, although biological factors may well shape helping, many other social and cognitive factors are also influential.

Aggression

Commonsense understandings also attribute aggressive behavior to biological factors. It is widely believed that people are aggressive because of their genes, their hormones, their fight-or-flight instinct, their innate natures, their responses to pain or discomfort, or their unconscious urges. Biological explanations are particularly common in discussions of gender and aggression. Some theorists argue, for example, that men tend to be more aggressive than women because it is evolutionarily useful for them to be so: aggressive males are likely to mate with more females than nonaggressive males and will therefore produce more offspring. Others argue that men tend to be more aggressive than women because of their higher concentrations of testosterone. Correlational studies assess testosterone levels among male prison inmates and military veterans and find that high testosterone levels are positively associated with violent records both before and during imprisonment for inmates, and with histories of delinquency, drug use, sexual promiscuity, and going AWOL among veterans (Dabbs and Dabbs 2000).

Biology clearly plays some part in human aggression. Physiological arousal—excitement generated by physical activity, danger, emotional interaction, or the use of alcohol—can generate aggression. Most social psychologists agree, however, that biological factors alone cannot explain human aggression. Biological influences on aggression are filtered through social situations and structures. For example, alcohol increases aggression by reducing inhibitions against aggression and increasing both attention to potential threats and vulnerability to social pressures to aggress (Taylor and Sears 1988). These inhibitions, cues, and pressures are socially, rather than biologically, defined. Recent research on hormones has demonstrated that their effects are quite complex: Some studies have found no differences in testosterone (or other hormone) levels between aggressive and nonaggressive people (e.g., Constantino et al. 1993); other studies have found that aggressive behavior may increase testosterone levels rather than the other way around (Rose, Bernstein, and Gordon 1975). Given that testosterone levels vary depending on stimuli in one's social environment, the relationships among hormones, the social setting, and behavior should be conceptualized as multi- rather than unidirectional (Freese, Li, and Wade 2003). Together, these results suggest that hormones are not the sole source of aggression but, rather, interact with other factors in shaping human behavior (see Sapolsky 1997 for a fuller discussion of these issues).

Another essentialist perspective, *frustration-aggression theory* (Dollard et al. 1939), argues that individuals are likely to behave aggressively when they have been prevented from achieving a goal. The emotional stimulation of frustration is presumed to trigger aggression. In one study, children who were forced to wait for a long time behind a wire screen before they were allowed to play with some enticing toys were very aggressive once they were admitted to the room—smashing the toys, throwing them across the room, and so

on—while children who had not had to wait played with the toys nondestruc-
tively (Barker, Dembo, and Lewin 1941). A recent application of these ideas
examines road rage among commuters. Hennessy and Wiesenthal (2001)
conclude that as frustration levels among drivers increase, they are more likely
to display road rage behaviors. We do not respond with aggression every time
we are frustrated, however. Wife abuse, for example, has been attributed by
some scholars to men's levels of frustration. Studies show, however, that men
who batter their wives are often quite unaggressive in situations such as their
workplaces (Kandel-Englander 1992). It is unlikely that they are frustrated
only in their marital relationships; it is far more likely that they channel their
frustration in different ways with different people, in accord with situational
norms.

Equally telling are overwhelming cross-cultural differences in aggression.
A recent United Nations survey on cross-cultural crime rates (2002) finds
enormous differences in murder rates across societies. Murder rates in South
Africa and El Salvador (47.5 and 31.5 per 100,000 people respectively), for
example, are consistently much higher than rates in the United Kingdom and
United States (2.0 and 5.6 per 100,000 people respectively). It is implausible
that biological factors account for this difference; indeed, there are clearly
cultural variations in what acts are even defined as murder, as in the case
of Neni Bai. In a recent cross-national comparison among students in the
United States and several European nations, McAlister and colleagues (2001)
observed significant cross-national variation in attitudes toward war, killing,
and the punishment of children. These large situational and cultural differences in aggression suggest that aggression is strongly influenced by social and
cultural factors.

Social Learning Theory

Altruism

Generosity and other forms of helping behavior increase as children age.
Most explanations for this trend derive from a social learning perspective. In
most societies, children are explicitly taught to share and to help others. This
behavior, like others, is learned through reinforcement principles and through
modeling: children consistently display greater generosity when they are exposed to generous as opposed to selfish models. Parents, other adults, and the
media are all effective models of helping (Piliavin and Charng 1990; Hastings
et al. 2007). Hoffman (2000, 2008) suggests that parents who actively discuss
kind or helpful acts with their children promote future prosocial behavior.
Children's attention to others' needs and the development of helping behavior

rapidly increase as the child moves from toddler to preschooler (Hastings, Zahn-Waxler, and McShane 2006). Adults also learn to help via reinforcement and modeling: a simple statement of gratitude for an act of generosity strongly increases both adults' (Moss and Page 1972) and children's (Hastings et al. 2007) tendencies to repeat this behavior. Learning to help, in other words, continues throughout life.

Social norms reinforce helping behavior. The norm of social responsibility is pervasive: we should help those who are dependent upon us. Parents help their children (and the law will take the children away if they fail this responsibility); in turn, children are supposed to care for their parents when they become elderly. A norm of reciprocity dictates that we should help those who help us. Norms of social justice proscribe violations of equity, as we noted in chapter 3. Cultures clearly vary in the intensity and perhaps even the content of these norms. Baron and Miller (2000; see also Miller, Bersoff, and Harwood 1990), for example, report that a general sense of responsibility for others is appreciably higher in India than in the United States. They attribute this difference to a greater stress on interpersonal interdependence and social obligations in Hindu Indian culture. Similarly, definitions of social justice vary within nations and communities.

Aggression

Social learning theorists suggest that children learn aggression, like altruism, through reinforcement and modeling. Bandura's Bobo doll experiments (discussed in chapter 3) demonstrated that children imitate the aggressive behavior they see adults perform, especially if they identify with the adults or see them rewarded for their aggression. Research on intergenerational family violence supports the predictions of social learning theory: children who observed abuse in their families of origin, or who were abused themselves, are far more likely to abuse their own intimate partners and/or children (Gelles 1994). Children who are physically disciplined by their parents also have a greater risk of delinquency as adolescents and of committing violence both inside and outside the home as adults (Straus et al. 1991). Numerous studies also connect aggressive behavior to exposure to violent media (Boxer et al. 2009; Comstock and Scharrer 1999). Observing violent behavior on television leads children to behave more aggressively toward other people, especially when they have also witnessed parental abuse (Heath, Kruttschnitt, and Ward 1986). Children in these situations learn that aggression is an effective way to solve problems and later use this behavior when they confront similar problems in their own lives.

Social learning also helps explain adult aggression. In one study, Black and Bevan (1992) measured aggression levels in people waiting to see both aggressive and nonaggressive movies, as well as in people who had just viewed these movies. People who had just viewed an aggressive film had higher levels of aggression than the other groups. Moreover, people who chose to see the aggressive film had higher levels of aggression even before entering the movie theater. These researchers conclude that "films featuring violence attract an audience with a propensity for aggression, [and] that viewing these films heightens this tendency" (42–43). We should note, however, that Ferguson and Kilburn's (2009) recent meta-analysis questions whether the size of such media effects is substantively meaningful.

Do these increased levels of aggressive feelings translate into real-world behavior? Ethical concerns prevent researchers from investigating this question directly; indirect evidence, however, suggests that media coverage may indeed increase actual aggression. Phillips (1983, 1986), for example, found that the daily rate of homicide in the United States nearly always increased during the week after a heavyweight boxing match, when the match was well publicized. These patterns had racialized and gendered implications: After white boxers lost fights, there was a corresponding increase in murders of white (but not black) men; conversely, after black boxers lost fights, there was an increase in murders of black (but not white) men (Aronson, Wilson, and Akert 1994). Violence has also been found to increase after hijackings (Bandura 1973), riots (Myers 1997), uprisings at sporting events (Dunand 1986; Rime and Leyens 1988) and wars (Archer and Gartner 1976, 1984).

Research on pornography also suggests that viewing violent material may increase the likelihood of behaving aggressively. One study asked undergraduate men whether they would "force a woman to have sex against her will" if they knew they would not be caught. More than half (57 percent) said they would do so, after they had viewed violent pornography. Even when they had not viewed violent pornography, 25–30 percent reported they would do so (Donnerstein 1983; Briere and Malamuth 1983).[1] The most negative effects of pornography are associated with viewing materials that combine sexual content with violence. Carr and VanDeusen (2004) found that the consumption of violent or rape-themed pornography is associated with propensity for rape and attitudes favorable for rape. Another study of widely available video pornography found that four-fifths of the films contained sexually explicit scenes depicting male domination or exploitation of women. Three-fourths of these videos depicted male physical aggression against women; half of them showed rape (Cowan et al. 1988). Thus, the pornography that is most common is also potentially the most dangerous. Kingston and colleagues (2008) documented that both the frequency of pornography consumption and its content are associated with recidivism among sex offenders. Representations of violence do not affect all people equally; they have stronger effects on those predisposed to aggression.

Social Exchange

Altruism

Social exchange theorists view at least some acts of helping as exchanges: when one person provides help to another, resources are transferred. Several of the social norms mentioned above are based on principles of social exchange. The reciprocity norm, for example, prescribes equality of exchange. Norms of social justice are also guided by equity principles. Overbenefited people may give some of their resources to someone who has been shortchanged (a restoration of justice). Even those who are not involved in a direct exchange may transfer resources to others; people donate to charities, which in turn distribute those resources to people in need.

The social exchange perspective is particularly relevant to the reactions of those who receive help. When the provision of help is largely one way, the recipient becomes indebted to the helper. Unidirectional helping threatens equity, creates a power imbalance, and may lower the recipient's self-esteem (and, conversely, heighten the donor's self-esteem). Thus, people are more likely to ask for help if they think they can repay it (Fisher, Nadler, and Whitcher-Alagna 1982; Penner et al. 2005). In real-world relationships between social equals, the possibilities for eventual repayment are considerably greater than in the brief interactions in laboratory studies. When participants in a helping encounter differ in their structural power, however, unidirectional helping is more problematic. *Oleanna*'s John explicitly breaks the academic rules (starting the class over) in order to help Carol. His certainty that he can do this with impunity communicates his status and legitimacy and underscores Carol's lack of power. The same act that is intended to help Carol also reinforces John's power over her. This ostensibly unidirectional helping in fact has benefits for John and costs for Carol.

People do weigh the costs and benefits of action and inaction. Among the costs of helping are the possibility of looking foolish, physical danger, messiness of possible blood or vomit, lost time, legal complications, contact with an undesirable other, and so forth. Benefits of action include the psychological reward of feeling good about one's self and social approval. The intensifying need of the other party is a primary cost of inaction; guilt or disapproval by others are also highly likely. The overall profile of costs and benefits eventually determines what one decides to do.

Perceived costs and benefits are particularly important in shaping gendered patterns of helping (Penner et al. 2005; Piliavin and Unger 1985). Many of the empirical differences between women and men in giving and receiving help relate to differences in their perceptions of the costs and benefits of helping. Providing physical help is often more costly for women, for example, because women tend to be physically smaller than men and because gender norms attest to the physical dominance of men over women. Reliance on the principles of social exchange in helping behavior may also differ by sex and class: middle-class boys, for example, are more likely than less advantaged boys or girls of any class to consider whether gifts will be reciprocated when deciding whether to offer gifts (Dreman 1976; Dreman and Greenbaum 1973). The principles of social exchange thus explain helping more adequately for some groups of actors than others.

Aggression

As we noted in chapter 3, social exchange research has rarely addressed aggression. Indeed, the theory's focus on individual choice directs attention away from interactions that may be involuntary for one or more of the participants, or that are based on emotion rather than on rational choice. Moreover, as Molm (2006) notes, research on social exchange has generally been restricted to the exchange of resources and rewards; her exploration of the use of punishment is a first step in the application of social exchange theory to studying aggression. She finds that the use of punishment varies according to the structural situations of the exchange partners: those actors with less access to reward power are more likely to punish their exchange partners (Molm 1989a, 1989b). Note, however, that "punishment" in these experiments is operationalized as taking a few cents away from one's experimental partner—a far cry from aggression outside the laboratory.

We suggest that exchange theory could be fruitful for understanding coercive situations. If aggression is viewed as a resource that actors may use to achieve their goals, then coercive interactions can be conceptualized as situations in which the power imbalance between the actors is extreme. Interestingly, many researchers working outside social psychology have used an implicit exchange perspective to understand aggression and violence. Gelles (1985, 1999), for example, examines wife battering as a rational strategy used by men to maintain dominance over their wives. He hypothesizes that men weigh the costs and benefits of possible actions and choose to beat their wives, because this promises high rewards and relatively low costs. Similarly, much criminal justice theory is based on the idea that aggressive crimes can be deterred by making the perceived costs of crime higher than the perceived benefits. (However, research shows that punishment acts as a deterrent only when it is both certain and nearly immediate—circumstances rarely realized in our criminal justice system [Bower and Hilgard 1981]. In the real world, even the death penalty does not deter violent crime, perhaps because only rarely are homicides punished by death.)

Some researchers have also used exchange theory to explain reactions to violence, such as the reactions of women to battering. When discussing an abusive relationship, people may ask, "Why didn't she just leave?" Exchange theory predicts that a woman will decide whether to leave or stay in an abusive relationship based on the costs and benefits associated with each choice. Leaving or reporting the act might entail a risk of incurring greater injury, the possibility of becoming homeless, and the risk of losing custody of one's children, although it also has the benefit of escaping from repeated abuse. Staying might provide the benefit of love and affection when violence is not imminent, financial support for oneself and one's children, and social status, but at the risk of further assault. Erez (2000) notes that these calculations are particularly challenging for immigrant women, who have the added risk of having their husband and possibly themselves deported. According to exchange theory, the balance of these perceived costs and benefits determines the woman's decision to stay or leave.

Social Cognition

Altruism

Helping behavior is the outcome of a cognitive decision-making process. First, we must notice that something is happening that might require help and then we must decide whether help is required. When we are in a hurry, tired, sick, or preoccupied, we are less likely to attend to the environment around us and thus to notice potential crises. Defining the situation as one that requires help is also not as straightforward as it might appear. People tend not to offer help in ambiguous situations, because of their concerns about appearing foolish. In one often-cited study, students sitting with others in a room rapidly filling up with smoke just continued to sit there, afraid of reacting inappropriately (Latane and Darley 1968). Normative conventions also affect the likelihood of intervention. In a study by Shotland and Straw (1976), strangers were much less likely to intervene in a fight between a man and a woman when they thought the two were married. Presumably both general norms of privacy about intimate relationships and patriarchal conceptions about the rights of husbands over their wives discouraged these strangers from intervening.

If help is required, we must decide whether we are capable of helping. This also entails deciding what sort of help is needed and how to provide it. We also assess our own sense of responsibility to provide help. One factor in assessing personal responsibility is the number of other available bystanders. The greater the number of others available who might help, the less likely any given person is to act (Schwartz and Gottlieb 1980). Blair, Foster-Thompson, and Wuensch (2005) find that even the virtual presence of others in online situations can impede responsiveness. In the murder of Kitty Genovese, the incident with which we began this book, this diffusion of responsibility is likely the major reason why her neighbors waited so long to call the police. Each thought someone else would take action. Once we have decided that intervention is called for and that we are capable of such action, we engage in the cost-benefit analyses suggested by social exchange theory. Social cognition and social exchange models thus intersect in the individual calculations of costs and benefits.

The social positions of those in need of help and those who offer help shape the cognitive assessment of costs and benefits of helping. Perceptions and judgments about who needs help, who is more capable of providing help, and whose need is legitimate, derive from the structural positions of those involved. Accordingly, the costs and benefits of both helping and inaction are gendered. Both socialization and social norms suggest that looking foolish might be more troublesome for men than women, that men may feel they have more of the physical and technical skills necessary for some forms of intervention, and that women might feel more concern about the welfare of others and thus feel more guilt should they fail to intervene.

Structural constraints on helping are not always straightforward. As we have noted, gender stereotypes cast women as less competent and more dependent than men. Consequently, women are offered more assistance than men in some situations. This also means, however, that women are expected to take precautions to avoid being in need. Because of their perceived greater physical and sexual vulnerability, women are expected to avoid walking alone at night, to avoid interacting with strangers, and so forth. When they are assaulted in such situations, both women and men are more likely to blame them. In one study, subjects attributed considerably more blame to women who were assaulted when they had been hitchhiking than to women assaulted while jogging or to men assaulted while engaging in either activity (Howard 1984a). Thus, stereotypes of women's greater vulnerability can generate both sympathy and blame, depending on attributions about their behavior.

Aggression

Cognition also plays an important role in aggression. One influential cognitive process involves the *priming* effects of aggressive cues. The presence of objects symbolizing aggression can provoke aggressive behavior. In one study, for example, college students who had seen a gun behaved more aggressively than those who had seen a badminton racket (Berkowitz and LePage 1967). The presence of objects associated with aggression primes aggressive behavior by making aggressive thoughts and feelings more accessible, even if the objects themselves are not used.

Words may also prime aggression: another study found that participants exposed to words related to aggression (e.g., *insult*, *stab*, or *anger*) wrote stories containing more aggression, anger, and violence and expressed more interest in watching violent films than those exposed to nonaggressive words (Langley et al. 1992). This process may help explain the effects of viewing media violence on aggressive behavior. These materials may indeed provide models of aggression for viewers to imitate, as social learning theory argues. However, they may also prime aggressive thoughts and memories that make aggressive behavior more cognitively accessible to individuals.

Priming effects also occur through the activation of social schemas. For example, "one common television script is that the bad guy provokes the good guy, who retaliates. The child who has learned this script from television might in later life be too quick to retaliate to minor insults" (Taylor, Peplau, and Sears 1994:451). Similarly, the finding that children who experience or witness abuse are more likely to abuse as adults could also be explained by the transmission not of specific behaviors but of scripts about the proper roles of women and men and the appropriate responses to frustration in intimate relationships.

Attribution is another cognitive process that helps explain aggression. Individuals are far more likely to respond aggressively to attacks they perceive to be intentional, for instance, than to attacks they perceive to be accidental or beyond the control of the instigator (Berkowitz 1986). Apologizing for provocative behavior, however, reduces aggressive responses (Schwartz et al. 1978). The apology presumably alters the attribution. Other evaluations are also significant. As discussed in chapter 3, many social behaviors stimulate cognitive calculations of equity and justice. Not getting what one expects or feels one deserves can result in perceptions of unfairness. In particular, provocation that is perceived to be unfair produces stronger aggressive reactions than provocation perceived as legitimate.

Stereotypes also influence aggression. Who would you expect to be more aggressive: a football player or a librarian? A young person or a very old person? A man or a woman? A black man or a white man? A white woman or an Asian American woman? A straight man or a gay man? A middle-class woman or a working-class woman? Most people have expectations about whom they expect to be aggressive. These expectations likely depend on one's own and others' social positions; a white man might expect that a black man would be more likely to aggress, whereas a black man might expect more aggression from a white man. In one study, for example, white participants character-ized women as passive and men as aggressive far more than black participants did (Smith and Midlarsky 1985). Thus, expectations about aggression are conditioned by membership in and stereotypes about different social groups.

Stereotypes also influence social psychological research on aggression. Despite the fact that men as well as women can be sexually assaulted, for ex-ample, there were no studies of male sexual assault victims until fairly recently (Howard 1984a; Mezey and King 2000). The reason that scholars have only recently begun to explore this issue is likely due to prevailing stereotypes of men as victimizers and protectors rather than as victims. Similarly, stereo-types of women as nonaggressive victims inhibit analysis of the ways in which women do aggress, as we discuss in greater depth below.

Symbolic Interaction

Altruism

The concepts of symbolic interaction seem well suited to explaining help-ing encounters. How we define situations through interaction is clearly re-lated to the resolution of those ambiguous situations in which helping might be required. Negotiating the identities we want to perform and the identities we want others to adopt is a major task in potential helping situations; the identity implications of needing help, of being helped, and of offering help are not trivial. In one scene in *Little Women*, for example, the March girls have spent Christmas morning gathering together their presents for each other and eagerly awaiting their holiday breakfast. Just as they gather at the table, their mother returns from a last-minute errand with an announcement:

"Merry Christmas, little daughters! . . . But I want to say one word before we sit down. Not far away from here lies a poor woman with a little newborn baby. Six children are huddled into one bed to keep from freezing, for they have no fire. There is nothing to eat over there; and the oldest boy came to tell me they were suffering hunger and cold. My girls, will you give them your breakfast as a Christmas present?"

They were all unusually hungry, having waited nearly an hour, and for a min-ute no one spoke; only a minute, for Jo exclaimed impetuously:

"I'm so glad you came before we began!"

"May I go and help carry the things to the poor little children?" asked Beth eagerly.

"I shall take the cream and the muffins," added Amy, heroically giving up the articles she most liked. (Alcott 1924:27)

In that long minute between Mrs. March's question and the girls' responses, we can well imagine the sorts of identity debates going on in their private thoughts: they must choose between the self-satisfaction of a fine meal and the costs of seeming, judging themselves as, and being judged by others in their family as selfish.

The consequences of social encounters depend on these situational definitions. In *Oleanna,* John and Carol fail to achieve a common working definition of their situation. From John's perspective, he provided help to a student. From Carol's perspective, he took advantage of her vulnerability. Their failure to achieve a mutual definition has disastrous consequences: John loses tenure and physically assaults Carol. The consequences for John are explicit in the play; the negative consequences for Carol, although not articulated, are not hard to imagine. Students who file complaints of sexual harassment, even when those complaints are judged valid, often are ostracized by faculty and other students alike; their academic and working environments may become so aversive that they drop out of school.

Symbolic interactionists maintain that the ability to take the role of the generalized other is partly a function of one's position in social structures (Schwalbe 1991; Stryker and Vryan 2003). Actors located in relatively complex social structures, such as bureaucratic organizations, are exposed to a greater variety of roles and therefore have more opportunities to take the role of a generalized other. Greater opportunity does not necessarily translate into use of those opportunities, however. John has clearly had the experience of being a student—and one who struggled academically—as well as the experience of being a professor. Nonetheless, he fails to reflect on Carol's perspective. One's social power shapes how much one has to take the perspective of others, and therefore, how likely one is to recognize others' needs and to offer help.

In addition, the symbolic interactions through which helping encounters are performed are themselves deeply social. Social norms of "appropriate" gendered and racialized behavior guide self-presentation and impression management. In one field experiment, white female students high in racial prejudice helped black victims in an emergency more slowly than white victims, but only when there were passive bystanders present. When there were no bystanders, all subjects helped the victims equally quickly (Gaertner,

Dovidio, and Johnson 1982). Furthermore, studies suggest that the implied presence of others (e.g., bringing a subject's group affiliations to mind before an experiment or doing an exercise with a virtual partner) can impact helping behavior (see Penner et al. 2005). The self-presentation of respondents appears to be based on concerns about the appraisals of others.

Eagly and Crowley (1986) argue that gender differences in patterns of helping are derived from the symbolic meanings of masculinity and femininity. Agency and a sense of self as a "good provider" are fundamental elements of traditional masculinity; chivalry, therefore, is part of the successful portrayal of masculinity. Chivalry depends on having someone to help, however: women. Being helpless and passive are fundamental elements of traditional femininity. The performance of both chivalry and the "damsel in distress" entail identity management. Management of femininity is particularly complex, as it also requires care for the personal and emotional needs of others.

Aggression

Symbolic meaning and interpretation are central to aggression. The priming effect of guns is a case in point: although the subjects in the Berkowitz and LePage study did not use the gun in their aggressive behavior, its symbolic connotation of aggression prompted them to behave aggressively. Interestingly, symbolic interaction has rarely addressed aggression, perhaps because its model of humans downplays the role of power and hierarchy in interaction. The theory describes individuals actively interpreting the world around them, an image at odds with the realities of coercion and force. Nonetheless, the few symbolic interactionist studies of aggression do demonstrate the rich potential of this theory.

Felson's (1978) provocative analysis of the impression management of aggression, for example, suggests that aggression is often an "attempt to seek or restore face, self-esteem, status, or power" (205). Actions that are perceived to attack the identity of another person—for example, calling someone dishonest or unkind—threaten that person's identity. One strategy for preventing or repairing that damage is to respond aggressively: "A successful counterattack is one effective way of nullifying the imputed negative identity by showing one's strength, competence, and courage" (207). Felson's (1997) more recent work illustrates this process in love triangles. While female partners of adulterers are more likely to attack their cheating partner, male partners are more likely to attack the rival lover in order to preserve their honor and sense of self.

This kind of identity work is deeply gendered. Consider the effects of being called a "girl": a woman may bristle at or be complimented by such a term, but a man or boy may feel compelled to fight, to resist what he perceives as a stigmatizing identity. Indeed, many male high school coaches frequently call their players "girls" or "ladies" to pump them up before a game. Aggression is a central theme of many cultural stereotypes of masculinity: "A 'real man' is a strong, heterosexual protector, capable of taking care of himself and, if necessary, guarding his and others' safety aggressively" (Stanko 1990:110). Many men report that, as boys, they were compelled to fight or bully other boys in order to prove their masculinity in their own and the eyes of other boys (Martino and Pallotta-Chiarolli 2003). Recent analyses of sports and war link men's participation in these activities to the need to prove their masculine identity (Connell 1995; Enloe 1993; Kreager 2007; Martino and Meyenn 2002; Messner and Sabo 1994).

Masculine identity rests on two contradictory forms of aggressive behavior. Many men establish a masculine identity by protecting and defending—sometimes aggressively—"their" women and children, and, often, others as well. In this case, aggression is perceived to be prosocial behavior. However, some men also confirm their masculine identity through antisocial aggressive behavior, such as crime and violence. A number of authors have suggested that gang rape, for example, is as much an interaction between men (on the symbolic level) as an act of violence against a woman (Fox and Thomson 2007). In their study of gang rape in college fraternities, Martin and Hummer (1993) conclude that "fraternity norms and practices influence members to view the sexual coercion of women, which is a felony crime, as a sport, a contest, or a game. . . . This sport is played not between men and women but between men and men. Women are the pawns or prey in the interfraternity rivalry game; they prove that a fraternity is successful or prestigious" (128).

Murnen and Kohlman's (2007) meta-analysis of twenty-nine studies reports a moderate relationship between membership in an all-male fraternity or sports team and rape-supportive attitudes. The association between membership in one of these groups and self-reported sexual aggression is smaller but still positive. Furthermore, both Herek's (2009) discussion of heterosexual men's violent aggression against lesbians and gay men and Kimmel and Mahler's (2003) analysis of random school shootings by rural, white boys similarly suggest that this violence is often an attempt to reaffirm their heterosexuality, one central component of hegemonic masculinity. Thus, aggression can be a strategy for constructing a valued masculine identity (see also Harry 1990).

Unlike men, women rarely manage their identities by enacting aggression. Cultural stereotypes locate women as the targets, not the perpetrators, of aggression or protection. Hollander's (2009) work on cultural resistance to women's self-defense suggests that people's deeply held beliefs about gender keep them from recognizing women's self-defense or perceiving women as strong and competent. Cultural stereotypes may themselves increase women's vulnerability: because some women do not believe that they can defend themselves, they may not try to do so, instead relying upon men for protection (see also Hollander 2001, 2002). Their inaction then confirms both the stereotype of women as needing protection and women's own identities as feminine. Unfortunately, women's inaction may be misinterpreted as consent, as seen in some instances of sexual assault (Jackman 2002).

Women and men may also differ in their interpretation of the events precipitating aggression. Shotland and Craig (1988) found that women interpreted behaviors such as smiling or speaking in a low voice as friendly, whereas men perceived these behaviors as indicating sexual interest. Similarly, Muehlenhard (1988) found that women perceived initiating a date, wearing sexy clothes, drinking alcoholic beverages, allowing the man to pay dating expenses, and going to his apartment as normative behaviors, while men interpreted them as signs of sexual interest. Men also rated force (having sex with a woman against her wishes) as more justifiable than did women. It is easy to see how these conflicting interpretations could facilitate date rape (and contradictory definitions of this situation).

Summary

As we have emphasized in this discussion, each of the major social psychological theories can be used to explain some aspects of both helping and aggressive behaviors. No one of these theories is sufficient by itself, but taken together, they can account for much of the variability in these forms of behavior. There are, however, systematic omissions in the sorts of questions these theories address. In particular, each of them tends to minimize the role of structural factors and power in helping and aggression. We turn to these topics in the next section.

Structural Patterns of Helping and Aggression

In the preceding review of theories of helping and aggression, we have deliberately highlighted what is at best a minor theme in this research: the effects of social structural positions. In the following section we offer a systematic analysis of the demographics of altruism and aggression. We focus on a few key questions: Who is more or less likely to offer help? Who is more or less likely to receive help? Who is more or less likely to be aggressive? Who is more or less likely to be the target of aggression? What kinds of situational factors and what kinds of individual differences make altruism or aggression more or less likely?

Who Provides Help?

According to gender stereotypes, helping encounters should be gendered. As competent, active, and strong, men should be more likely to provide help; as helpless, passive, and weak, women should be more in need of and likely to receive help. Early studies of altruism consistently reported that, under similar conditions, men offer help more than women and women receive more help than men (Krebs 1970).

Research conducted since 1970, however, paints a different picture. Piliavin and Unger's (1985) extensive review of gender and helping suggests that gendered patterns of helping behavior are not so clear-cut. There is consistent evidence that women respond more empathically than men to the distress of others. Because women are also more willing to report affective responses than are men, due to differential socialization, it is difficult to interpret this finding. Women report providing their friends with more personal favors, emotional support, and counseling about personal problems. In laboratory studies, women donate more money than do men (Lerner and Frank 1974). Women also seem to value helping more than do men (e.g., Hales and Fenner 1973). The subtleties of these patterns are intriguing: Calabrese and Cochran (1990) report, for example, that although women (and Asian men) are less likely to cheat than white men, they are more likely to cheat when their cheating helps others succeed, whereas white men are more likely to cheat for their own personal gain.

Women do not always provide more help than men, however. Men are more likely to provide help than women when women perceive helping as more dangerous, an audience witnesses the act, and other potential helpers are available (see Piliavin and Charng 1990). Men are more likely to provide help that requires physical strength, such as lifting someone who has collapsed. Differential expertise is also relevant, and assumptions about expertise vary along explicitly gendered lines. Men are more likely to offer help for car problems (West, Whitney, and Schnedler 1975); women are more likely to offer help to children (Wunderlich and Willis 1977) or to assist with laundry (Dovidio et al. 1978).

Social positions and situational factors may combine to influence the provision of help. We noted above that involvement in more complex social structures enhances opportunities to role-take and thus those in more advantaged financial circumstances might be more helpful. When we consider low-cost helping, there is some support for this prediction:

Upper-middle-class residents of two cities were more likely than lower-middle-class residents to return unstamped lost letters (Lowe and Ritchey 1973); "middle-class" people (as assessed by their clothes) were more likely to return a dropped wallet than were "lower-class" people (Diener et al. 1973). Opposite patterns have been found in higher-cost helping, however, both in semicontrolled studies (Yarrow, Scott and Waxler 1973) and in real-world patterns. Poorer people give higher proportions of their incomes to charities, for example, than those who are wealthy. Indeed, contributions of the wealthy steadily declined during the Reagan era of the 1980s, while contributions of those with lower incomes steadily increased. Reports following the September 11 terrorist attacks on the World Trade Center and Pentagon, the tsunami in Asia, and Hurricane Katrina, however, suggest that these events stimulated considerable increases in the amount of charitable giving in recent years (*Giving USA* 2010). Charitable giving reached a record high in 2007, and despite small declines attributed to poor economic times, approximately 82 percent of all households continue to give. While recent tax returns consistently find that those who earn less give larger percentages of their earnings, those who give the largest donations tend to be college educated and married and have higher incomes (*Giving USA* 2005). Common motivations for helping include the existence of urgent need, religious values, and the beliefs that those with more should help those with less and that everyone should give back to society.

Who Receives Help?

There are also gendered patterns in the receipt of help. Following logically from patterns of who provides help, women are helped more (by men) in situations involving automobile mishaps, thefts, or dropped goods. Men are helped more (by women) in situations involving children or household tasks. In less gender-typed circumstances, such as lending money or stapling questionnaires, gender differences in the receipt of help disappear (see Piliavin and Unger 1985; Penner et al. 2005).

Other social positions also affect the receipt of help. Predictions about these effects are based on intergroup dynamics. Ingroup favoritism, majority bias against a minority group, or majority support of a minority group have all been found—more evidence that the effects of social positions depend on situation and context. In some public situations, racial dynamics seem to play little role. Both black and white shoppers, for example, provided assistance to both black and white shoppers who spilled a bag of groceries (Wispe and Freshley 1971). Helpers (race unidentified) did not distinguish between Mexican and English surnames in returning unstamped lost letters (Lowe and Ritchey 1973). Biases against racial minority groups are found in other public situations, however. In one study, both male and female white adults performed a small favor more often for white than Asian requestors, and in another, whites predominantly helped other whites whose cars were disabled, whereas blacks did not show a racial preference (West et al. 1975).

Some of these contradictions are due to situated costs and benefits. One field experiment found, for example, that a minor helping gesture was offered more to blacks than to whites (by helpers whose race was not identified) when it was cost free, but more to whites than blacks when there was a small financial cost (Brown and Reed 1982). Not surprisingly, racial prejudice is more evident in anonymous helping. Whites were more likely to mail a "lost" application for graduate school, for example, when the enclosed photograph showed a white rather than a black applicant (Benson, Karabenick, and Lerner 1976). Political nuances are also significant: in one study blacks were assisted more if they identified themselves with the older, conservative label "Negro" rather than the (then) radical label "black" (Katz, Cohen, and Glass 1975). Although the terms in this study are dated, the patterns are likely not.

More recently Kunstman and Plant (2008) studied the impact of race on helping behavior in emergency situations. Their findings parallel other studies suggesting that racial biases surface at the most critical moments (Saucier, Miller, and Doucet 2005; Hodson, Dovidio, and Gaertner 2002). These researchers set up emergency situations to explore whether variation in the severity of the need for help impacted how quickly individuals offered help to black and white victims. Results indicated that severe emergencies involving black victims triggered increased levels of aversion in white helpers. This aversion, in turn, led to slower response rates for black than for white victims. Gaertner and Dovidio (2005) argue the decision to act requires a balancing of the motive to be seen as egalitarian with the motive to avoid contact with members of other groups. Saucier, Smith, and McManus (2007) suggest this very process may account for the slow governmental response and lack of aid provided to the primarily poor and African American victims of Hurricane Katrina. Unfortunately, the pattern that emerges from both these older and newer studies of helping behavior suggests that racist attitudes may bear more on those decisions where helping is most critical.

Because of this resilience of racial prejudice, there is a good deal of evidence that blacks help each other. Blacks were particularly likely to provide low-cost assistance to other blacks on a predominantly white college campus, for example, where they may have felt a special solidarity with and responsibility to other minority students (Wegner and Crano 1975). Recent research on volunteerism reports that black volunteers tend to concentrate their efforts on issues they consider important to the black community (Wilkie, Ferree, and

Ratcliff 1998; Musick, Wilson, and Bynum 2000). Studies of racial patterns in the effectiveness of volunteer counselors suggest that among both blacks and whites, intraracial helping is characterized by more contact between the counselor and client and by improved client satisfaction (Morrow-Howell, Lott, and Ozawa 1990). To fully understand the racialized patterns of helping, scholars must consider how race, gender, social class, sexuality, and other statuses intersect to impact assessments of vulnerability and need, levels of commitment to helping, and attributions by and about those who need help (Mattis et al. 2008; Penner et al. 2005).

Underscoring the influence of social prejudices, studies show that sexual orientation also determines the receipt of help. Both women and men (whose sexual orientation was not assessed) were more likely to do a favor for a male heterosexual than homosexual caller (Shaw, Borough, and Fink 1994). Both women and men (again, whose sexual orientation was not assessed) were more likely to provide change for heterosexual than homosexual requestors of either gender; this pattern did not change when an explanation for the request was provided (Gray, Russell and Blockley 1991; Tsang 1994). The fact that the sexual orientation of the actors was assessed in neither of these studies, even though the effect of sexual orientation was the key independent variable, speaks volumes about the pervasive assumption of heterosexuality.

Cultural context also shapes the provision and receipt of helping. The tendency to favor one's ingroup is considerably stronger in collectivist than in individualist cultures. Because the interests of the individual in collectivist cultures are often subordinated to the needs of the group, members of collectivist cultures are more likely to share resources with ingroup members. Chinese and Japanese respondents offered more help than did U.S. respondents to others whom they perceived to be members of their own national group, for example; these same respondents were less likely than U.S. respondents to help those perceived to be from a different national group (Leung and Bond 1984).

The receipt of help based on gender differs in (at least) one significant respect from the receipt of help based on race, class, sexuality, or nationality. Social psychologists generally interpret the latter in terms of intergroup conflicts and intragroup favoritism. Research on gendered patterns in helping does not suggest even the possibility of intergroup conflict: that is, that women or men might discriminate against each other in the provision and receipt of help. Rather, researchers treat women and men as members of a common group, differing only in their abilities and styles of helping and vulnerabilities to needing help. In contrast, researchers assume potential ingroup preferences based on other social positions. Thus, a systematic structural analysis is at least partially evident in analyses of the effects of race, class, sexuality, or nationality on helping behavior, in contrast to the consistent focus on individual traits in analyses of the effects of gender.[2]

Who Is Aggressive?

Sociobiologists argue that sex differences in aggression result from innate differences between women and men. To support their arguments, these theorists point to a large body of evidence that suggests that men tend to engage in more real-world physical aggression than do women. According to the Uniform Crime Report, for example, women and girls were charged with only 10.4 percent of the murders and nonnegligent manslaughters and 21.5 percent of the aggravated assaults in the United States in 2007.[3] Laboratory experiments also have found that men, on average, behave more physically aggressively than women, as Maccoby and Jacklin (1974) concluded in their influential review of such research. Others, however, have challenged the conclusion that there are large, stable sex differences in aggression. Hyde (1986), for example, found that sex category accounted for only 5 percent of the variation in aggression in the 143 studies she analyzed. Moreover, most of the studies in Maccoby and Jacklin's review involved children; sex differences among adults are far smaller than among children (Eagly and Steffen 1986). Recent meta-analyses of aggression research demonstrate that if differences do exist, they are not nearly as large as prior analyses suggest (Knight et al. 2002). Laboratory studies completed subsequent to Maccoby and Jacklin's review corroborate these meta-analyses, demonstrating that women and men have similar capacities for aggression (Macaulay 1985; White and Kowalski 1994). Thus, if there are sex differences in aggression, they are far smaller than stereotypes suggest (Knight et al. 2002). Moreover, it is clear that the sexes are more similar than they are different: most men, like most women, commit little aggressive violence.

Gender has not been a central theoretical construct in most other social psychological theories of aggression, although all have discussed sex differences in aggressive behavior. Most theories are gender neutral: frustration-aggression theory, for example, posits that women and men will respond similarly to frustration. Examining this theory with a gendered lens, however, suggests some problems. If aggression results from frustration, then what are we to make of the fact that women tend to engage in far less real-world physical aggression than do men? It is unlikely that women's lives are less frustrating than men's. How then can social psychology explain gender differences in aggressive behavior?

Social learning theory provides one answer: women may be equally capable of violence, but these capacities are encouraged in men and inhibited in women. Girls rarely observe women modeling aggressive behavior and are punished more harshly than boys for behaving aggressively. These gendered consequences of aggression continue into adulthood. A businessman who behaves aggressively may be labeled a "star" or a "go-getter," for example, while a woman who behaves similarly may be labeled "pushy," "bitchy," or "abrasive" (Correll and Ridgeway 2003; Foschi 2000). Women may learn that indirect aggression will serve them better than direct physical aggression. Eagly and Steffen's (1986) meta-analysis of sixty-three studies of adult aggression found that more than one-third of the sex differences observed in aggression could be accounted for by differences in guilt, anxiety, and concern about retaliation. Thus, whereas the principles of social learning theory are gender neutral, social norms and expectations are not, resulting in different patterns of aggressive behavior for women and men.

This analysis implies that if social norms and reactions to women's aggression were different, women would behave differently. Bandura's (1965) Bobo doll experiments support this hypothesis. Boys in these experiments behaved more aggressively than girls. However, when the children were rewarded for aggressive behavior, the girls' aggression increased to match the boys' level. Other studies show that women may act as aggressively as men when aggression is perceived as prosocial. Thus, "sex" differences might be due not to differences in aggressive tendencies but to societal norms that lead women and men to define situational cues differently and lead people in general to respond more negatively to women's aggression. In other words, these are gender differences, not sex differences. Because women are less frequently rewarded for aggression, they may choose other means to achieve their goals— not because of an innate aversion to aggression but because aggression is not a rewarding strategy for them.

The size of sex differences in aggression also varies by social situations. In one study, female and male undergraduates read vignettes in which one student prevented another from preparing for an examination in dance (a feminine context) or in body building (a masculine context) (Towson and Zanna 1982). The male participants advocated responding more aggressively than the female subjects did, but only in the masculine situation. In the feminine situation, the sex difference disappeared. Franchina, Eisler, and Moore (2001) found similar results when they asked a sample of 107 men to listen to tape-recorded conversations regarding dating situations: men in the masculine context displayed more negative attributions and verbal aggression when their masculinity was threatened by a female partner compared to men in the gender-neutral dating context. Again, the important factor is not sex, but gender. Kogut, Langley, and O'Neal (1992) found that respondents' adherence to masculine or feminine expectations predicted aggression in some

circumstances: "Women possessing more stereotypically masculine traits ag-
gressed more following insult than did women less masculine in their gender
role orientation" (365). Similarly, Nirenberg and Gaebelein (1979) found that
men with gender-traditional attitudes were more likely to aggress against both
women and men. The important distinction, then, is not one's sex per se, but
how well one has learned to perform the traits and characteristics considered
appropriate for one's sex category.

Moreover, when women are aggressive, gender stereotypes suggest that
they will act suddenly and emotionally, out of an instinct to preserve themselves or their children. Chronic domestic violence is expected from men
but not from women; women may respond to domestic violence and kill an
abuser in self-defense during an episode of battering, but they are not expected to premeditate retaliation or to behave aggressively when the abuser
is helpless. In the well-publicized 1993 case of John and Lorena Bobbitt, for
example, his chronic physical abuse of her did not seem to shock the nation,
but her response—severing his penis with a knife while he slept—did.

Thus, cognitive stereotypes, expectations, and social norms condition
reactions to women's and men's aggression. Although violence by all actors is nominally disapproved, in practice, men's aggression is more readily
accepted than women's. Boys are rewarded for fighting because it fits with
gender expectations; girls are not (Thorne 1993; see also Kimmel 2006). As
adults, gender (and race and class) expectations continue to shape reactions to women's aggression. The criminal justice system treats women who
violate gender expectations more harshly than those who do not. Women
who murder their husbands typically receive far harsher punishments than
men who murder their wives (White and Kowalski 1994). Reactions to the
violence of others also varies by sex: women have more favorable attitudes
toward rape victims and attribute more blame to rapists than do men, for
example. Nonetheless, both women and men tend to hold female victims
more responsible in rape cases than in other types of crime (White and
Sorensen 1992).

These patterns are especially evident in reactions to women who kill their
children. Consider the case of Susan Smith, the South Carolina mother who
in 1994 strapped her two young sons into their car seats and allowed the car to
roll into a lake, resulting in the boys' deaths. Later, she said she had intended
to drown herself as well. Although Smith committed a dreadful crime, her actions were less physically violent than those of many murderers, and according to her account she sought relief from pain and misery, not harm to her
sons. Yet she was publicly vilified in the press and called a "monster" by reporters and the public alike (Bragg 1995:A4), who clamored for her to receive
the death penalty. Why? Because her behaviors did not match widespread

stereotypes of what a "mother" should be like. The vehement public reaction to the drowning of her sons resulted not only from the fact that she caused the death of two young boys, but from the fact that she did so *as a woman and a mother*—violating gender norms as well as more general moral norms (see Gartner and McCarthy 2005). It may be useful to speculate what reaction would have ensued had the boys' father committed this act. Ironically, gender may also explain why Smith was sentenced to life imprisonment rather than the death penalty; the United States has historically been reluctant to execute women (Sullivan 1995:A2). The 2008 case of Casey Anthony, a young Florida mother accused of killing her two-year-old daughter, Caylee, has come under similar public scrutiny (Edwards 2010).

Other social positions also influence aggression and social reactions to it. The connection between race and real-world aggression is dramatically illustrated by crime statistics. According to the 2007 Uniform Crime Report, African Americans were charged with nearly 23.1 percent of total offenses reported, yet this group makes up only about 12.4 percent of the U.S. population. African Americans make up 40 percent of the prison population, with nearly a third of all young black men currently under the supervision of the correctional system (Pager 2007; Pettit and Western 2004). In contrast, some experimental studies have found no racial differences in aggression or have found blacks to be less aggressive than whites (e.g., Finn 1986; Luchterhead and Weller 1976). There are several explanations for the disparity between experimental findings and arrest patterns. First, there are racial inequities in criminal justice responses to violence: blacks are more likely to be arrested than whites for the same crime and are more likely to be imprisoned if convicted (Bridges and Crutchfield 1988; Crutchfield et al. 1995). These patterns also reflect social class biases. "Violent street crime tends to be committed by powerless men, but powerful men also commit crimes, although they are less likely to be charged or convicted of them" (Basow 1992:312). Wealthier men tend to commit white collar, rather than violent, crimes. Yet, as Schanzenbach and Yaeger (2006) find, racial disparities in case outcomes continue to occur even when racial minorities are implicated in white collar crimes. (That white collar crimes are not thought of as aggressive is itself worth noting.)

Race is also crucial in the interpretation of violence. Duncan (1976) showed white undergraduates a videotape of an ambiguous situation (one person shoving another) and asked subjects to assess the violence of the shove. The students judged the behavior to be more violent when the perpetrator was black rather than white. They also attributed the violence to the person when the perpetrator was black but to the situation when the perpetrator was white. Similar results were obtained with black respondents in a later study. Duncan suggests that the concept of violence was more accessible when a black person was seen committing the same act; research on implicit stereotyping supports this analysis (Greenwald, Oakes, and Hoffman 2003).

Research by Howard and Pike (1986) suggests that the effects of race on attributions about aggression are not as straightforward as stereotypes (and some laboratory studies) might suggest. Research participants (white and Asian American college students) were asked to describe their reactions to an interview with a man who had been arrested on a disorderly conduct charge. Some subjects were told the man was black; others, that he was white. The race of the actor affected attributions of blame, but in an unexpected way: "Subjects were more likely to blame the actor when he was white than when he was black, and to blame society when the actor was black as opposed to white" (163). The authors' speculative explanation is that these college students' (a liberal segment of the overall population) knowledge of racism and discrimination in the criminal justice situation influenced their attributions.

Class stereotypes also influence aggression and social reactions to it. Many people believe that poor and working-class people are more likely to be aggressive than are members of upper classes. The reasoning behind this assumption is economic: because financial problems often cause frustration, and because the poor presumably have more financial problems than the rich, the poor must be more aggressive. There is some evidence that violence is more frequent in poorer families and neighborhoods. A study by Roff (1992) found that social class during childhood was the second most significant predictor of adolescent delinquency, after childhood measures of aggression; subjects in low or middle social classes were most at risk for delinquency.

On the other hand, some forms of aggression occur fairly consistently across social classes, especially those that occur within families, such as domestic violence and child sexual abuse. What is not consistent is aggressors' treatment by the criminal justice system: in general, middle- and upper-class offenders are treated more leniently than poor or working-class offenders (see Reiman 1995). The prevalence of *private* violence across all classes suggests that social class affects the forms in which aggression is expressed, but not the tendency to aggress. Messerschmidt's (1993, 1997) research on crime among different race and class groups supports this point. Crime exists across all social categories, but takes different shapes for men from different racial and socioeconomic groups because these groups have different resources, different opportunities for aggression, and different stakes in the mainstream culture.

Cultural norms may underlie the relationship between ethnicity and aggression. Kaufman, Gregory, and Stephan (1990) studied differences in the reactions of Anglo and Hispanic students to being an ethnic minority in their schools. Hispanic students were more moody, but not more aggressive, in classrooms where they were a minority. Anglo students, however, were more aggressive in parallel situations. Kaufman and colleagues attribute this difference to cultural norms: they maintain that Hispanic culture emphasizes individual effort to be likable and easygoing, while Anglo culture permits more overt aggression. Similarly, Moghaddam, Taylor, and Wright (1993) note that Japanese children are taught to avoid or withdraw from potentially aggressive situations, while Western children are taught to confront and retaliate against aggression:

> In Japanese culture, parents actively discourage quarreling and encourage their children to yield rather than fight on. When Japanese children are faced with an argument or a fight, their mother will likely tell them "Makeru ga kachi," which means "To lose is to win." In the Japanese household, the child who yields is honored. (Moghaddam et al. 1993:124)

Recently, Bear, Manning, and Shiomi (2006) interviewed two hundred American and Japanese fifth grade students to identify the reasons they refrain from aggressive acts toward others. They found that children in the United States were more likely than Japanese children to give self-focused justifications. While both groups of children mentioned concern with others in their justifications, a majority of American children also mentioned justifications centered on avoiding punishment (92 percent) or avoiding retaliation (79 percent). Such responses were less common in the Japanese sample (10 percent and 42 percent respectively). Thus, an individual's rationale for either choosing or avoiding aggression is marked by cultural variation.

Similarly, Lambert (1971, cited in Moghaddam et al. 1993) suggests that Mexican and U.S. parents respond differently to children's aggression because of different degrees of interdependence in their respective extended families. One Mexican mother explained her punishment of her child's aggression in this way: "I cannot permit my son to fight with the child next door in the Mexican town, because he is my brother's child and if our children don't get along, then my brother and I may come to a parting of the ways and that may lead to great problems" (Lambert 1971:51). In contrast, an American mother said, "If he can't get along with one child, he can always play with someone else. There are many children around to *choose* from." In this Mexican community, families are so interdependent that conflict would be devastating; this interdependence was not found in the U.S. community. The place of the family in the larger community, which varies cross-culturally, thus affects parental responses to aggression.

Who Are the Targets of Aggression?

Social positions such as gender, race, sexuality, and class also affect patterns of victimization (both actual and stereotypic). Stereotypes suggest that women are not only nonaggressive bystanders, but are also disproportionately the victims of violence. Women are believed to need protection (from men) against violence (paradoxically, also from men). Indeed, women's fear of being victimized by violence is greater than men's in every racial, ethnic, age, and social class group (Gordon and Riger 1989), despite the fact that men are more likely to be the targets of every kind of violence except rape (Koss 1993). Experimental research reports the same results: research participants are likely to aggress more against men than women in experimental settings (Eagly and Steffen 1986). Gender stereotypes mask men's victimization, however, facilitating a sense of vulnerability in women and a sense of self-sufficiency in men (Hollander 2001). Part of the reason for men's greater victimization, of course, lies in lifestyle differences. Men are far less likely than women to restrict their activities because of fear or to take safety precautions in their homes or on the street (Gordon and Riger 1989). Social norms also make men more legitimate targets for many forms of aggression. Again, however, social context is crucial: women may be chivalrously protected from aggression in public places, but domestic violence statistics suggest that these normative restrictions do not apply in private.

Most aggression is also intraracial (LaFree 1995), in part because of the extensive everyday segregation of racial groups in the United States (Krivo, Peterson, and Kuhl 2009; Massey and Denton 1993). Interracial violence, however, has received far more social psychological attention. Interracial (and interethnic) aggression are also topics of great social concern, because these have been the basis for wars and riots, as well as much everyday violence. Cognitive social psychologists suggest that the targets of violence are often dehumanized by aggressors—a process in which different beliefs and values are attributed to an individual or group, making them seem less than human and rationalizing aggression against them. Dehumanization is particularly easy when the target is a member of an easily definable outgroup, such as a different racial or ethnic group. Moreover, dehumanization may prevent us from defining the suffering of outgroup members as a reason for intervention. Cuddy, Rock, and Norton (2007), for example, asked white and nonwhite individuals whether they would step in to assist a particular black or white victim and found that individuals characterized ingroup victims as having more "humanly" emotions (e.g., anguish) than outgroup victims. Those respondents who did not dehumanize outgroup victims were more likely to help. Although many people would like to believe that racism and discrimination have largely disappeared, unobtrusive studies of white and black helping behavior, aggression, and nonverbal communication indicate that whites' behavior often appears antiblack, despite survey data reporting a decrease in expressed antiblack attitudes (Crosby, Bromley, and Saxe 1980; Hutchings 2009; Schuman et al. 1997).

Because of the greater likelihood that people of color are poor, they also have a far greater risk of being victimized by violence than do whites. The relationship between social class and the risk of victimization has not been studied extensively by social psychologists, but it is well known that poorer people are more likely to be the targets of crime because they tend to live in more vulnerable neighborhoods and have fewer resources with which to defend themselves (e.g., by installing security systems, driving rather than walking or taking public transportation, or working in safe environments).

Sexual orientation also affects individuals' risk of violence. Violence against lesbians and gay men appears to be escalating (Herek 2009; Herek and Berrill 1992), and those who are more visibly homosexual are at greater risk (Harry 1990; Renfrow 2008). In a recent survey, Lyons (2006) compared student attributions of blame in biased crime scenarios. Whereas individuals appear to display sympathy for black victims of a hate crime, individuals are less likely to display sympathy for gay and lesbian victims. In fact, these victims are often held accountable for their own victimization. This kind of violence, as well as the homophobic attitudes that support it, are closely linked to gender norms: "Although gender identity is distinct from socioerotic identity, the two are closely related. Heterosexuality is equated ideologically with 'normal' masculinity and 'normal' femininity, whereas homosexuality is equated with violating norms of gender." As a result, "gay people are stigmatized not only for their erotic behavior, but also for their perceived violation of gender norms" (Herek 1992:97).

Coda: Helping and Harming—Lessons from Opposition

As we noted at the beginning of this chapter, altruism and aggression are assumed to be opposite behaviors. As is often true with opposites, however, their dynamics are more similar than they might at first appear. In the concluding section of this chapter, we consider what the research traditions on altruism and aggression share and where they differ. This analysis reveals important insights about the assumptions underlying social psychological research, as well as the structural contexts of these behaviors. We focus in particular on the implications of prevailing methodological strategies and thematic issues that crosscut these two fields of research.

Research versus Reality

The methodological approaches of these two literatures are very similar. Both have relied heavily on the experimental paradigm dominant in most social psychological research. This paradigm requires random assignment of subjects to experimental conditions, strict control of extraneous factors, and tight manipulation of independent variables—requirements that are not easily adapted to studying real-life situations or long-term relationships between family members, romantic partners, or coworkers. Instead, most research has been conducted in short-term laboratory settings, often with unacquainted college students as participants.

A common scenario in a laboratory study of aggression entails exposing subjects to aggressive cues (or not exposing them to such cues, in control conditions). Participants might enter a waiting room in which guns are present or watch a film about boxing. Participants then experience some sort of provocation from a confederate of the experimenter, followed by an opportunity to administer electric shocks or some other form of punishment, supposedly to the person who has provoked them. (Often the person is ostensibly in another room, so participants do not see the target receive their aggression.) This sort of laboratory scenario is far removed from "real-world" aggression such as murder, assault, or verbal confrontations between friends, coworkers, or family members. Most of us are never asked to administer electric shocks to others, especially to strangers whom we have never met. Thus, "the social psychologist curious about the violent phenomena of murder, riots, and war may well end up studying and understanding the shock-setting behavior of deceived college students, the Bobo doll hammerings of TV-watching children, and the horn-honking of frustrated motorists" (Lubek 1979:266). Situations in studies of helping, such as picking up a stranger's dropped parcels or giving someone the change for a phone call, are, not surprisingly, more common in everyday life, although even these are hardly the most common forms of everyday helping. Laboratory situations also constrain the possibility of retaliation for aggression or reciprocation of altruism. Because results of these laboratory studies are often generalized to real-world situations, it is important to ask what patterns are missed by these approaches, a topic we take up below.

Everyday Helping

Findings that men provide more help and women receive more help are due in part to the experimental research tradition, which focuses on the forms of help performed more often by men, such as physical labor and help with male-typed tasks. There has been much less attention to patterns of emotional support and indirect helping (especially with female-typed tasks, forms of behavior that women may be more likely than men to perform). Only when we consider real-world helping relationships do these patterns emerge.

What sorts of help are provided in everyday life? In a socioeconomic context in which most people experience substantial demands both at work and at home, the occasional necessity of both receiving and offering help is ubiquitous. What about the everyday patterns of caring, nurturing, and offering minor (sometimes major) but never-ending assistance to family, friends, or neighbors? (See Cancian and Oliker 2000.) As the U.S. population is steadily aging and the economic circumstances of adult children are relatively worse than in recent generations, patterns of intergenerational assistance have received increasing attention from demographers and public policy analysts (Lye 1996).

Do structural circumstances shape the provision or receipt of such assistance? Like behavior studied in experimental contexts, everyday helping is systematically patterned by gender, race, class and other structural positions (Hogan, Eggebeen and Clogg 1993). Helping in daily family life is pervasively gendered, as DeVault's (1991) ethnography *Feeding the Family* reveals. DeVault demonstrates that virtually all tasks of home maintenance and support are differentially allocated by sex. Intergenerational support is also deeply gendered: older adults with one or more daughters are far more likely to receive assistance in old age than those with only sons (Spitze and Logan 1990). Adult women are three times as likely as adult men to live with an aging parent and are more likely to exchange, rather than just receive, support. Controlling for resources, needs, family structure, and closeness of ties across generations, gender persistently affects the provision, but not the receipt, of aid (Hogan et al. 1993).

Lye and colleagues (1995) suggest that the origins of these patterns lie at least partially in childhood. American men invest less time and emotional resources in their children than do women, and after a divorce they contribute considerably fewer financial resources to their children. These patterns persist throughout the life span; even as grandparents, men provide less support to their adult children and their grandchildren than do women. Both girls and boys thus learn that the provision of support is more appropriate for women than for men. The type of assistance is also gendered: sons are more likely to give financial or household assistance (e.g., with repairs, transportation, or work around the house) to their parents, whereas daughters are more likely to provide advice and homecare (e.g., physical care, cooking, or cleaning). To fail to consider everyday helping is to miss the major and asymmetric contribution of women.

Research on racial patterns of intergenerational helping shows contradictory results. It is a common assumption that families of minority racial groups exchange more support (based most often on ethnographic studies, e.g., Stack 1974). Hogan and colleagues (1993) assert, however, that large-scale representative surveys do not find stronger support networks among minority families than among white families. Based on data from the 1987–1988 National Survey of Families and Households, for example, Hogan and colleagues report that blacks are consistently less likely than whites to engage in any form of intergenerational assistance. The number of children in a family, however, is crucial to interpreting these patterns. Black families tend to have more children than white families. One reason that black adult children receive comparatively less assistance than do whites from their parents is because more siblings compete for this support. Moreover, black parents are likely to have less disposable income to share with their children than are white parents. Roschelle's (1997) *No More Kin* suggests that men and women of all ethnicities participate in support networks. Their participation tends to follow traditional stereotypes, with women being responsible for child care. She also concludes that white men are more likely than others to receive assistance from their kin. Across racial groups, however, she finds that kin networks are not a primary source of giving and receiving child care. Roschelle's analysis points to a decline in the support individuals receive from their kin networks. It is important to note, however, that exchanges of practical and financial assistance are not necessarily indicators of emotional ties.

Intragroup solidarity is a powerful factor in shaping patterns of real-world support. Thus, support comes not only from family, but also from friends and coworkers. Black professionals, for example, are likely both to have had and to have served as mentors to other black professionals (Kalbfleish and Davies 1991). Similarly, in the 1980s and 1990s in the United States, when gay men were the primary population living with HIV/AIDS, most providers of daily help for these individuals were gay men and lesbians. Salais and Fischer's (1995) research remains one of the few studies to explicitly assess the connection between one's sexual preferences and prosocial behavior. They find that homosexual men display more empathy—an important precursor to helping—than do heterosexual men. (Interestingly, the few experimental studies that address effects of sexual orientation have focused on receiving rather than providing help, despite the fact that lesbians and gay men are active agents in real-world helping.)

Considering everyday altruism is also crucial for understanding cross-cultural patterns of helping others. A set of studies comparing patterns of helping across six countries (Kenya, Mexico, the Philippines, the United States, Japan, and India) found considerable differences in levels of children's helping behavior (Whiting and Edwards 1988; Whiting and Whiting 1975). Kenyan, Mexican, and Filipino children showed the highest levels of helping, with Indian and Japanese children in the middle range; U.S. children showed the lowest levels of helping. These cross-cultural differences in helping behavior are correlated with children's daily responsibilities. Helping was least likely in communities in which children competed in school and were rarely responsible for farm or household chores. Helping was most common where children had to cooperate with other family members in performing many chores, especially where older siblings were required to share in the care and raising of other children. Thus, contextual factors—together with cultural factors—are instrumental in shaping children's everyday helping behavior (see also de Guzman, Edwards, and Carlo 2005).

Recent scholarship suggests that social psychological studies of helping behavior may have had a real-world impact on displays of prosocial and helping behaviors. Holmes, Miller, and Lerner (2002) argue that psychological models of humans as self-interested actors have spilled over into the lay theories that everyday actors use to guide their actions and make sense of social processes. The end result is that although people want to act on feelings of compassion for others, they must first reconcile compassion with their self-interest before being able to act (see also Simpson, Irwin and Lawrence 2006). Thus, the assumptions social psychologists make about social actors' intentions may come to bear on the everyday behaviors we wish to understand, as these assumptions become widely accepted outside of the academy.

Everyday Aggression

Unlike helping behavior, physical aggression is not an everyday event in the lives of most individuals. Although the newspapers are filled with incidents of physical violence, and social psychologists have emphasized physical aggression in their research, the forms of aggression most individuals are likely to encounter in their daily lives are verbal arguments. As with altruism, focusing on extreme forms of aggressive behavior has diverted attention from other types of aggression, which may show different patterns by gender, race, class, and sexuality.

Researchers have implied, for example, that women do not engage in active, physical aggression—indeed, perhaps in any aggression at all. Many early studies did not even include women as participants, assuming that aggression in women was too infrequent to study. Moreover, most studies have focused on physical violence, which has skewed findings about the relationship between aggression and gender. As discussed above, studies have found significant, albeit small, sex differences in physical aggression (Björkqvist et al. 1992; Eagly and Steffen 1986). Sex differences in indirect and verbal aggression (such as spreading rumors or ignoring a person) are even smaller (Eagly and Steffen 1986; Lagerspetz, Björkqvist, and Peltonen 1988). Scholarly emphasis on physical aggression has thus minimized those situations in which men's and women's aggression may be more similar.

The dominance of the experimental paradigm that has so shaped research on altruism has also contributed to these patterns of findings about aggression. Eagly and Steffen (1986) maintain that experimental situations "manifest the four conditions associated with larger sex-of-subject and sex-of-target effect sizes: A laboratory setting, physical aggression, a semiprivate context, and required aggressive behavior." The result is that "the best known and most popular methods for studying human aggression . . . happen to be those that are most likely to elicit greater aggression in men than women and greater aggression toward men than women" (325–26).

Women are more likely to be aggressive in private contexts such as the home than in less private situations such as laboratory experiments. Research on child abuse, for example, shows that women commit a considerable amount of such abuse (although men's rate of abuse is higher when time spent with children is controlled [Gelles 1994; Margolin 1992]). Ignoring everyday aggression also makes invisible the many situations in which women are more frequent targets of aggression: domestic violence, sexual harassment in the workplace and on the street, bullying in schools, and child sexual abuse. These patterns have been explored more by sociologists and social workers than by social psychologists.

Some empirical studies on domestic abuse have reported that women engage in a considerable amount of aggression against their partners (e.g., Heimer and Kruttschnitt 2006; Straus and Gelles 1986; Straus, Gelles, and Steinmetz 2006). Some researchers go so far as to contend that wives and husbands have equal levels of aggression (e.g., Steinmetz 1977/1978), although this assertion has triggered intense critiques. Recent research also reports a considerable amount of battering in lesbian relationships (Lockhart et al. 1994; Renzetti 1988, 1992). The issue of female aggression is contentious: some scholars (and activists) fear that examining women's aggression may detract attention from the fact that women are overwhelmingly the targets, rather than the perpetrators, of aggression. They point out, for example, that studies that find reciprocal battering often ignore the frequency, motivations, or consequences of violence. A single episode of self-defense may be counted as equivalent to an ongoing pattern of instigation. These writers contend that when these factors are taken into account, women suffer far greater victimization than do men (Carney, Buttell, and Dutton 2007; DeLeon-Granados, Wells, and Binsbacher 2006; Dobash et al. 1992).

Research clearly does show that women are capable of aggression, and do engage in aggressive behavior in certain situations. Women and men do not appear to differ on personality measures of aggressivity or hostility (Frodi, Macaulay, and Thorne 1977; Hyde 1986) or everyday anger (Averill 1982; Tavris 1989). The laboratory studies show that when there is no risk of being recognized (and therefore no risk of retaliation), women may behave as aggressively as men (Björkqvist and Niemelä 1992:14). In most real-world situations, however, women are not as physically aggressive as men. Why? First, men's aggression tends to have more damaging consequences, because men tend to be larger and stronger than women and are generally taught how to use their bodies more effectively than women. Second, women tend to believe that behaving aggressively is more dangerous to themselves than men do; this belief is an important mediator of sex differences in aggression (Eagly and Steffen 1986). Third, men's physical violence tends to be ongoing, while women's tends to be episodic and more frequently in self-defense. (Ironically, this may mean that women are more likely to engage in severe violence, because that may be the only way they believe they can overcome men's perceived physical advantages.) Fourth, men's violence is facilitated by expectations for masculinity (and women's violence is restrained by expectations for femininity). One important reason for the relative persistence of men's aggression, toward both women and other men, is that when conflict arises, backing down risks the loss of masculinity. Being aggressive, in other words, is performing masculinity (Katz 2006). Finally, men's aggression is reinforced by greater social power, both within a relationship and in the broader social environment. Compare the situation of a traditional wife, who is dependent on her husband for financial survival and who risks losing her children if she leaves the marriage, with that of her husband, who has the financial and professional resources to support himself. In this context, wife battering has a very different meaning than husband battering.

Thus, women and men may have the same capacity for aggression, but this capacity is tempered by socialization, structural circumstances, and the symbolic meanings associated with aggression (Heimer and Kruttschnitt 2006). Ultimately, these differences result in women's subordination. The stereotype that men are more aggressive than women permits men to maintain power and dominance over women by fostering fear and dependence in women and by restricting access to the competitive realms of the economy, polity, and military (White and Kowalski 1994). Indeed, some have argued that domestic violence represents not a "breakdown of social order," but "the reflection of a power struggle for the maintenance of a certain kind of social order" (McGrath, discussed in Breines and Gordon 1983:511).

Instrumentality and Expressiveness

The distinction between goal-directed behavior, on the one hand, and behavior motivated by emotions, on the other, also cuts across altruism and aggression. As we have noted, helping behavior can be instrumental: people can provide help to others in order to meet their own goals. Helping behavior can also be provoked by the rush of adrenaline in observing an emergency or by the depth of compassion from seeing someone in pain. Similarly, aggressive behavior can be either instrumental or expressive. People may hurt others in order to bring about desired ends, or they may lash out in anger or fear. Indeed, the line between aggression and altruism disappears in some forms of instrumental aggression: prosocial aggression, such as fighting a war, entails aggression toward some people while helping others.

The distinction between instrumental and expressive behavior is gendered. At the level of stereotypes, instrumentality is more closely related to the male stereotype of rationality, whereas emotional expression is a central component of the female stereotype (Shields 2002; Smith-Lovin 1995). Thus, stereotypes suggest that men should behave more instrumentally and women more emotionally, both when they help and when they harm others. Research suggests a more complex picture, however. The altruism literature portrays women more often as emotional, compassionate, expressive helpers, and men as thoughtful, organized, goal-oriented helpers. The literature on aggression also presents women as emotional aggressors (e.g., they might aggress in defense of their children), consistent with these stereotypes. Men's aggression is also portrayed as expressive, but as driven by hormonal, biological urges rather than as instrumental. Indeed, in one of the many fascinating contradictions of gender, women are often held responsible for controlling the aggressive behavior of "their" men. Hastings and colleagues (2007) urge scholars to be careful when making generalizations, because sex differences may in fact stem from the cognitive availability of feminine and masculine stereotypes within a researcher's mind (e.g., gender) rather than actual differences among participants.

Just as we have questioned the assumption of sex differences in aggression, we also question the validity of a distinction between instrumental and expressive behavior. Is helping expressive or instrumental when a head of household spends a good deal of his or her time at home planning, preparing, and cleaning up after meals for the family? Is aggression expressive or instrumental when that same head of household speaks sharply to a child who has transgressed family rules? Goal-oriented behavior can be laden with feeling, as a participant in DeVault's (1991) study of family caring indicates: "If you have a real discussion at the dinner table, you can give a person a chance to let you in on their life. . . . It's a time when you can show that you really care about that person in more than just a caretaking role" (33–34).

Similarity, Difference, and Power

We have argued that the capacities of women and men to help others, the occasional vulnerabilities of women and men to needing help, the capacities of women and men to engage in aggressive behavior, and the capacities of women and men to be victimized by others are not inherently different. Both women and men share these strengths and these vulnerabilities. Yet much research in these areas (and in social psychology more generally) appears to assume that there are innate or at least deeply rooted differences between women and men in both helping behavior and aggression. By conducting research in situations and with methods most likely to elicit sex differences, social psychological researchers themselves have contributed to the widespread cultural belief in sex difference (held even by those who struggle to escape these stereotypes). Because beliefs shape behavior, social psychological research (and cultural practices more generally) contributes to a self-perpetuating system that creates, affirms, and entrenches sex difference. We have emphasized that social structural factors shape these potentials and possibilities into the gendered patterns researchers have not only discovered, but, in part, created. Difference enters in through the location of women and men in their particular social structural circumstances and is deepened by the cultural traditions that ossify these circumstances into the regularities of individual lives and the histories of social groups. Difference is exaggerated; similarity is made invisible.

Power

The gaps in these (and other social psychological) areas indicate a larger pattern: widespread inattention to issues of power and dominance in research on both helping behavior and aggression. Power relationships structure who can offer help to whom, who can request help from whom, who can receive help from whom, and who cannot refuse to be helped when help is offered. Power defines what constitutes helping and who legitimizes the definition. Who determines whether help is necessary? Who determines the means of help? Is an act helping when it reproduces social dependencies? Are recipients of help more visible if they are women, poor, people of color, or some combination of these? Are agents of helping more acclaimed if they are wealthy, men, or white? Similarly, power shapes who aggresses against whom, who are the targets of aggression, what forms aggressive behavior takes, and what is defined as aggression.

Sprague's (1995:19) distinction between forms of helping that encourage independence and forms of helping that sustain dependence illustrates how the act of helping someone can reaffirm one's own power. People who provide help often do so (likely unintentionally) in a way that perpetuates their own role as helper rather than teaching others how to provide for themselves. The perspective of both parties is crucial. We can assume that *Oleanna*'s John views his gesture of helping as benign. Carol will not pass the class without his help, and he thinks that making her come to his office regularly for private tutoring sessions is the best way to help her. From Carol's perspective, however, this form of helping is intrusive. John's mode of tutoring enforces Carol's reliance on him; he does not show her better study strategies, suggest she join study groups of other students, or show her other techniques that would allow her to develop her study skills. In short, John ensures that Carol will continue to depend on him.

This example also suggests that the boundary between helping and aggression is fragile. Why are some forms of public assistance defined as helping? Why is the fact that seventeen million children in this country lack decent nutrition not an indication of societal aggression? Why is helping rarely analyzed in terms of the structural advantages of the helper and the structural disadvantages of those who are given assistance? Indeed, the transfer of resources from those who are wealthy to those who are poor is an excellent case in point. When those with resources contribute money to those with less, it is celebrated as charity. That such contributions provide tax write-offs is often unremarked. When we consider the profile of research in altruism and aggression, the centrality of power is inescapable—yet it is too often unacknowledged.

Summary

We have analyzed research on helping behavior and aggression through a gendered lens. Research in each of these areas has been deeply influenced by prevailing cultural assumptions about gender, as well as about race, class, and sexuality, yet in large part these assumptions have been neither acknowledged nor incorporated in these analyses. Thus, these assumptions have framed the nature of the questions asked—and the questions not asked—about both helping behavior and aggression. We have shown, in contrast, that gender is a central organizing principle of these types of social behaviors. Moreover, the embeddedness of both research traditions in cultural stereotypes about gender, race, ethnicity, social class, and sexuality underlies structural similarities in the emphases and omissions of each line of research. Thus, although helping and harming others may seem to be polar opposites, a gendered analysis reveals their interdependence.

Notes

1. See Segal (1993) for discussion of problems with this research, however.

2. While inequalities clearly exist between women and men, we should emphasize that a heterosexual presumption underlies most analyses of these societal inequalities. Society is organized so that virtually all social groups are assumed to include similar numbers of women and men, and they are presumed to be allied in pairs—pairs that are inscribed by inequality, to be sure. Social groups are not assumed to include similar numbers of blacks and whites, old and young, or rich and poor—or even some set ratio of these groups. That is a profound difference between gender and the other systems of inequalities.

3. We must be cautious, however, in using arrest data as a measure of aggression, because arrests are influenced by factors such as the opportunity to participate in criminal activity (Eagly and Steffen 1986) and the biases of the criminal justice system (Visher 1983).

7

Conclusions

Reprising a Gender Lens on Social Psychology

A Case in Point

IN THE PRECEDING CHAPTERS, WE HAVE discussed in detail why social psychological theories need to integrate gender into their analyses and how they might do so. In this final chapter, we summarize the key themes of a gendered lens on social psychology and show how the various social psychological theories might work together to explain patterns of social interaction. The implications of a gender lens might be better understood through example. We have cited a good deal of experimental work throughout the book, but we deliberately chose our example from everyday life rather than from the lab. Why? The many constraints of experimental work—the barrenness of the social context, the deliberate removal of effects often found in everyday life, the strict control over the circumstances—have limited the generalizability of findings of social psychological research, as we have stressed throughout the book. The experimental method provides a degree of rigor available in no other method, and therefore we can feel confident about the internal validity of such research. But because we are interested in asking the sorts of questions less amenable to the laboratory context, we turn now to broader arenas. And so, we trace the circumstances of a contemporary couple as they negotiate the demands of everyday life.[1]

Eve and Adam have known each other for ten years. They have lived together for seven years; when they moved in together they allocated household work relatively evenly, although Eve did a bit more cooking and cleaning, whereas

Adam did more of the outside maintenance work. They married when they decided to move to a new city and pursue graduate degrees. They both brought strongly egalitarian beliefs and expectations to the relationship; they identify as feminist and generally progressive (in contrast to many members of both their families). When they married, she retained her own name, a decision that both sets of parents greeted with consternation.

Time passed. Both graduated from their programs, she with a master's degree in social work, he with a law degree. He secured a prestigious clerkship; she located a position with a local well-respected counseling center. With all the years it took for them to attain this point in their professional careers, they became cognizant of a decision they had put off—having children. They decided to get pregnant and during the first year of their postdegree jobs, Eve had a baby. She took a six-month maternity leave and then returned to work.

In another year and a half, Eve became pregnant again. Both Eve and Adam had long felt that it is not fair to raise a child without siblings, and they preferred their children to be fairly close in age. Both agreed that two children were enough, recognizing both the financial and the emotional costs of having more children. At this point, Eve was well ensconced in her job. She was the assistant director of one branch of the center and poised to take over the directorship when the current director retired in a few more years. Adam was also doing well at the firm he joined when he completed his clerkship. In a few more years, he had a good chance of earning a partnership.

But now they would have two children. Eve planned to take a maternity leave again, but this time they had some serious talks about just how much attention kids need. In addition, they weighed their relative incomes, noting that Adam earned far more as an attorney (and had the potential for far greater future earnings) than Eve did at the counseling center. Reluctantly, Eve decided to take an open-ended leave from her position to become a full-time parent. She reasoned that she could still take clients on an ad hoc basis and bring in some income to the household and that she would have a good deal more control over her time and much more time to spend with her children. This too would free up more time for Adam, for whom the pressures of a potential partnership were growing intense. Both felt pleased with this decision and thought it best for the entire family.

Let's check in five years later. Eve and Adam have two children, ages seven and five (plus a few pets now). Eve has elected not to return to her position. The director did retire, and another younger member of the group took her position. Eve is seeing a few clients in the room they remodeled in the basement. Adam has become a partner in his law firm and now finds himself busier than ever at work. Eve is responsible for primary child care. She also contributes a small but fairly steady income to the family through her counseling activities. Adam contributes the bulk of the income, considerably more than Eve could have done in her profession. Adam spends time with the kids on Sundays, his dedicated day off. He also arranges to work at home on evenings when Eve is seeing clients.

Eve and Adam are content with this arrangement. It seems fair to all, it clearly provides an excellent income for the family, and the kids always have a parent available to them.

Eve and Adam's story illustrates many of the points of the theories we have presented throughout this volume. A close analysis of this vignette reveals a host of ways in which gender dynamics shape social behavior. A closer look also reveals how systems of class and sexuality shape social behavior.

Traces of Social Psychological Theories

Let's look at Eve and Adam through the lenses of the several social psycho-logical theories. The basic tenet of social exchange and related theories is that social behavior is motivated by self-interest and the desire to gain rewards (and avoid punishments). Eve and Adam move to a new city in order to pursue graduate work; we can assume that the costs of moving were not as considerable as the advantages to them of studying in this particular com-munity. When they have a second baby, Eve leaves her job; Adam does not. Cost-efficiency is one component of their decision calculus: the family will have a good deal more money if Adam continues to work. This same cost-benefit logic may also explain why Eve, rather than Adam, took a parental leave. Without further information, we cannot know whether they made any explicit exchanges. But we can assume that Eve's adoption of more parenting responsibility was part of an exchange for cutting back so heavily on her paid work. Similarly, Adam's restriction of his structured parenting responsibilities to one day probably reflects an exchange for his many hours of paid work. These exchanges were likely based in part on the relative resources of the two partners: time, skills, money, and so on. This analysis of cost-benefit differen-tials is one of the core principles of exchange theory.

Exchange theory argues that individuals choose to behave in particular ways as a function of their resources and alternatives. What exchange theory does not address, however, are the dynamics of these choice processes. Under-standing these processes requires another social psychological theory—social cognition. One important backdrop for understanding Eve and Adam's nego-tiations about work and family is that both partners strongly endorse feminist and progressive social and political beliefs. Presumably these convictions shape many of their behavioral decisions: to pursue careers, to work in fields where they can help others. On the other hand, both live (and have grown up) in a culture that has particular gender expectations and stereotypes; these presumably also influence Eve and Adam's ideas about the appropriate roles of men and women—for example, about who might be a better primary care-taker of their children.

In addition, Eve and Adam have to make a number of difficult decisions. They have to weigh information in order to decide where to go to graduate school, whether to have a first child, whether to have a second child, whether either of them should stop working for pay. (Note that each of these decisions will underlie future exchanges they make in their relationship.) We might speculate that a bit of selective memory also comes into play. Would the Eve and Adam who began graduate school with their strong beliefs have believed they would be where they ended up seven years later, and happily so? We as readers also make attributions about Eve and Adam and the reasons for their choices. We construct our own explanations for why they made the choices they did and our own evaluations that follow from these attributions.

Social comparisons are also crucial to how each person deals with these conflicts—indeed, to how they define them. Because truly egalitarian relationships are still a rarity (see Schwartz 1994; Wilcox and Nock 2006), Adam can feel good about himself for being willing to share tasks in their early years together. Even if the sharing is not quite equal, the fact that he does some of the cooking, even some of the laundry, makes him stand out by comparison from some of the men in couples they know. Both Eve and Adam may feel that their objectively unequal work allocations are fair, due to gendered expectations of even greater asymmetry and social comparisons with other couples whose work allocations are less equal.

Eve and Adam's attitudes and stereotypes are important in their choices about work and family. But how do these beliefs and attitudes develop? How, in everyday interaction, do situations become defined, identities negotiated, meanings shared? This is the realm of symbolic interaction. Much symbolic interaction also underlies this vignette, although we have not presented the details of these interactions. Both Eve and Adam have strongly developed senses of themselves and the sort of lives they want to lead. In making decisions, they rely on a host of culturally significant symbol systems. Spouse, professional, and parent are all symbols, and the meaning that each of these symbols has for Eve and Adam is a strong influence on the life choices they make. *Professional* may now be a symbol available to both women and men, but the symbol *parent* has historically had different meanings for women and men. (Consider, for example, the different connotations of the words *mothering* and *fathering*: fathering a child implies little more than participating in the child's conception; mothering a child implies a far greater investment of time, energy, and care.) As a result, women may experience a certain tension between these positions of *professional* and *parent*. And, of course, there are undoubtedly many negotiations and situations that have needed defining to get Eve and Adam to this point. Although we cannot eavesdrop on their conversations, their situation is familiar enough to many readers that we can likely imagine some of the identity management and altercasting that has gone on. And lest we forget their own parents, it is clear that a great deal of negotiation and impression management must have been involved in providing accounts to their parents and in-laws for Eve's decision to keep her own surname, possibly about how they chose their children's surnames, probably about her decision to return to work after their first child was born.

Thus, these three social psychological theories offer three different lenses, or ways of viewing the world. Social exchange sees a world full of rational decision-makers: individuals weighing the costs and benefits of different lines of action, assessing the resources and alternatives available to the relevant players in an interaction, and behaving in the ways they perceive will be most beneficial. Social cognition sees a world of information-processors: individuals struggling to deal with the mass of stimuli available in the world, using tools such as categories, schemas, and stereotypes to guide behavior. Symbolic interactionism sees a world of meaning-makers: individuals making sense out of the world by developing symbols and identities, managing impressions, and defining situations through negotiation with others.

Which of these lenses is correct? Each lens offers a valid picture of the world. People are decision-makers, information-processors, and meaning-makers all at the same time. None of these perspectives offers the *only* valid picture of the world, however. Looking at the world through only one of these lenses is like using only one sense to perceive the world. What we hear when we listen is true, but what we smell, taste, feel, and see is also true. Using all our senses together provides a more complete representation of reality than any one sense alone can provide.

We also believe that each social psychological lens has some significant gaps. In the preceding chapters, we have noted the specific blind spots associated with each theory. One critique applies equally to all three theories, however: none of the perspectives offers a satisfactory analysis of social structure and how it affects individual thoughts and behaviors. Social structure rarely enters explicitly into social cognitive and symbolic interactionist work. Structure plays a more prominent part in social exchange theory, but as we have pointed out in chapter 3, this theoretical emphasis rarely extends into empirical research. The distribution of resources—and therefore power—in society is highly structured: some people (men, whites, upper classes) tend to have many more resources, and therefore much more power, than others (women, people of color, working classes). For example, none of the theories addresses why it is that Adam is likely to make more money than Eve. One explanation involves gender socialization and ongoing expectations that push women and men to choose different types of work. But another equally important explanation involves the biases of the labor market (and the people who comprise it), which segregate women and men into different jobs despite their preferences and which pays women less than men even if they are performing the same tasks. Thus, the structure of the labor market makes it more financially feasible for Adam to continue working and Eve to stop, rather than vice versa. Although Eve and Adam treat this as a choice, it is clearly a constrained choice. Moreover, the class structure of the society is what allows them to make this choice at all. Couples who do not belong to the middle and upper classes do not have the luxury of such a choice; both partners in such couples must work for pay. Both Eve and Adam benefit from class privilege in ways they do not even seem to realize. Social psychologists have paid little attention to these kinds of structural factors and how they affect the patterning of power in relationships.

Because of this inattention to structure and power, social psychology has also generally failed to problematize social positions such as gender, race, and class. As we have discussed extensively in the preceding chapters, social psychologists have tended either to ignore gender, to view it as synonymous with biological sex, or to accept sex difference as an explanation in itself rather than as something to be explained. Although work on gender and social psychology is becoming both more widespread and more nuanced, the mainstream of social psychology continues without understanding how central gender is to the processes it describes. In contrast, our contention throughout this book is that no social psychological topic can be fully understood without seeing how deeply and pervasively it is gendered. Moreover, gender cannot be fully understood without analyzing its intersections with other social statuses.

Approaches to Gender

We have identified four basic perspectives that dominate scholarship on gender: essentialist, socialization, social constructionist, and structural. Each would analyze Eve and Adam's situation differently. In this section, we briefly reprise these four perspectives, using the vignette above to elaborate some central gendered themes. We also note how these perspectives on gender might map onto the three social psychological theories discussed above.

Essentialism argues that Eve and Adam make the choices they do because child care, maintenance work, breadwinning, and so on are built into their genes, their hormones, or some other part of their "natures." We do not repeat our critiques of this theory here; we simply note that these theories take as explanation the very phenomena we consider it crucial to explain. Moreover, they cannot adequately explain the considerable historical, cross-cultural, and interpersonal differences in these sorts of behaviors. Essentialist assumptions can be found in both the social exchange literature and the social cognition literature, but this perspective is entirely incompatible with symbolic interaction, which sees gendered identity and behavior as negotiated, not fixed.

The other major social psychological theories argue that gender is learned, constructed, or structured, rather than innate. The socialization perspective suggests that Eve and Adam learned their various skills, behavioral tendencies, and personality patterns as they were growing up, by watching family members, friends and neighbors, or other models on television or in the movies. Adam learned that breadwinning is an important role for men, while Eve learned that caretaking is a valued occupation for women. These lessons may also have shaped their career choices, as well as their later decisions about the division of labor in their own home. Note that the socialization perspective draws from both social cognition (people learn particular schemas or scripts for behavior) and social learning theory (they learn through being rewarded for particular behaviors or watching others receive rewards). This perspective does not, however, provide an easy explanation for the fact that both Eve and Adam have developed ideological positions at odds with those of their parents.

The social constructionist approach, in contrast, looks at the ways in which both individuals construct gender (and other identities) through their actions. For Adam, becoming a lawyer and supporting his family may be a way of enacting his masculinity; on the other hand, his help with domestic work and his willingness to negotiate about family arrangements no doubt help to maintain his view of himself as progressive. For Eve, bearing and caring for children may be a way of constructing femininity; her continued (although greatly reduced) part-time work may help her maintain her view of herself as an independent woman. Both Eve and Adam—and others around them—must negotiate and redefine the situation at every stage in their relationship. For example, when they marry, Eve keeps her surname. Her choice is worthy of comment only in a world still structured by naming conventions—fundamental components of identity—that are asymmetric by gender. Her in-laws actually question the depth of the relationship because she would not take their name. In other words, these respective actors' definitions of the situation are dramatically different. To Eve's in-laws, the choice of surname indicates a tenuous commitment to their family; to Eve, it may symbolize personal identity and independence. The social constructionist perspective draws on both cognition and symbolic interaction to understand these kinds of choices.

The structural perspective on gender looks beyond individual character-istics and cognitions, and focuses instead on the structural positions and associated resources of the two partners. Adam is an attorney (a relatively well-paid and prestigious profession) and a man in a society that privileges masculinity. Eve, in contrast, is a social worker (a relatively poorly paid and low-prestige profession) and a woman. Structuralism notes the ways in which Eve and Adam's relative positions in the social structure result in gendered outcomes: Eve stays home with their two children and does the majority of the domestic work, and Adam brings home the money to support the family. We would expect that as a result, Adam would have more power than Eve in their relationship. Perhaps the most important point about this structural analysis is that it shows how gendered outcomes can occur even without conscious intentions on the part of the actors involved. Both Eve and Adam consider themselves progressive and feminist; they would argue that they have made practical rather than ideological choices and would no doubt be shocked to realize the degree to which their lives have become traditionally gendered. But a number of relatively minor decisions set in motion long ago have culminated in a highly traditional work/family arrangement because of the gender and class inequities of the social structure. Both social cognition and social exchange are central to this structural perspective.

As with the three social psychological theories, no one of these four ap-proaches to gender is complete by itself; again we must use more than one lens to fully understand social situations. To see these multiple lenses at work, consider Eve and Adam's decisions about parenting. Although most new par-ents these days believe that children benefit from having the attention of two parents, and expect that both fathers and mothers will be actively involved in parenting, it is the rare father who takes paternity leave when his child is born. Lest we attribute this to individual intransigence, the structure of the workplace rarely allows this. Many organizations now have maternity poli-cies in place; far fewer have paternity policies. And even when they do, social influence often dictates that men shouldn't use them or their careers will suffer (Bekkengen 2006; Olson 1997). Moreover, the occupational structure of society generates sex segregation and discrimination such that men gener-ally earn more than women; thus a man's taking paternity leave generally has economic as well as symbolic costs.

Even if Eve and Adam held identical jobs, however, others would likely see them, and their occupational and personal choices, differently. Consider this scenario: a male employer has just been told that one of his key male employ-ees is planning to get married. How would this employer respond? There is a good chance that he would respond with happiness, and perhaps relief that this long-term bachelor is finally "settling down." Now consider a slightly different scenario: the same employer has just heard the same news, but about a key *female* employee. Is his reaction the same? Probably not. The employer's mind may turn to the future; he may fear that she will have children and leave the company or at least demand maternity leave. Marriage for a female employee suggests instability; for a male employee it suggests maturity and increased stability. Thus, gender is invoked not only by the distribution of jobs and wages but also by the images and assumptions of those in the occupational sphere.

When Eve and Adam have their second child, the gendered norms come even more acutely into play. Adam compares himself to his law firm colleagues. They are working seventy-hour weeks; he, in contrast, has promised he will be home at least three nights a week for dinner and all day Sunday. Eve compares herself to other women who have chosen to leave potential careers or work part time in order to care for their kids. Both Eve and Adam have referential frameworks that are highly gendered because the structures of work and family life are highly gendered. It is worth noting that these gendered expectations are so fundamental that both Eve and Adam feel satisfied with their situation. This need not be a sort of self-serving blind spot on Adam's part or self-delusion on Eve's. Social structures shape each everyday decision about the allocation of work and family responsibilities. These decisions involve the jockeying of exchanges of time, money, and energy; they are based on frameworks of cultural schemas so familiar that most of us don't even remark on them; and they are negotiated between partners in an ongoing stream of symbolic interactions.

In our view, each of these perspectives has something to offer. Although we have found fault with essentialist perspectives throughout this book, the essentialist position does remind us that our lives are influenced (although not determined) by biological potentials. At a minimum, the physiological differences among people—the ability to bear children, or not; the ability to see and hear and move easily; the ability to overpower another person—affect the lives of individuals, and do so in patterned ways. We believe, however, that these biological potentials are filtered through cultural beliefs and understandings. How these potentials are understood and developed by individuals and groups has a far greater impact on our lives than does raw biology. Indeed, the pervasive cultural belief in the significance of biology may be as important a determinant of behavior as biology itself. The belief that women and men are predisposed by biology to prefer and excel at different tasks is as responsible for the gendered division of labor as any biological difference and has long served to justify gender inequality.

Although we believe the nonessentialist positions contribute more to our understanding of social life, each has its strengths and limitations as well. We agree with the socialization approach that gender is learned and maintained through modeling, rewards, and punishments; however, we believe that gender is more dynamic and fluid than most socialization perspectives suggest. We draw from the structural approach the insight that gender is structured by social position: much of what we understand to be gendered behavior is driven not by individual characteristics (whether innate or learned) but by one's positions in various social hierarchies. However, we also believe that it is necessary to combine this approach with the social constructionist perspective, which pays much greater attention to the ways in which gender is negotiated in interaction against a backdrop of cultural expectations. We suggest that in order to truly understand social interaction, we need a multilevel model of gender that incorporates the strengths of each approach.

We have also argued throughout this book that any approach to gender must incorporate the ways that other social positions, such as race, class, age, sexual orientation, and (dis)ability, intersect and interact with gender. The instances of political impression management that we have described, for example, occur within a social system that affords men far greater power than women. However, such situations are not reducible to sex, or to gender, alone. Barack Obama is not simply a man; he is a mixed-race man who is popularly perceived as a "black man," a relatively wealthy man, a famous man, a heterosexual man, a middle-aged man, an able-bodied man, and a father. Hillary Rodham Clinton is not simply a woman; she is a white woman, a wealthy woman, a heterosexual woman, an able-bodied woman, a mother, the wife of a former president, and the secretary of state. Similarly, the professor in Mamet's *Oleanna* is not only a man, but also a middle-aged man situated in a powerful position in the authority structure of the academy. The student, on the other hand, is not only a woman, but also a young woman situated in a less powerful position in the academy. These multiple statuses are always present; one is always all of one's statuses, and it is impossible to experience—or analyze—one status without the others. Thus, models of social life need to envision and incorporate the ways in which these statuses coexist and interact. Social scientists are only beginning to develop the tools to do this; we suggest that this is an urgent need in social psychology as well as in the study of gender and other social positions.

Before we close, there is a bit more to say about Eve and Adam. Some readers may find it difficult to identify with Eve and Adam. The referential groups tapped by this example will not accord with everyone's situations and experiences. Individuals without enough money or educational opportunities to obtain graduate degrees, to have careers available, or to have the choice to stop working even if they wanted, may find few similarities between Eve and Adam's professional dilemmas and their own. The following variation might be more resonant with these readers' experiences. Suppose that Eve and Adam are poor rather than relatively well-off, as they are in the original example. What if neither had attended college, let alone graduate school, and both were working in relatively low-prestige, low-paying jobs—he as a school bus driver, she as a waitress—when their first child was born? It is unlikely, first of all, that either employer would have offered them a paid or even an unpaid parental leave. It is true that the Family and Medical Leave Act mandates that companies with more than fifty employees offer unpaid leave to new parents. However, the majority of U.S. companies have fewer than fifty employees and therefore are not required to offer such leave. Those companies that offer the most generous leave policies—including paid or partially paid parental leave—are generally large, wealthy companies with many employees. Those people who have access to the most generous leave policies are also those people who are better off to begin with.

Even if Eve and Adam had had the option of taking an unpaid parental leave, it is unlikely that they would have been able to afford to do so. For a family that is barely scraping by on two incomes, adding a new baby and at the same time losing one income might mean financial disaster. The important decisions to be made might involve how to juggle shift work, rather than which income to keep.

Alternatively, suppose that the couple had the same economic and educational statuses as in the first example, but were both female or both male. In this case, the couple (call them Eve and Anna) cannot legally marry in most American states. Their decision to have a child will be considerably more complicated: they must either find a sperm donor or try to adopt a child, a goal that is prohibited in some states because of their sexual orientation. If they do succeed in having a child, on the other hand, they will have to deal not only with the usual pressures of parenthood but also with added pressures resulting from the stereotypes and prejudices of others. In each case, the active referential frameworks, choices, options, expectations, and stereotypes differ. These alternative versions of the saga of Eve and Adam remind us of the importance of the full array of social positions for understanding human behavior. All of these positions—economic resources, racial and ethnic histories, sexual orientation, gender—together shape actors' social behavior.

Final Messages for the Reader

We have summarized what we see as the most important themes of this volume. We have illustrated precisely what we mean by a gender lens in working with this example of Eve and Adam and their deliberations as they make

important life decisions. We close by suggesting questions we think it would
be useful to emphasize in your own future endeavors. Some of you are researchers, some of you are teachers, some of you are students, and we know
all of you are readers. We keep each of these roles in mind as we offer the
following questions and principles to consider when conducting, teaching, or
evaluating social psychological research.

About Theories
Assumptions: What assumptions are made? What possibilities are left out?
Implications: What are the implications of this perspective for those in
   varying social positions?
Historical Context: How have political and social trends shaped the ques-
   tions that are asked and the answers that are posed?

About Social Resources and Human Action
Inequality: What is the distribution of resources, access, opportunity,
   options, and consequences? Which groups are advantaged; which are
   disadvantaged?
Choice: Do individuals have choices? Which ones? Do some have more
   choices than others? Who structures whether choice is available?
Agency: In what realms do/can (some) people act as agents? Which people?

About Social Groups
Position: Be aware, always, of structural positions such as gender, race,
   class, sexuality, age, and (dis)ability. Explore how these positions work
   together, as well as separately. For example, how do gender and social
   class jointly determine Eve and Adam's choices about family and work?
   How would their experiences differ if they were people of color? If they
   were both the same sex?
Difference and Similarity: Always consider differences within groups, not
   just between groups. Be as aware of similarity as of difference. Where
   difference is emphasized, ask why. Where similarity is emphasized, also
   ask why.
Sex versus Gender: Keep in mind that sex and gender are distinct terms,
   based in distinctly different theories, with distinctly different implications. Be aware that gender is not fixed/homogenous/dichotomous/
   individual.

About Everything
Power: How is the behavior/pattern in question shaped by power? Who
   has power over whom? What is this power based on? How is this power

exercised and for what ends? Are power differences revealed or masked? Why?

These questions have often not been asked in traditional social psychology. As a result, much research and theorizing have left out important groups, perspectives, and questions. Nevertheless, recent trends in both sociology and psychology are stretching disciplinary boundaries and goals. Sociology is moving toward a *public sociology* that seeks to replace disinterested scholarship in the academy with practical research shared with a popular audience (e.g., Buroway 2005; Clawson et al. 2007). Psychology is moving toward a *positive psychology* that seeks to replace a focus on disorder and pathology with a focus on happiness, love, and justice (e.g., Compton 2005; Peterson and Seligman 2004; Seligman 2002). Both trends encourage the growth of a social psychology with a critical eye and an activist conscience—a social psychology that asks the unasked, examines the unexamined, applies the unapplied, and disseminates the undisseminated. Taking these issues seriously, we believe, will lead us to a fuller understanding of social life. This understanding, in turn, will help us better address some of the most important questions facing us as individuals, communities, and societies. How social psychologists will use this knowledge, which strategies they will employ, and what the outcomes will be remains to be seen. We encourage social psychologists—sociologists and psychologists alike—to use our research to promote the goals of social justice so crucial to the global future.

Note

1. We are indebted to Barbara Risman (1998) for the basic outlines of this example.

References

Akeret, Christian, and Julie McEwan. 2004. *Tomboys! Feisty Girls and Spirited Women.* Women Make Movies.

Alcott, Louisa May. 1924. *Little Women.* Akron, OH: Saalfield.

Allison, Dorothy. 1994. *Skin: Talking About Sex, Class, and Literature.* Ithaca, NY: Firebrand.

American Psychological Association, Office of Ethnic Minority Affairs. 2008. *Annual Report: ASA Committee on Ethnic Minority Affairs.* Washington, DC: American Psychological Association.

Anderson, Eric. 2005. "Orthodox and Inclusive Masculinity: Competing Masculinities Among Heterosexual Men in a Feminized Terrain." *Sociological Perspectives* 48(3):337–55.

Anderson, Margaret L., and Patricia Hill Collins, eds. 2004. *Race, Class, and Gender: An Anthology,* fifth ed. Belmont, CA: Wadsworth.

Anderson, Susan M., and Sandra Lipsitz Bem. 1981. "Sex Typing and Androgyny in Dyadic Interaction." *Journal of Personality and Social Psychology* 41:74–86.

Archer, Dane, and Rosemary Gartner. 1976. "Violent Acts and Violent Times: A Comparative Approach to Postwar Homicide Rates." *American Sociological Review* 41:937–63.

———. 1984. *Violence and Crime in Cross-National Perspective.* New Haven, CT: Yale University Press.

Archibald, W. Peter. 1978. *Social Psychology as Political Economy.* Toronto: McGraw-Hill.

Arendell, Terry. 1992. "The Social Self as Gendered: A Masculinist Discourse of Divorce." *Symbolic Interaction* 15:151–81.

———. 1995. *Fathers and Divorce.* Thousand Oaks, CA: Sage.

Argyle, Michael. 1994. *The Psychology of Social Class.* New York: Routledge.

Aronson, Elliot, Timothy D. Wilson, and Robin M. Akert. 1994. *Social Psychology: The Heart and the Mind.* New York: HarperCollins.

Ashmore, Richard D., and Frances K. Del Boca, eds. 1986. *The Social Psychology of Female-Male Relations: A Critical Analysis of Central Concepts.* New York: Academic Press.

Averill, James R. 1982. *Anger and Aggression: An Essay on Emotion.* New York: Springer-Verlag.

Bandura, Albert. 1965. "Influences of Models' Reinforcement Contingencies on the Acquisition of Imitative Responses." *Journal of Personality and Social Psychology* 1:589–93.

———. 1969. *Principles of Behavior Modification.* New York: Holt, Rinehart and Winston.

———. 1973. *Aggression: A Social Learning Analysis.* Englewood Cliffs, NJ: Prentice Hall.

———. 1977. *Social Learning Theory.* Englewood Cliffs, NJ: Prentice Hall.

———. 1986. *Social Foundations of Thought and Action.* Englewood Cliffs, NJ: Prentice Hall.

Bandura, Albert, Dorothea Ross, and Sheila A. Ross. 1963. "Imitation of Film-Mediated Aggressive Models." *Journal of Abnormal and Social Psychology* 66:3–11.

Bandura, Albert, and Richard H. Walters. 1963. *Social Learning and Personality Development.* New York: Holt, Rinehart and Winston.

Banse, Rainer, Jan Seise, and Nikola Zerbes. 2001. "Implicit Attitudes towards Homosexuality: Reliability, Validity, and Controllability of the IAT." *Zeitschrift für Experimentelle Psychologie* 48(2):145–60.

Barker, R., T. Dembo, and K. Lewin. 1941. "Frustration and Aggression: An Experiment with Young Children." *University of Iowa Studies in Child Welfare* 18:1–314.

Baron, Jonathan, and Joan Miller. 2000. "Limiting the Scope of Moral Obligations to Help." *Journal of Cross-Cultural Psychology* 31(6):703.

Baron, Reuben M., Linda Albright, and Thomas E. Malloy. 1995. "Effects of Behavioral and Social Class Information on Social Judgment." *Personality and Social Psychology Bulletin* 12:308–15.

Basow, Susan A. 1992. *Gender: Stereotypes and Roles.* Pacific Grove, CA: Brooks/Cole.

Baumeister, Roy F., and Kathleen D. Vohs. 2004. "Sexual Economics: Sex as Female Resource for Social Exchange in Heterosexual Interactions." *Personality and Social Psychology Review* 8(4):339–63.

Bayton, James A., Lois B. McAlister, and Jeston Hamer. 1956. "Race-Class Stereotypes." *Journal of Negro Education* 25:75–78.

Beal, Carole R. 1994. *Boys and Girls: The Development of Gender Roles.* New York: McGraw-Hill.

Bear, George G., Maureen A. Manning, and Kunio Shiomi. 2006. "Children's Reasoning About Aggression: Differences Between Japan and the United States and Implications for School Discipline." *School Psychology Review* 35(1):62–77.

Beauboeuf-Lafontant, Tamara. 2003. "Strong and Large Black Women? Exploring Relationships between Deviant Womanhood and Weight." *Gender and Society* 17(1):111–21.

Begley, Sharon. 1995. "Three Is Not Enough." *Newsweek*, February 13, 67–69.

Bekkengen, Lisbeth. 2006. "Men's Parental Leave: A Manifestation of Gender Equality or Child-Orientation?" Pp. 149–62 in *Gender Segregation: Divisions of Work in Post-Industrial Welfare States*, edited by Lena Gonäs and Jan Ch Karlsson. Burlington, VT: Ashgate.

Bell, Kanika. 2002. "Gender and Racial Identity Attitudes Among Black Female Students in Different Collegiate Environments." 8th International Interdisciplinary Congress on Women. Department of Women and Gender Studies, Makerere University, Kampala-Uganda.

Bem, Daryl J. 1970. *Beliefs, Attitudes, and Human Affairs*. Belmont, CA: Brooks/Cole.

Bem, Sandra L. 1974. "The Measurement of Psychological Androgyny." *Journal of Consulting and Clinical Psychology* 42:155–62.

———. 1975. "Sex Role Adaptability: One Consequence of Psychological Androgyny." *Journal of Personality and Social Psychology* 31:634–43.

———. 1993. *The Lenses of Gender: Transforming the Debate on Sexual Inequality*. New Haven, CT: Yale University Press.

Bem, Sandra Lipsitz, and Ellen Lenney. 1976. "Sex Typing and the Avoidance of Cross-Sex Behavior." *Journal of Personality and Social Psychology* 33:48–54.

Bemiller, Michelle. 2005. "Men Who Cheer." *Sociological Focus* 38(3):205–22.

Benson, P. L., S. A. Karabenick, and R. M. Lerner. 1976. "Pretty Pleases: The Effects of Physical Attractiveness, Race, and Sex on Receiving Help." *Journal of Experimental Social Psychology* 12:409–15.

Bergen, Elizabeth. 1991. "The Economic Context of Labor Allocation: Implications for Gender Stratification." *Journal of Family Issues* 12:140–57.

Berger, Joseph, Thomas L. Conner, and M. Hamit Fişek. 1974. *Expectation States Theory: A Theoretical Research Program*. Cambridge, MA: Winthrop.

Berger, Joseph, M. Hamit Fişek, Robert Z. Norman, and Morris Zelditch, Jr. 1977. *Status Characteristics in Social Interaction: An Expectation States Approach*. New York: Elsevier.

Berger, Michelle Tracy, and Kathleen Guidroz, eds. 2009. *The Intersectional Approach: Transforming the Academy Through Race, Class and Gender*. Chapel Hill: University of North Carolina Press.

Berk, Sarah Fenstermaker. 1985. *The Gender Factory: The Apportionment of Work in American Households*. New York: Plenum.

Berkowitz, Leonard. 1986. "Situational Influences on Reactions to Observed Violence." *Journal of Social Issues* 42(3):93–106.

Berkowitz, Leonard, and Anthony LePage. 1967. "Weapons as Aggression-Eliciting Stimuli." *Journal of Personality and Social Psychology* 7:202–7.

Bittman, Michael, Paula England, Liana Sayer, Nancy Folbre, and George Matheson. 2003. "When Does Gender Trump Money? Bargaining and Time in Household Work." *American Journal of Sociology* 109(1):184–214.

Björkqvist, Kaj. 1994. "Sex Differences in Physical, Verbal, and Indirect Aggression: A Review of Recent Research." *Sex Roles* 30:177–88.

Björkqvist, Kaj, Karin Österman, and Ari Kaukiainen. 1992. "The Development of Direct and Indirect Aggression Strategies in Males and Females." Pp. 51–64 in *Of Mice and Women: Aspects of Female Aggression*, edited by K. Björkqvist and P. Niemelä. San Diego, CA: Academic Press.

Björkqvist, Kaj, and Pirkko Niemelä. 1992. "New Trends in the Study of Female Aggression." Pp. 3–16 in *Of Mice and Women: Aspects of Female Aggression*, edited by K. Björkqvist and P. Niemelä. San Diego, CA: Academic Press.

Black, Katherine A., and David J. Gold. 2008. "Gender Differences and Socioeconomic Status Biases in Judgments About Blame in Date Rape Scenarios." *Violence & Victims* 23(1):115–28.

Black, Stephen L., and Susan Bevan. 1992. "At the Movies with Buss and Durkee: A Natural Experiment on Film Violence." *Aggressive Behavior* 18:37–45.

Blackless, Melanie, Anthony Charuvastra, Amanda Derryck, Anne Fausto-Sterling, Karl Lauzanna, and Ellen Lee. 2000. "How Sexually Dimorphic Are We?" *American Journal of Human Biology* 12(2):151–66.

Blair, C. A., L. F. Foster-Thompson, and K. L. Wuensch. 2005. "Electronic Helping Behavior: The Virtual Presence of Others Makes a Difference." *Basic and Applied Social Psychology* 27:171–78.

Blau, Peter M. 1964. *Exchange and Power in Social Life*. New York: Wiley.

Blinde, Elaine M., and Diane E. Taub. 1992. "Homophobia and Women's Sport: The Disempowerment of Athletes." *Sociological Focus* 25:151–66.

Blood, Robert O., Jr., and Donald M. Wolfe. 1960. *Husbands and Wives*. New York: Free Press.

Blumstein, Philip. 1991. "The Production of Selves in Personal Relationships." Pp. 305–22 in *The Self-Society Dynamic: Cognition, Emotion, and Action*, edited by J. A. Howard and P. L. Callero. New York: Cambridge University Press.

Blumstein, Philip, and Pepper Schwartz. 1983. *American Couples: Money, Work, and Sex*. New York: Morrow.

Bogle, Kathleen A. 2008. *Hooking Up: Sex, Dating, and Relationship on Campus*. New York: New York University Press.

Bonilla-Silva, Eduardo. 2006. *Racism Without Racists: Color-Blind Racism and the Persistence of Racial Inequality in the United States*, second ed. Lanham, MD: Rowman & Littlefield.

Bornstein, Kate. 1994. *Gender Outlaw: On Men, Women, and the Rest of Us*. New York: Vintage.

Boswell, A. Ayres, and Joan Z. Spade. 1996. "Fraternities and Collegiate Rape Culture: Why Are Some Fraternities More Dangerous Places for Women?" *Gender and Society* 10(2):133–47.

Boyle, D. Ellen, Nancy L. Marshall, and Wendy W. Robeson. 2003. "Gender at Play." *American Behavioral Scientist* 46(10):1326.

Bower, Gordon H., and Ernest R. Hilgard. 1981. *Theories of Learning*. Englewood Cliffs, NJ: Prentice Hall.

Boxer, Paul, L. Rowell Huesmann, Brad J. Bushman, Maureen O'Brien, and Dominic Morceri. 2009. "The Role of Violent Media Preference in Cumulative Developmental Risk for Violence and General Aggression." *Journal of Youth and Adolescence* 38(3):417–28.

Bragg, Rick. 1995. "Susan Smith: Victim or Monster? Image Is a Life-or-Death Matter to Mother Who Drowned Two Sons." *Seattle Times*, July 9, AI.

Bramel, Dana, and Ronald Friend. 1981. "Hawthorne, the Myth of the Docile Worker, and Class Bias in Psychology." *American Psychologist* 36:867–78.

Breines, Winnie, and Linda Gordon. 1983. "The New Scholarship on Family Violence." *Signs: Journal of Women in Culture and Society* 8:490–531.

Brewer, Marilynn B. 1988. "A Dual Process Model of Impression Formation." In *Advances in Social Cognition*, vol. 1, edited by T. K. Srull and R. S. Wyer. Hillsdale, NJ: Erlbaum.

Brewer, Marilynn B., Valerie Dull, and Layton Lui. 1981. "Perceptions of the Elderly: Stereotypes as Prototypes." *Journal of Personality and Social Psychology* 41:656–70.

Brewer, Marilynn B., Hing-Kay Ho, Ju-Young Lee, and Norman Miller. 1987. "Social Identity and Social Distance among Hong Kong Schoolchildren." *Personality and Social Psychology Bulletin* 13:156–65.

Bridges, George S., and Robert D. Crutchfield. 1988. "Law, Social Standing, and Racial Disparities in Imprisonment." *Social Forces* 66:699–724.

Briere, John, and Neil M. Malamuth. 1983. "Self-Reported Likelihood of Sexually Aggressive Behavior: Attitudinal Versus Sexual Explanations." *Journal of Research in Personality* 17:315–23.

Brines, Julie. 1993. "The Exchange Value of Housework." *Rationality and Society* 5:302–40.

———. 1994. "Economic Dependency, Gender, and the Division of Labor at Home." *American Journal of Sociology* 100:652–88.

Brines, Julie, and Kara Joyner. 1999. "The Ties That Bind: Principles of Cohesion in Cohabitation and Marriage." *American Sociological Review* 64(3):333–56.

Brodkin, Karen. 1998. *How Jews Became White Folks and What That Says About Race in America.* Piscataway, NJ: Rutgers University Press.

Broverman, Inge K., Susan R. Vogel, Donald M. Broverman, Frank E. Clarkson, and Paul S. Rosenkrantz. 1972. "Sex-Role Stereotypes: A Current Appraisal." *Journal of Social Issues* 28(2):59–78.

Brown, Clifford E., and Mark D. Reed. 1982. "Race, Cost, and Car-Status: Interacting Variables Using the Lost-Letter Technique." *Psychological Reports* 51:303–8.

Bryson, Seymour. 1998. "Relationship Between Race and Attitudes Toward Black Men." *Journal of Multicultural Counseling and Development* 26(4):282–93.

Buchanan, Tom. 2008. "The Same-Sex-Referent Work Satisfaction Relationship Assessing the Mediating Role of Distributive Justice Perceptions." *Sociological Focus* 41(2):177–200.

Buckley, Tamara R., and Robert T. Carter. 2005. "Black Adolescent Girls: Do Gender Role and Racial Identity Impact Their Self-Esteem?" *Sex Roles* 53(9/10):647–61.

Buroway, Michael. 2005. "2004 ASA Presidential Address: For Public Sociology." *American Sociological Review* 70(1):4–28.

Bussey, Kay, and Albert Bandura. 1984. "Influence of Gender Constancy and Social Power on Sex-Linked Modeling." *Journal of Personality and Social Psychology* 47:1292–1302.

Butler, Dore, and Florence L. Geis. 1990. "Nonverbal Affect Responses to Male and Female Leaders: Implications for Leadership Evaluations." *Journal of Personality and Social Psychology* 58:48–59.

Butler, Judith. 2004. *Undoing Gender*. New York: Routledge.

Byrd, Stephanie Ellen. 2006. "Life Happens: Understanding Specialization and Adaptation of Women Transitioning Between Traditional and Dual-Career Families." Annual Meeting of the American Sociological Association, Montreal.

———. 2009. "The Social Construction of Marital Commitment." *Journal of Marriage and Family*. 71(2):318–36.

Cahill, Spencer. 1986. "Childhood Socialization as a Recruitment Process." *Sociological Studies of Child Development* 1:163–86.

Calabrese, Raymond L., and John T. Cochran. 1990. "The Relationship of Alienation to Cheating among a Sample of American Adolescents." *Journal of Research and Development in Education* 23(2):65–72.

Callahan, Sara B. Dykins. 2008. "Academic Outings." *Symbolic Interaction* 31(4):351–75.

Campbell, Donald T. 1967. "Stereotypes and the Perception of Group Differences." *American Psychologist* 22:817–29.

Cancian, Francesca, and Stacey Oliker. 2000. *For Love and Money: A Gendered View of Caring*. Thousand Oaks, CA: Pine Forge Press.

Cantor, Muriel G. 1987. "Popular Culture and the Portrayal of Women: Content and Control." Pp. 190–214 in *Analyzing Gender*, edited by B. B. Hess and M. M. Ferree. Newbury Park, CA: Sage.

Carli, Linda L. 1990. "Gender, Language, and Influence." *Journal of Personality and Social Psychology* 50:941–51.

———.1991. "Gender, Status, and Influence." Pp. 89–113 in *Advances in Group Processes*, vol. 8, edited by E. J. Lawler, B. Markovsky, C. Ridgeway, and H. A. Walker. Greenwich, CT: JAI.

Carlson, Rae. 1971. "Sex Differences in Ego Functioning: Exploratory Studies of Agency and Communion." *Journal of Consulting and Clinical Psychology* 37:267–77.

Carney, Michelle, Fred Buttell, and Don Dutton. 2007. "Women Who Perpetrate Intimate Partner Violence: A Review of the Literature With Recommendations for Treatment." *Aggression and Violent Behavior* 12(1):108–15.

Carpenter, Sandra, and Susan Trentham. 2001. "Should We Take 'Gender' Out of Gender Subtypes? The Effects of Gender, Evaluative Valence, and Context on the Organization of Person Subtypes." *Sex Roles* 45(7/8):455–80.

Carr, Joetta L., and Karen M. VanDeusen. 2004. "Risk Factors for Male Sexual Aggression on College Campuses." *Journal of Family Violence* 19(5):279–89.

Carrigan, Tim, R. W. Connell, and John Lee. 1985. "Toward a New Sociology of Masculinity." *Theory and Society* 14:551–604.

———. 1987. *Toward a New Sociology of Masculinity*. Boston: Allen and Unwin.

Carrington, Christopher. 1999. *No Place Like Home: Relationships and Family Life Among Lesbians and Gay Men*. Chicago: University of Chicago Press.

Carter, Scott J., Mamadi Corra, and Shannon K. Carter. 2009. "The Interaction of Race and Gender: Changing Gender Role Attitudes, 1974–2006." *Social Science Quarterly* 90:193–208.

Cast, Alicia D., Jan E. Stets, and Peter J. Burke. 1999. "Does the Self-Conform to the Views of Others?" *Social Psychology Quarterly* 62:68–82.

Chambliss, William J. 1995. "Crime Control and Ethnic Minorities: Legitimizing Racial Oppression by Creating Moral Panics." Pp. 235–58 in *Ethnicity, Race, and Crime: Perspectives across Time and Place*, edited by D. F. Hawkins. Albany: State University of New York Press.

Charon, Joel M. 2004. *Ten Questions: A Sociological Perspective.* Belmont, CA: Wadsworth.

Chasteen, Alison L., Sudipa Bhattacharyya, Michelle Horhota, Raymond Tam, and Lynn Hasher. 2005. "How Feelings of Stereotype Threat Influence Older Adults' Memory Performance." *Experimental Aging Research* 31(3):235–60.

Cherry, Frances. 1995. *The "Stubborn Particulars" of Social Psychology: Essays on the Research Process.* New York: Routledge.

Childers, Kevin. 2000. "Status Characteristics Theory and Sexual Orientation: Explaining Gender Differences in Responses to Sexual Orientation." *Current Research in Social Psychology* 5(11).

Chisholm, Shirley. 1973. *The Good Fight.* Harper Collins.

Chodorow, Nancy. 1978. *The Reproduction of Mothering: Psychoanalysis and the Sociology of Gender.* Berkeley: University of California Press.

Chow, Esther Ngan-Ling. 1985. "The Acculturation Experiences of Asian American Women." Pp. 238–51 in *Beyond Sex Roles*, second ed., edited by A. Sargent. St. Paul, MN: West.

Chozick, Amy. 2008. "Obama's Pin Flag Reappears." Washington Wire. *Wall Street Journal.* May 14.

Clawson, Dan, Robert Zussman, Joya Misra, Naomi Gerstel, Randall Stokes, Douglas L. Anderton, and Michael Buroway. 2007. *Public Sociology: Fifteen Eminent Sociologists Debate Politics and the Profession in the Twenty-First Century.* Berkeley: University of California Press.

Clarey, Christopher. 2010. "Two Comebacks Unlike Any Others." *New York Times,* April 2.

Clark, R., and A. Nunes. 2008. "The Face of Society: Gender and Race in Introductory Sociology Books Revisited." *Teaching Sociology* 36(3):227–39.

Cline, Rebecca J., and Karen E. Musolf. 1985. "Disclosure as Social Exchange: Anticipated Length of Relationship, Sex Roles, and Disclosure Intimacy." *Western Journal of Speech Communication* 49:43–56.

Cohen, Claudia E. 1981. "Person Categories and Social Perception: Testing Some Boundaries of the Processing Effects of Prior Knowledge." *Journal of Personality and Social Psychology* 40:441–52.

Cohen, E. G. 1982. "Expectation States and Interracial Interaction in School Settings." *Annual Review of Sociology* 8:209–35.

Coleman, Richard Patrick, Lee Rainwater, and Kent A. McClelland. 1978. *Social Standing in America: New Dimensions of Class.* New York: Basic Books.

Collins, Patricia Hill. 1990. *Black Feminist Thought: Knowledge, Consciousness, and the Politics of Empowerment.* London: HarperCollins.

——. 2000. *Black Feminist Thought: Knowledge, Consciousness, and the Politics of Empowerment,* second ed. London: HarperCollins.

Coltrane, Scott. 2000. "Research on Household Labor: Modeling and Measuring the Social Embeddedness of Routine Family Work." *Journal of Marriage and the Family* 62:1208–33.

Compton, William C. 2005. *Introduction to Positive Psychology.* Belmont, CA: Wadsworth.

Comstock, G., and E. Scharrer. 1999. *Television: What's On, Who's Watching, and What It Means.* San Diego, CA: Academic Press.

Connell, R. W. 1987. *Gender and Power: Society, the Person, and Sexual Politics.* Stanford, CA: Stanford University Press.

——. 1995. *Masculinities.* Berkeley: University of California Press.

——. 2002. *Gender.* Malden, MA: Blackwell Publishers.

——. 2009. *Gender: Short Introductions,* second ed. Malden, MA: Polity Press.

Constantino, John N., Daniel Grosz, Paul Saenger, and Donald W. Chandler. 1993. "Testosterone and Aggression in Children." *Journal of the American Academy of Child and Adolescent Psychiatry* 32:1217–22.

Cook, Karen S., Gary Alan Fine, and James S. House, eds. 1995. *Sociological Perspectives on Social Psychology.* Boston: Allyn and Bacon.

Cook, Karen S., and Karen A. Hegtvedt. 1986. "Justice and Power: An Exchange Analysis." Pp. 19–41 in *Justice in Social Relations,* edited by H. W. Bierhoff, R. L. Cohen, and J. Greenberg. New York: Plenum.

Cook, Karen S., Jodi O'Brien, and Peter Kollock. 1990. "Exchange Theory: A Blueprint for Structure and Process." Pp. 158–81 in *Frontiers of Social Theory: The New Syntheses,* edited by G. Ritzer. New York: Columbia University Press.

Cook, Karen S., and Eric Rice. 2003. "Social Exchange Theory." Pp. 53–76 in *Handbook of Social Psychology,* edited by John DeLamater. New York: Kluwer Plenum.

Correll, Shelley J., and Cecilia L. Ridgeway. 2003. "Expectation States Theory." Pp. 29–52 in *Handbook of Social Psychology,* edited by John DeLamater. New York: Kluwer Plenum.

Cota, Albert A. and Kenneth L. Dion. 1986. "Salience of Gender and Sex Composition of Ad Hoc Groups: An Experimental Test of Distinctiveness Theory." *Journal of Personality and Social Psychology* 50:770–76.

Cowan, Gloria, Carole Lee, Daniella Levy, and Debra Snyder. 1988. "Dominance and Inequality in X-Rated Videocassettes." *Psychology of Women Quarterly* 12:299–311.

Crane Betsy, and Jesse Crane-Seeber. 2003. "The Four Boxes of Gendered Sexuality: Good Girl/Bad Girl and Tough Guy/Sweet Guy." In *Sexual Lives: A Reader on the Theories and Realities of Human Sexualities,* edited by R. Heasley and B. Crane. New York: McGraw-Hill.

Crocker, Jennifer, and Brenda Major. 1989. "Social Stigma and Self-Esteem: The Self-Protective Properties of Stigma." *Psychological Review* 96:608–30.

Croizet, J. C., and T. Clare. 1998. "Extending the Concept of Stereotype Threat to Social Class: The Intellectual Underperformance of Students from Low Socioeconomic Backgrounds." *Personality and Social Psychology Bulletin* 24:588–94.

Crosby, Faye J. 1982. *Relative Deprivation and Working Women.* New York: Oxford University Press.

Crosby, Faye, Stephanie Bromley, and Leonard Saxe. 1980. "Recent Unobtrusive Studies of Black and White Discrimination and Prejudice: A Literature Review." *Psychological Bulletin* 87:546–63.

Crouter, A. C., S. D. Whiteman, S. M. McHale, and D. W. Osgood. 2007. "Development of Gender Attitude Traditionality Across Middle Childhood and Adolescence." *Child Development* 78:911–26.

Crutchfield, Robert D., Joseph L. Weis, Rodney L. Engen, and Randy R. Gainey. 1995. *Racial and Ethnic Disparities in the Prosecution of Felony Cases in King County.* Final Report to the Washington State Minority and Justice Commission, November.

Cuddy, A. J. C., M. Rock, and M. I. Norton. 2007. "Aid in the Aftermath of Hurricane Katrina: Inferences of Secondary Emotions and Intergroup Helping." *Group Processes and Intergroup Relations* 10:107–118.

Cunningham, Mick. 2007. "Influences of Women's Employment on the Gendered Division of Household Labor Over the Life Course: Evidence from a 31-Year Panel Study." *Journal of Family Issues* 28(3):422–44.

Dabbs, J. M., Jr., and M. G. Dabbs. 2000. *Heroes, Rogues, and Lovers: Testosterone and Behavior.* New York: McGraw-Hill.

Dar-Nimrod, Ilan, and Steven J. Heine. 2006. "Exposure to Scientific Theories Affects Women's Math Performance." *Science* 314(5768):435.

Davis, Shannon N., Theodore N. Greenstein, and Jennifer P. Gerteisen Marks. 2007. "Effects of Union Type on Division of Household Labor: Do Cohabiting Men Really Perform More Housework?" *Journal of Family Issues* 28(9):1246–72.

Deaux, Kay. 1976. *The Behavior of Women and Men.* Monterey, CA: Brooks/Cole.

———.1984. "From Individual Differences to Social Categories: Analysis of a Decade's Research on Gender." *American Psychologist* 39:105–16.

———. 1995. "How Basic Can You Be? The Evolution of Research on Gender Stereotypes." *Journal of Social Issues* 51(1):11–20.

Deaux, Kay, and Brenda Major. 1990. *A Social-Psychological Model of Gender.* New Haven, CT: Yale University Press.

Deaux, K., and M. LaFrance. 1998. "Gender." Pp. 788–827 in *Handbook of Social Psychology,* fourth ed., edited by D. Gilbert, S. T. Fiske, and G. Lindzey. New York: Random House.

Deaux, Kay, and Laurie L. Lewis. 1984. "The Structure of Gender Stereotypes: Interrelationships among Components and Gender Labels." *Journal of Personality and Social Psychology* 46:991–1004.

de Guzman, Maria Rosario, Carolyn P. Edwards, and Gustavo Carlo. 2005. "Prosocial Behaviors in Context: A Study of the Gikuyu Children of Ngecha, Kenya." *Journal of Applied Developmental Psychology* 26:542–58.

DeLamater, John, ed. 2003. *Handbook of Social Psychology.* New York: Kluwer-Plenum.

DeLeon-Granados, William, William Wells, and Ruddyard Binsbacher. 2006. "Arresting Development: Trends in Female Arrests for Domestic Violence and Proposed Explanations." *Violence Against Women* 12:355–71.

Della Fave, L. Richard. 1980. "The Meek Shall Not Inherit the Earth: Self-Evaluations and the Legitimacy of Stratification." *American Sociological Review* 45:955–71.

Deutsch, Francine M. 2007. "Undoing Gender." *Gender and Society* 21(1):106–27.

Deutsch, Morton. 1975. "Equity, Equality, and Need: What Determines What Value Will Be Used as the Basis for Distributive Justice?" *Journal of Social Issues* 31(3):137–50.

DeVault, Marjorie L. 1991. *Feeding the Family: The Social Organizational of Caring as Gendered Work.* Chicago: University of Chicago Press.

Devine, Patricia G. 1989. "Stereotypes and Prejudice: Their Automatic and Controlled Components." *Journal of Personality and Social Psychology* 56:5–18.

Devine, Patricia G., and Sara M. Baker. 1991. "Measurement of Racial Stereotype Subtyping." *Personality and Social Psychology Bulletin* 17:44–50.

Devine, Patricia G., and Andrew J. Elliot. 1995. "Are Racial Stereotypes Really Fading? The Princeton Trilogy Revisited." *Personality and Social Psychology Bulletin* 21:1139–50.

Diener, Edward, Karen L. Westford, Scott C. Fraser, and Arthur L. Bearman. 1973. "Selected Demographic Variables in Altruism." *Psychological Reports* 33:226.

Dobash, Russell P., R. Emerson Dobash, Margo Wilson, and Martin Daly. 1992. "They Myth of Sexual Symmetry in Martial Violence." *Social Problems* 39:71–91.

Dollard, John, Leonard William Doob, Neal E. Miller, Orval Herbert Mowrer, and Robert R. Sears. 1939. *Frustration and Aggression.* New Haven, CT: Yale University Press.

Domhoff, G. William. 2009. *Who Rules America? Challenges to Corporate and Class Dominance,* sixth ed. New York: McGraw-Hill.

Donnerstein, Edward. 1983. "Erotica and Human Aggression." In *Aggression: Theoretical and Empirical Views,* vol. 1, edited by R. G. Geen and E. Donnerstein. New York: Academic Press.

Dovidio, J. F., J. C. Campbell, S. Rigaud, J. Yankura, L. Rominger, and R. Pine. 1978. "Androgyny, Sex-Roles, and Helping." Unpublished manuscript, Colgate University, Hamilton, NY.

Dozier, Raine. 2005. "Beards, Breasts, and Bodies: Doing Sex in a Gendered World." *Gender and Society* 19(3):297–316.

Dreman, S. B. 1976. "Sharing Behavior in Israeli Schoolchildren: Cognitive and Social Learning Factors." *Child Development* 47(1):186–94.

Dreman, S. B., and Charles W. Greenbaum. 1973. "Altruism or Reciprocity: Sharing Behavior in Israeli Kindergarten Children." *Child Development* 44:61–88.

Duerst-Lahti, Georgia. 2006. "Presidential Elections: Gendered Space and the Case of 2004." Pp. 12–42 in *Gender and Elections: Shaping the Future of American Politics,* edited by Susan J. Carroll and Richard L. Fox. New York: Cambridge University Press.

Dugatkin, Lee. 1999. *Cheating Monkeys and Citizen Bees: The Nature of Cooperation in Animals and Humans.* New York: Free Press.

Dunand, Muriel A. 1986. "Violence et Panique dans le Stade de Football de Bruxelles en 1985: Approche Psychosociale des Evénements" [Violence and Panic in the Brussels Football Stadium in 1985: A Psychosocial Approach to These Remarkable Events]. *Cahiers de Psychologie Cognitive* 6:235–66.

Duncan, Birt L. 1976. "Differential Social Perception and Attribution of Inter-Group Violence: Testing the Lower Limits of Stereotyping Blacks." *Journal of Personality and Social Psychology* 34:590–98.

Duneier, Mitchell. 2000. *Sidewalk*. New York: Farrar, Straus, and Giroux.

Duneier, Mitchell, and Harvey Molotch 1999. "Talking City Trouble: Interactional Vandalism, Social Inequality, and the 'Urban Interaction Problem.'" *American Journal of Sociology* 104(5):1263–95.

Eagly, Alice H., and Linda L. Carli. 1981. "Sex of Researchers and Sex-Typed Communications as Determinants of Sex Differences in Influenceability: A Meta-Analysis of Social Influence Studies." *Psychological Bulletin* 90:1–20.

Eagly, Alice, and M. Crowley. 1986. "Gender and Helping Behavior: A Meta-Analytic Review of the Social Psychological Literature." *Psychological Bulletin* 100:282–308.

Eagly, Alice H., and Steven J. Karau. 1991. "Gender and the Emergence of Leaders: A Meta-Analysis." *Journal of Personality and Social Psychology* 60:685–710.

Eagly, Alice H., and Valerie J. Steffen. 1986. "Gender and Aggressive Behavior: A Meta-Analytic Review of the Social Psychological Literature." *Psychological Bulletin* 100:309–30.

Eccles, Jacquelynne S., and Janis E. Jacobs. 1986. "Social Forces Shape Math Attitudes and Performance." *Signs: Journal of Women in Culture and Society* 11:367–89.

Eckhoff, Torstein. 1974. *Justice: Its Determinants in Social Interaction*. Rotterdam, Netherlands: Rotterdam University Press.

Edmondson, Madeleine, and Alden Duer Cohen. 1976. *The Women of Watergate*. New York: Pocket Books.

Edwards, Amy L. 2010. "Casey Anthony Jailhouse Letters Started with a Wave." *Orlando Sentinel* (Orlando, FL), April 8.

Egelko, Bob. 1994. "The Rich Don't Live on Death Row." *Seattle Times*, September 6, A3.

Emerson, Joan P. 1970. "Behavior in Private Places: Sustaining Definitions of Reality in Gynecological Examinations." Pp. 74–97 in *Recent Sociology*, no. 2, edited by P. Dreitsel. New York: Macmillan.

Emerson, Richard M. 1972a. "Exchange Theory, Part I: A Psychological Basis for Social Exchange." Pp. 38–57 in *Sociological Theories in Progress*, vol. 2, edited by J. Berger, Jr., M. Zelditch, and B. Anderson. Boston: Houghton Mifflin.

———. 1972b. "Exchange Theory, Part II: Exchange Relations and Networks." Pp. 58–87 in *Sociological Theories in Progress*, vol. 2, edited by J. Berger, Jr., M. Zelditch, and B. Anderson. Boston: Houghton Mifflin.

England, Paula, and George Farkas, 1986. *Households, Employment, and Gender: A Sociological, Economic, and Demographic View*. New York: Aldine de Gruyter.

England, Paula, and Barbara Stanek Kilbourne. 1990. "Feminist Critiques of the Separatist Model of Self." *Rationality and Society* 2:156–71.

England, Paula, Emily Fitzgerald Shafer, and Alison C. Fogarty. 2009. "Hooking Up and Forming Romantic Relationships on Today's College Campuses." Pp. 531–47 in *The Gendered Society Reader*, third ed., edited by Michael S. Kimmel and Amy Aronson. New York: Oxford University Press.

Enloe, Cynthia. 1993. *The Morning After: Sexual Politics at the End of the Cold War*. Berkeley: University of California Press.

Epstein, C. F. 2007. "Great Divides: The Cultural, Cognitive, and Social Bases of the Global Subordination of Women." *American Sociological Review* 72(2):1–22.

Erez, Edna. 2000. "Immigration, Culture Conflict and Domestic Violence/Woman Battering." *Crime Prevention and Community Safety: An International Journal* 2: 27–36.

Espiritu, Yen Le. 2007. *Asian American Women and Men: Labor, Laws, and Love*, second ed. Thousand Oaks, CA: Sage.

Esposito, J. L. 1998. "Introduction: Women in Islam and Muslim Societies." Pp. ix–xxvii in *Islam, Gender, and Social Change*, edited by Y. Y. Haddad and J. L. Esposito. New York: Oxford University Press.

Evans, M. D. R., Jonathan Kelley, and Tamas Kolosi. 1992. "Images of Class: Public Perceptions in Hungary and Australia." *American Sociological Review* 57:461–82.

Fausto-Sterling, Anne. 1985. *Myths of Gender: Biological Theories About Women and Men*. New York: Basic Books.

———. 1993. "The Five Sexes: Why Male and Female Are Not Enough." *Sciences* 32(2):20–5.

———. 2000. *Sexing the Body: Gender Politics and the Construction of Sexuality*. New York: Basic Books.

Feagin, Joe R., and K. McKinney. 2003. *The Many Costs of Racism*. Lanham, MD: Rowman & Littlefield.

Felson, Richard B. 1978. "Aggression as Impression Management." *Social Problems* 41:205–13.

———. 1997. "Anger, Aggression and Violence in Love Triangles." *Violence and Victims* 12:345–62.

Fenstermaker, Sarah, and Candace West. 2002. *Doing Gender, Doing Difference: Inequality, Power, and Institutional Change*. New York: Routledge.

Ferguson, C. J., and J. Kilburn. 2009. "The Public Health Risks of Media Violence: A Meta-Analytic Review." *Journal of Pediatrics* 154(5):759–63.

Ferree, Myra Marx. 1991. "The Gender Division of Labor in Two-Earner Marriages: Dimensions of Variability and Change." *Journal of Family Issues* 12:158–80.

Ferree, Myra Marx, and Elaine J. Hall. 1996. "Rethinking Stratification from a Feminist Perspective: Gender, Race and Class in Mainstream Textbooks." *American Sociological Review* 61(6):929–50.

———. 2000. "Gender Stratification and Paradigm Change: A Reply to Manza and Van Schyndel." *American Sociological Review* 65(3):475–81.

Festinger, Leon. 1957. *A Theory of Cognitive Dissonance*. Stanford, CA: Stanford University Press.

Festinger, Leon, and J. M. Carlsmith. 1959. "Cognitive Consequences of Forced Compliance." *Journal of Abnormal and Social Psychology* 58(2).

Fetner, Tina. 2008. *How the Religious Right Shaped Lesbian and Gay Activism.* Minneapolis: University of Minnesota Press.

Fine, Michelle, and Susan M. Gordon. 1989. "Feminist Transformations Of/Despite Psychology." Pp. 147–74 in *Gender and Thought: Psychological Perspectives,* edited by M. Crawford and M. Gentry. New York: Springer-Verlag.

Finn, J. 1986. "The Relationship Between Sex Role Attitudes and Attitudes Supporting Marital Violence." *Sex Roles* 14(5/6):235–42.

Fisher, Jeffrey D., Arie Nadler, and S. Whitcher-Alagna. 1982. "Recipient Reactions to Aid." *Psychological Bulletin* 91:33–54.

Fiske, Susan T., and Steven L. Neuberg. 1990. "A Continuum of Impression Formation, from Category-Based to Individuating Processes: Influences of Information and Motivation on Attention and Interpretation." Pp. 1–74 in *Advances in Experimental Social Psychology,* vol. 23, edited by M. P. Zanna. San Diego, CA: Academic Press.

Fiske, Susan T., and Shelley E. Taylor. 1991. *Social Cognition,* second ed. New York: McGraw-Hill.

———. 2008. *Social Cognition, From Brains to Culture.* New York: McGraw-Hill.

Fitzgerald, Louise F. 1993. "Sexual Harassment: Violence Against Women in the Workplace." *American Psychologist* 48:1070–76.

Fong, Stanley L., and Harvey Peskin. 1969. "Sex-Role Strain and Personality Adjustment of China-Born Students in America: A Pilot Study." *Journal of Abnormal Psychology* 74:563–67.

Forbes, Jack D. 1992. "The Hispanic Spin: Party Politics and Governmental Manipulation of Ethnic Identity." *Latin American Perspectives* 19(4):59–78.

Ford, Clellan S., and Frank A. Beach. 1951. *Patterns of Sexual Behavior.* New York: Harper.

Form, William, and Christine Hanson. 1985. "The Consistency of Stratal Ideologies of Economic Justice." *Research in Social Stratification and Mobility* 4:239–69.

Forry, N., L. Leslie, and B. Letiecq. 2007. "Marital Quality in Interracial Relationships: The Role of Sex Role Ideology and Perceived Fairness." *Journal of Family Issues* 28(12): 1538–52.

Foschi, Martha. 1989. "Status Characteristics, Standards, and Attributions." Pp. 58–72 in *Sociological Theories in Progress: New Formulations,* edited by J. Berger, M. Zelditch, and B. Anderson. Newbury Park, CA: Sage.

———. 1991. "Gender and Double Standards for Competence." Pp. 181–207 in *Gender, Interaction, and Inequality,* edited by C. Ridgeway. New York: Springer-Verlag.

———. 2000. "Double Standards for Competence: Theory and Research." *Annual Review of Sociology* 26:21–42.

Fothergill, Alice, and Lori Peek. Forthcoming. *Children of Katrina.* Austin: University of Texas Press.

Fox, Greer Litton. 1977. "'Nice Girl': Social Control of Women through a Value Construct." *Signs: Journal of Women in Culture and Society* 2:805–17.

Fox, Marie, and Michael Thomson. 2007. "Pack-Sex? Masculinity/Sport/Sex." Annual Meeting of the Law and Society Association. Berlin, Germany.

Franchina, J. J., R. M. Eisler, and T. M. Moore. 2001. "Masculine Gender Role Stress and Intimate Abuse: Effects of Masculine Gender Relevance of Dating Situations and Female Threat on Men's Attributions and Affective Responses." *Psychology of Men and Masculinity* 2(1):34–41.

Frankenberg, Ruth. 1993. *White Women, Race Matters: The Social Construction of Whiteness.* Minneapolis: University of Minnesota Press.

Fraser, Steven, ed. 1995. *The Bell Curve Wars: Race, Intelligence, and the Future of America.* New York: Basic Books.

Frederickson, B., and K. Harrison. 2005. "Throwing Like a Girl: Self-Objectification Predicts Adolescent Girls' Motor Performance." *Journal of Sport and Social Issues* 29:79–101.

Freese, Jeremy, Jui-Chung Li, and Lisa Wade. 2003. "The Potential Relevances of Biology to Social Inquiry." *Annual Review of Sociology* 29:233–56.

Friedman, Debra, and Carol Diem. 1993. "Feminism and the Pro- (Rational-) Choice Movement: Rational-Choice Theory, Feminist Critiques, and Gender Inequality." Pp. 91–114 in *Theory on Gender/Feminism on Theory*, edited by P. England. Hawthorne, NY: Aldine de Gruyter.

Frodi, Ann, Jacqueline Macaulay, and Pauline R. Thorne. 1977. "Are Women Always Less Aggressive Than Men? A Review of the Experimental Literature." *Psychological Bulletin* 84:634–60.

Fuwa, M. 2004. "Macro-Level Gender Inequality and the Division of Household Labor in 22 Countries." *American Sociological Review* 69:751–67.

Gaertner, S. L., and J. F. Dovidio. 2005. "Categorization, Recategorization and Intergroup Bias." In *Reflecting on the Nature of Prejudice*, edited by J. F. Dovidio, P. Glick, and L. Rudman. Philadelphia, PA: Psychology Press.

Gaertner, Samuel L., John F. Dovidio, and Gary Johnson. 1982. "Race of Victim, Nonresponsive Bystanders, and Helping Behavior." *Journal of Social Psychology* 117:69–77.

Gager, C. T., and B. E. Hohmann-Marriott. 2006. "Distributive Justice in the Household: A Comparison of Alternative Theoretical Models." *Marriage and Family Review* 40(2/3):5–42.

Gallant, Mary J. 1992. "Slave Runaways in Colonial Virginia: Accounts and Status Passage as Collective Process." *Symbolic Interaction* 15:389–412.

Gardner, Carol Brooks. 1989. "Analyzing Gender in Public Places: Rethinking Goffman's Vision of Everyday Life." *American Sociologist* 20(1):42–56.

———.1990. "Safe Conduct: Women, Crime, and Self in Public Places." *Social Problems* 37:311–28.

Gartner, Rosemary, and Bill McCarthy. 2005. "Killing One's Children: Maternal Infanticide and the Dark Figure of Homicide." Pp. 91–114 in *Gender and Crime: Patterns in Victimization and Offending*, edited by Karen Heimer and Candace Kruttschnitt. New York: New York University Press.

Garfinkel, Harold. 1967. *Studies in Ethnomethodology.* Englewood Cliffs, NJ: Prentice Hall.

Geer, James H., and Gloria G. Robertson. 2005. "Implicit Attitudes in Sexuality: Gender Differences." *Archives of Sexual Behavior* 34(6):671–77.

Geiger, W., J. Harwood, and M. L. Hummert. 2006. "College Students' Multiple Stereotypes of Lesbians: A Cognitive Perspective." *Journal of Homosexuality* 52:165–82.

Gelles, Richard J. 1985. "Family Violence: What We Know and What We Can Do." In *Unhappy Families,* edited by E. N. Newberger and R. Bourne. Littleton, MA: PSG Publishing.

———. 1994. "Family Violence, Abuse, and Neglect." Pp. 262–80 in *Families and Change: Coping with Stressful Events,* edited by P. C. McKenzy and S. J. Price. Thousand Oaks, CA: Sage.

———. 1999. "Male Offenders: Our Understanding From the Data." Pp. 36–48 in *What Causes Men's Violence Against Women,* edited by M. Harway and J. O'Neil. Thousand Oaks, CA: Sage.

Giddens, Anthony. 1991. *Introduction to Sociology.* New York: Norton.

Gillespie, Joan B. 2005. "The Phenomenon of the Public Wife: An Exercise in Goffman's Impression Management." Pp. 379–98 in *Life as Theater: A Dramaturgical Sourcebook,* second ed., edited by Dennis Brissett and Charles Edgley. New Brunswick, NJ: Transaction.

Gilligan, Carol. 1982. In a *Different Voice: Psychological Theory and Women's Development.* Cambridge, MA: Harvard University Press.

Giménez, Martha E. 1992. "U.S. Ethnic Politics: Implications for Latin Americans." *Latin American Perspectives* 19(4):7–17.

Giving USA. 1986. New York: American Association of Fund-Raising Council, Inc.

———. 2005. New York: American Association of Fund-Raising Council, Inc.

———. 2010. New York: American Association of Fund-Raising Council, Inc.

Glick, P., and S. T. Fiske. 1996. "The Ambivalent Sexism Inventory: Differentiating Hostile and Benevolent Sexism." *Journal of Personality and Social Psychology* 70(3):491–512.

Goar, Carla, and Jane Sell. 2005. "Using Task Definition to Modify Racial Inequality Within Task Groups." *Sociological Quarterly* 46(3):525–43.

Goffman, Erving. 1959. *The Presentation of Self in Everyday Life.* New York: Doubleday.

———. 1961. *Asylums: Essays on the Social Situation of Mental Patients and Other Inmates.* Garden City, NY: Anchor.

———. 1963. *Stigma.* Englewood Cliffs, NJ: Prentice Hall.

———. 1976. *Gender Advertisements.* New York: Harper and Row.

———. 1977. "The Arrangement between the Sexes." *Theory and Society* 4:301–31.

Gordon, Margaret T., and Stephanie Riger. 1989. *The Female Fear: The Social Cost of Rape.* Urbana: University of Illinois Press.

Graham, Sandra. 1992. "Most of the Subjects Were White and Middle Class: Trends in Published Research on African Americans in Selected APA Journals, 1970–1989." *American Psychologist* 47:629–39.

Gray, Colin, Phil Russell, and Stephanie Blockley. 1991. "The Effects upon Helping Behaviour of Wearing Pro-Gay Identification." *British Journal of Social Psychology* 30:171–78.

Green, Raymond J., Richard D. Ashmore, and Robert Manzi, Jr. 2005. "The Structure of Gender Type Perception: Testing the Elaboration, Encapsulation, and Evaluation Framework." *Social Cognition* 23(5):429–64.

Green, Raymond J., and Robert Manzi. 2002. "A Comparison of Methodologies for Uncovering the Structure of Racial Stereotype Subgrouping." *Social Behavior and Personality* 30(7):709–28.

Greenberg, Jerold. 1978. "Effects of Reward Value and Retaliative Power on Allocation Decisions: Justice, Generosity, or Greed?" *Journal of Personality and Social Psychology* 36:367–79.

Greenstein, Theodore N. 1996. "Gender Ideology and the Perceptions of the Fairness of the Division of Household Labor: Effects on Marital Quality." *Social Forces* 74:1029–42.

———. 2000. "Economic Dependence, Gender, and the Division of Labor in the Home: A Replication and Extension." *Journal of Marriage and Family* 62:322–35.

Greenwald, Anthony G., M. R. Banaji, L. A. Rudman, S. D. Farnham, B. A. Nosek, and D. S. Mellott. 2002. "A Unified Theory of Implicit Attitudes, Stereotypes, Self-Esteem, and Self-Concept." *Psychological Review* 109:3–25.

Greenwald, Anthony, Mark A. Oakes, and Hunter G. Hoffman. 2003. "Targets of Discrimination: Effects of Race on Responses to Weapons Holders." *Journal of Experimental Social Psychology* 39:399–405.

Greenwald, Anthony G., T. Andrew Poehlman, Eric Luis Uhlmann, and Mahzarin R. Banaji. 2009. "Understanding and Using the Implicit Association Test." *Journal of Personality and Social Psychology* 97(1):17–41.

Greenwald, Anthony G., Colin Tucker Smith, N. Sriram, Yoav Bar-Anan, and Brian Nosek. 2009. "Implicit Race Attitudes Predicted Vote in the 2008 U.S. Presidential Election." *Analyses of Social Issues and Public Policy* 9(1):241–53.

Grossman, J. M., and L. Charmaraman. 2009. "Race, Context, and Privilege: White Adolescents' Explanations of Racial-Ethnic Centrality." *Journal of Youth Adolescence* 37:1–11.

Gurin, Patricia, Arthur H. Miller, and Gerald Gurin. 1980. "Stratum Identification and Consciousness." *Social Psychology Quarterly* 43:30–47.

Gustav-Wrathall, John Donald. 1998. *Take the Young Stranger By the Hand.* Chicago: University of Chicago Press.

Halberstam, Judith. 1998. *Female Masculinity.* Durham, NC: Duke University Press.

Hales, Loyde W., and Bradford J. Fenner. 1973. "Sex and Social Class Differences in Work Values." *Elementary School Guidance and Counseling* 8:26–32.

Hall, Peter M. 2005. "The Presidency and Impression Management." Pp. 365–78 in *Life as Theater: A Dramaturgical Sourcebook,* second ed., edited by Dennis Brissett and Charles Edgley. New Brunswick, NJ: Transaction.

Hansen, Ronald D., and Virginia E. O'Leary. 1983. "Actors and Actresses: The Effects of Sex on Causal Attributions." *Basic and Applied Social Psychology* 4:209–30.

Harlow, R. 2003. "'Race Doesn't Matter, But . . .': The Effect of Race on Professors' Experiences and Emotion Management in the Undergraduate College Classroom." *Social Psychology Quarterly* 66(4):348–63.

Harnois, Catherine E. 2009. "Imagining a 'Feminist Revolution': Can Multiracial Feminism Revolutionize Quantitative Social Science Research." Pp. 157–72 in *The Intersectional Approach: Transforming the Academy Through Race, Class and Gender,* edited by Michele Berger and Kathleen Guidroz. Chapel Hill: University of North Carolina Press.

Harry, Joseph. 1990. "Conceptualizing Anti-Gay Violence." *Journal of Interpersonal Violence* 5:350–58.

Hartmann, Heidi. 1993. "Comment on Brines and Fiorentine." *Rationality and Society* 5:375–85.

Hartsock, Nancy C. M. 1985. "Exchange Theory: Critique from a Feminist Standpoint." *Current Perspectives in Social Theory* 6:57–70.

Hastings, Paul, Kelly McShane, Richard Parker, and Farriola Ladha. 2007. "Ready to Make Nice: Parental Socialization of Young Sons' and Daughters' Prosocial Behaviors With Peers." *Journal of Genetic Psychology* 168(2).

Hastings, P. D., C. Zahn-Waxler, and K. E. McShane. 2006. "We Are, By Nature, Moral Creatures: Biological Bases of Concern for Others." Pp. 483–516 in *Handbook of Moral Development*, edited by Melanie Killen and Judith Smetana. Mahwah, NJ: Lawrence Erlbaum Associates.

Healy, Joseph F. 1995. *Race, Ethnicity, Gender, and Class: The Sociology of Group Conflict and Change.* Thousand Oaks, CA: Pine Forge Press.

Heath, Linda, Candace Kruttschnitt, and David Ward. 1986. "Television and Violent Criminal Behavior: Beyond the Bobo Doll." *Violence and Victims* 1:177–90.

Hegtvedt, Karen A., and Barry Markovsky. 1995. "Justice and Injustice." Pp. 257–280 in *Sociological Perspectives on Social Psychology*, edited by K. S. Cook, G. A. Fine, and J. S. House. Boston: Allyn and Bacon.

Heilbrun, Carolyn. 1973. *Toward a Recognition of Androgyny.* New York: Knopf.

Heimer, Karen, and Candace Kruttschnitt. 2006. *Gender and Crime: Patterns in Victimization and Offending.* New York: New York University Press.

Hendrick, Susan, Clyde Hendrick, Michelle J. Slapion-Foote, and Franklin H. Foote. 1985. "Gender Differences in Sexual Attitudes." *Journal of Personality and Social Psychology* 48:1630–42.

Hennessy, D. A., and D. L. Wiesenthal. 2001. "Gender, Driver Aggression, and Driver Violence: An Applied Evaluation." *Sex Roles* 44:661–76.

Herbert, Melissa. 1995. "Frederick the Great or Frederick's of Hollywood? The Accomplishment of Gender among Women in the Military." Annual Meeting of the Pacific Sociological Association. San Francisco.

———. 2000. *Camouflage Isn't Only For Combat: Gender, Sexuality, and Women in the Military.* New York: New York University Press.

Herdt, Gilbert. 1998. *Same Sex, Different Cultures.* Nashville, TN: Westview.

Herek, Gregory M. 1992. "The Social Context of Hate Crimes: Notes on Cultural Heterosexism." Pp. 89–104 in *Hate Crimes: Confronting Violence against Lesbians and Gay Men*, edited by G. M. Herek and K. T. Berrill. Newbury Park, CA: Sage.

———. 2009. "Hate Crimes and Stigma-Related Experiences Among Sexual Minority Adults in the United States: Prevalence Estimates From a National Probability Sample." *Journal of Interpersonal Violence* 24:54–74.

Herek, Gregory M., and Kevin T. Berrill, eds. 1992. *Hate Crimes: Confronting Violence against Lesbians and Gay Men.* Newbury Park, CA: Sage.

Herrnstein, Richard J., and Charles Murray. 1994. *The Bell Curve*. New York: Free Press.

Hess, B. B., and Myra Marx Ferree. 1987. *Analyzing Gender*. Newbury Park, CA: Sage.

Higgins, E. Tory. 1997. "Beyond Pleasure and Pain." *American Psychologist* 52:1280–1300.

Higgins, E. Tory, and Daniel C. Molden. 2003. "How Strategies for Making Judgments and Decisions Affect Cognition: Motivated Cognition Revisited." Pp. 211–36 in *Foundations of Social Cognition*, edited by G.V. Bodenhausen and A. J. Lambert. Mahwah, NJ: Lawrence Erlbaum Associates.

Hoburg, Robin, Julie Konik, Michelle Williams, and Mary Crawford. 2004. "Bisexuality Among Self-Identified Heterosexual College Students." *Journal of Bisexuality* 4(1/2):25–36.

Hochschild, Arlie Russell. 1983. *The Managed Heart: Commercialization of Human Feeling*. Berkeley: University of California Press.

Hodson, G., J. F. Dovidio, and S. L. Gaertner. 2002. "Processes in Racial Discrimination: Differential Weighting of Conflicting Information." *Personality and Social Psychology Bulletin* 28:460–71.

Hoffman, M. L. 2000. *Empathy and Moral Development: Implications for Caring and Justice*. New York: Cambridge University Press.

———. 2008. "Empathy and Prosocial Behavior." Pp. 440–55 in *Handbook of Emotions*, edited by Michael Lewis, Jeannette M. Haviland-Jones, and Lisa Feldman Barrett. New York: Guilford Press.

Hoffman, Curt, and Nancy Hurst. 1990. "Gender Stereotypes: Perception or Rationalization?" *Journal of Personality and Social Psychology* 58:197–208.

Hogan, Dennis P., David J. Eggebeen, and Clifford C. Clogg. 1993. "The Structure of Intergenerational Exchanges in American Families." *American Journal of Sociology* 98:1428–58.

Hollander, Jocelyn A. 1998. "Doing 'Studs': The Performance of Gender and Sexuality on Late-Night Television." Pp. 43–71 in *Everyday Inequalities: Critical Inquiries*, edited by Jodi O'Brien and Judith A. Howard. Cambridge, MA: Basil Blackwell.

———. 2001. "Vulnerability and Dangerousness: The Construction of Gender Through Conversation About Violence." *Gender and Society* 15:83–109.

———. 2002. "Resisting Vulnerability: The Social Reconstruction of Gender in Interaction." *Social Problems* 49:474–96.

———. 2009. "The Roots of Resistance to Women's Self-Defense." *Violence Against Women* 15(4):574–94.

Hollander, Jocelyn A., and Judith A. Howard. 2000. "Social Psychological Theories on Social Inequality." *Social Psychology Quarterly* 63:338–51.

Holmes, John G., Dale T. Miller, and Melvin J. Lerner. 2002. "Committing Altruism Under the Cloak of Self-Interest: The Exchange Fiction." *Journal of Experimental Social Psychology* 38(2).

Homans, George C. 1974. *Social Behavior: Its Elementary Forms*. New York: Harcourt Brace and World.

Hook, Jennifer L. 2006. "Care in Context: Men's Unpaid Work in 20 Countries, 1965–2003." *American Sociological Review* 71(4):639–60.

hooks, bell. 2006. *Outlaw Culture: Resisting Representations*. New York: Routledge.

Hossain, Ziarat, and Jaipaul L. Roopnarine. 1993. "Division of Household Labor and Child Care in Dual-Earner African-American Families with Infants." *Sex Roles* 29:571–83.

Howard, Judith A. 1984a. "Societal Influences on Attribution: Blaming Some Victims More Than Others." *Journal of Personality and Social Psychology* 47:494–505.

———. 1984b. "The 'Normal' Victim: The Effects of Gender Stereotypes on Reactions to Victims." *Social Psychology Quarterly* 47:270–81.

———. 1988. "Gender Differences in Sexual Attitudes: Conservativism or Powerlessness?" *Gender and Society* 1:103–114.

———. 1994. "A Social Cognitive Conception of Social Structure." *Social Psychology* 57:210–27.

Howard, Judith A., Phillip Blumstein, and Pepper Schwartz. 1986. "Sex, Power, and Influence Tactics in Intimate Relationships." *Journal of Personality and Social Psychology* 51:102–9.

Howard, Judith A., and Kenneth C. Pike. 1986. "Ideological Investment in Cognitive Processing: The Influence of Social Statuses on Attribution." *Social Psychology Quarterly* 49:154–67.

Howard, Judith A., and Daniel G. Renfrow. 2003. "Social Cognition." Pp. 259–82 in *Handbook of Social Psychology*, edited by John DeLamater. New York: Kluwer-Plenum.

Hubler, M., B. Hauser, V. N. Meyer-Whalen, and S. Arnold. 1999. "SRY-Negative XX True Hermaphrodite in a Basset Hound." *Theriogenology* 55:1391–1403.

Hughes, J. R. 2006. "A General Review of Recent Reports on Homosexuality and Lesbianism." *Sexual Disabilities* 24:185–205.

Hughes, Michael, and David H. Demo. 1989. "Self-Perceptions of Black Americans: Self-Esteem and Personal Efficacy." *American Journal of Sociology* 95:132–59.

Hummert, M. L., T. A. Garstka, A. G. Greenwalk, D. S. Mellot, and L. T. O'Brien. 2002. "Using the Implicit Association Test to Measure Age Differences in Implicit Social Cognitions." *Psychology and Aging* 17:482–95.

Hurtado, Aida, Patricia Gurin, and Timothy Peng. 1994. "Social Identities: A Framework for Studying the Adaptations of Immigrants and Ethnics: The Adaptations of Mexicans in the United States." *Social Problems* 41:129–51.

Hutchings, Vincent L. 2009. "Change or More of the Same? Evaluating Racial Attitudes in the Obama Era." *Public Opinion Quarterly* 73(5):917–42.

Hyde, Janet S. 1986. "Gender Differences in Aggression." Pp. 51–66 in *The Psychology of Gender: Advances through Meta-Analysis*, edited by J. S. Hyde and M. C. Linn. Baltimore, MD: Johns Hopkins University Press.

———. 2005. "The Gender Similarities Hypothesis." *American Psychologist* 60(6).

Hyde, J. S., E. Fennema, S. J. Lamon. 1990. "Gender Differences in Mathematics Performance: A Meta-Analysis." *Psychological Bulletin* 107(2):139–55.

Irvine. Leslie. 2004. *If You Tame Me*. Philadelphia, PA: Temple University Press.

Jackman, Mary. 2002. "Violence in Social Life." *Annual Review of Sociology* 28:387–415.

Jaffee, S., and J. S. Hyde. 2000. "Gender Differences in Moral Orientation." *Psychological Bulletin* 126:703–26.

James, William. 1890/1991. *The Principles of Psychology*, vol. 1. Cambridge, MA: Harvard University Press.

Johnson, Cathryn, Timothy Dowd, and Cecilia Ridgeway. 2006. "Legitimacy as a Social Process." *Annual Review of Sociology* 32:53–78.

Jones, Tricia S., and Martin S. Remland. 1992. "Sources of Variability in Perceptions of and Responses to Sexual Harassment." *Sex Roles* 27:121–42.

Jost, John T., and Mahzarin R. Banaji. 1994. "The Role of Stereotyping in System-Justification and the Production of False Consciousness." *British Journal of Social Psychology* 33:1–27.

Kahn, Arnold, R. E. Nelson, and William P. Gaeddert. 1980. "Sex of Subject and Sex Composition of the Group as Determinants of Reward Allocation." *Journal of Personality and Social Psychology* 38:737–50.

Kahn, Arnold, and William P. Gaeddert. 1985. "From Theories of Equity to Theories of Justice: The Liberating Consequences of Studying Women." Pp. 129–148 in *Women, Gender, and Social Psychology*, edited by V. E. O'Leary, R. K. Unger, and B. Strudler Wallston. Hillsdale, NJ: Lawrence Erlbaum.

Kalbfleisch, Pamela J., and Andrea B. Davies. 1991. "Minorities and Mentoring: Managing the Multicultural Institution." *Communication Education* 40:266–71.

Kandel-Englander, Elizabeth. 1992. "Wife Battering and Violence Outside the Family." *Journal of Interpersonal Violence* 7:462–70.

Kanter, Rosabeth Moss. 1977. *Men and Women of the Corporation.* New York: Basic Books.

Karlins, Marvin, Thomas L. Coffman, and Gary Walters. 1969. "On the Fading of Social Stereotypes: Studies in Three Generations of College Students." *Journal of Personality and Social Psychology* 13:1–16.

Karp, David A. 1986. "'You Can Take the Boy Out of Dorchester, But You Can't Take Dorchester Out of the Boy': Toward a Social Psychology of Mobility." *Symbolic Interaction* 9:19–36.

Karraker, Katherine Hildebrandt, Dena Ann Vogel, and Margaret Ann Lake. 1995. "Parents' Gender-Stereotyped Perceptions of Newborns: The Eye of the Beholder Revisited." *Sex Roles* 33:687–701.

Kashima, Yoshihisa, Michael Siegal, Kenichiro Tanaka, and Hiroko Isaka. 1988. "Universalism in Lay Conceptions of Distributive Justice: A Cross-Cultural Examination." *International Journal of Psychology* 23:51–64.

Katz, Daniel, and Kenneth W. Braly. 1933. "Racial Stereotypes of One Hundred College Students." *Journal of Abnormal and Social Psychology* 28:280–90.

Katz, Irwin, Sheldon Cohen, and David Glass. 1975. "Some Determinants of Cross-Race Helping Behavior." *Journal of Personality and Social Psychology* 32:964–70.

Katz, Jackson. 2006. *The Macho Paradox.* Naperville, IL: Sourcebooks.

Kaufman, Karen, W. Larry Gregory, and Walter G. Stephan. 1990. "Maladjustment in Statistical Minorities within Ethnically Unbalanced Classrooms." *American Journal of Community Psychology* 18:757–65.

Keita, Gwendolyn Puryear, Leslie Cameron, and Tanya Burrwell. 2006. *Women in the American Psychological Association.* Washington, DC: American Psychological Association.

Kelley, Johnathan, and M. D. R. Evans. 1995. "Class and Class Conflict in Six Western Nations." *American Sociological Review* 60:157–78.

Kendall, Frances E. 2006. *Understanding White Privilege.* New York: Routledge.

Kenrick, D. T., J. Ackerman, and S. Ledlow. 2003. "Evolutionary Social Psychology." Pp. 103–24 in *Handbook of Social Psychology,* edited by John DeLamater. New York: Kluwer-Plenum.

Kerbo, Harold R. 1976. "The Stigma of Welfare and a Passive Poor." *Sociology and Social Research* 60:173–87.

Kessler, Suzanne J., and Wendy McKenna. 1978. *Gender: An Ethnomethodological Approach.* New York: John Wiley.

Kessler-Harris, Alice. 2003. *Out to Work: A History of Wage-Earning Women in the United States.* New York: Oxford University Press.

Kilty, Keith, and Maria Vidal de Haymes. 2004. "What's in a Name? Racial and Ethnic Classifications and the Meaning of Hispanic/Latino in the United States." *Ethnic Studies Review* 27(1):32–56.

Kimmel, Michael. 2006. *Manhood in America,* second ed. New York: Oxford University Press.

Kimmel, Michael, and Abby Ferber, eds. 2003. *Privilege: A Reader.* Nashville, TN: Westview.

Kimmel, Michael S., Jeff R. Hearn, and Robert W. Connell. 2004. *Handbook of Studies on Men and Masculinities.* New York: Sage.

Kimmel, Michael S., and Matthew Mahler. 2003. "Adolescent Masculinity, Homophobia, and Violence: Random School Shootings, 1982–2001." *American Behavioral Scientist* 46(10):1439–58.

Kimura, Aya. 2007. "Self-Esteem and Perceived Racial Discrimination: Variations in the Moderation Effect of Racial Identity." Annual meeting of the American Sociological Association, New York.

Kingston, Drew A., Paul Fedoroff, Philip Firestone, Susan Curry, and John M. Bradford. 2008. "Pornography Use and Sexual Aggression: The Impact of Frequency and Type of Pornography Use on Recidivism Among Sexual Offenders." *Aggressive Behavior* 34(4):241–51.

Kirchmeyer, Catherine. 1996. "Gender Roles and Decision-Making in Demographically Diverse Groups." *Sex Roles* 34(9/10):649–63.

Kluegel, James R., and Eliot R. Smith. 1986. *Beliefs About Inequality.* New York: Aldine.

Knight, J. R., H. Wechsler, M. Kuo, M. Seibring, E. R. Weitzman, and M. Schuckit. 2002. "Alcohol Abuse and Dependence Among U.S. College Students." *Journal of Studies of Alcohol* 63(3):263–70.

Knudson, Knud, and Kari Wærness. 2008. "National Context and Spouses' Housework in 34 Countries." *European Sociological Review* 24(1):97–113.

Koenig, A. M., and A. H. Eagly. 2005. "Stereotype Threat in Men on a Test of Social Sensitivity." *Sex Roles* 52:489–96.

Kogut, Diane, Travis Langley, and Edgar C. O'Neal. 1992. "Gender Role Masculinity and Angry Aggression in Women." *Sex Roles* 26:355–68.

Kollock, Peter, Philip Blumstein, and Pepper Schwartz. 1985. "Sex and Power in Interaction: Conversational Privileges and Duties." *American Sociological Review* 50:34–46.

Kollock, Peter, and Jodi O'Brien. 1992. "The Social Construction of Social Exchange." Pp. 89–112 in *Advances in Group Processes*, edited by E. J. Lawler, B. Markovsky, C. Ridgeway, and H. A. Walker. Greenwich, CT: JAI.

———. 1994. *The Production of Reality: Essays and Readings in Social Psychology.* Thousand Oaks, CA: Pine Forge Press.

Koss, Mary P. 1993. "Rape: Scope, Impact, Interventions, and Public Policy Responses." *American Psychologist* 48:1062–69.

Kreager, Derek A. 2007. "Unnecessary Roughness? School Sports, Peer Networks, and Male Adolescent Violence." *American Sociological Review* 75(5).

Krebs, D. L. 1970. "Altruism: An Examination of the Concept and a Review of the Literature." *Psychological Bulletin* 73:258–302.

Krivo, L. J., R. D. Peterson, and D. C. Kuhl. 2009. "Segregation, Racial Structure, and Neighborhood Crime." *American Journal of Sociology* 114(6):1765–1802.

Kuhn, Manfred H., and Thomas S. McPartland. 1954. "An Empirical Investigation of Self-Attitudes." *American Sociological Review* 19:68–76.

Kunstman, J. W., and E. A. Plant. 2008. "Racing to Help: Racial Bias in High Emergency Helping Situations." *Journal of Personality and Social* Psychology 95:1499–1510.

Kurdek, Lawrence A. 1993. "The Allocation of Household Labor in Gay, Lesbian, and Heterosexual Married Couples." *Journal of Social Issues* 49:127–39.

———. 2004. "Are Gay and Lesbian Cohabiting Couples *Really* Different from Heterosexual Married Couples?" *Journal of Marriage and Family* 66:880–900.

———. 2005. "What Do We Know About Gay and Lesbian Couples?" *Current Directions in Psychological Science* 14(5).

LaFree, Gary. 1995 "Race and Crime Trends in the United States, 1946–1990." Pp. 169–193 in *Ethnicity, Race, and Crime: Perspectives Across Time and Place*, edited by D. F. Hawkins. Albany: State University of New York Press.

Lagerspetz, Kristi M. J., Kaj Björkqvist, and Tarja Peltonen. 1988. "Is Indirect Aggression Typical of Females? Gender Differences in Aggressiveness in 11–12-year-old Children." *Aggressive Behavior* 14:303–15.

Lamb, Sharon. 2004. "Sexual Tensions in Girls' Friendships." *Feminism and Psychology* 14(3):376–82.

Lambert, W. W. 1971. "Cross-Cultural Background to Personality Development and the Socialization of Aggression: Findings from the Six Culture Study." Pp. 49–61 in *Comparative Perspectives on Social Psychology*, edited by W. W. Lambert and R. Weisbrod. Boston: Little, Brown.

Landrine, Hope. 1985. "Race X Class Stereotypes of Women." *Sex Roles* 13:65–75.

Landry, Bart. 2000. *Black Working Wives.* Berkeley: University of California Press.

Langer, Ellen J. 1989. *Mindfulness.* Reading, MA: Addison-Wesley.

Langer, Ellen J., A. Blank, and Benzion Chanowitz. 1978. "The Mindlessness of Ostensibly Thoughtful Action: The Role of 'Placebic' Information in Interpersonal Interaction." *Journal of Personality and Social Psychology* 36:635–42.

Langer, Ellen J., Susan Fiske, Shelley E. Taylor, and Benzion Chanowitz. 1976. "Stigma, Staring and Discomfort: A Novel-Stimulus Hypothesis." *Journal of Experimental Social Psychology* 12:451–63.

Langley, Travis, Edgar C. O'Neal, K. M. Craig, and Elizabeth A. Yost. 1992. "Aggression Consistent, Inconsistent, and Irrelevant Priming Effects on Selective Exposure to Media Violence." *Aggressive Behavior* 18:349–56.

Lareau, Annette, and Dalton Conley, eds. 2008. *Social Class: How Does It Work?* New York: Russell Sage Foundation.

Lassiter, G. D., A. L. Geers, I. M. Handley, P. E. Weiland, and P. J. Munhall. 2002. "Videotaped Interrogations and Confessions: A Simple Change in Camera Perspective Alters Verdicts in Simulated Trials." *Journal of Applied Psychology* 87:867–74.

Lassiter, G. D., S. S. Diamond, H. C. Schmidt, and J. K. Elek. 2007. "Evaluating Videotaped Confessions: Expertise Provides No Defense Against Camera Perspective Effect." *Psychological Science* 18:224–26.

Latane, Bibb, and John M. Darley. 1968. "Group Inhibition of Bystander Intervention in Emergencies." *Journal of Personality and Social Psychology* 10:215–21.

———. 1970. *The Unresponsive Bystander: Why Doesn't He Help?* Englewood Cliffs, NJ: Prentice Hall.

Leahey, Erin, and Guang Guo. 2001. "Gender Differences in Mathematical Trajectories." *Social Forces* 80(2):713–32.

Lerner, R. M., and P. Frank. 1974. "Relation of Race and Sex to Supermarket Helping Behavior." *Journal of Social Psychology* 94:201–3.

Leung, Kwok, and Michael H. Bond. 1984. "The Impact of Cultural Collectivism on Reward Allocation." *Journal of Personality and Social Psychology* 47:793–804.

Leventhal, Gerald S., Jurgis Karuza, Jr., and William Rick Fry. 1980. "Beyond Fairness: A Theory of Allocation Preferences." Pp. 167–218 in *Justice and Social Interaction*, edited by G. Mikula. New York: Springer-Verlag.

Lips, Hilary, and Katie Lawson. 2009. "Work Values, Gender, and Expectations About Work Commitment and Pay." *Sex Roles* 61(9/10):667–76.

Litzler, Elizabeth, and Julie Brines. 2005. "A Fair Bargain? Breadwinning Arrangements, Interpersonal Comparisons, and the Risk of Divorce." Annual Meeting of the American Sociological, Philadelphia.

Lockhart, Lettie L., Barbara W. White, Vicki Causby, and Alicia Isaac. 1994. "Letting Out the Secret: Violence in Lesbian Relationships." *Journal of Interpersonal Violence* 9:469–92.

Loftus, Jeni. 2001. "American's Liberalization in Attitudes Toward Homosexuality: 1973–1998." *American Sociological Review* 66(5).

Logel, Christine, Emma C. Iserman, Paul G. Davies, Diane M. Quinn, and Steven J. Spencer. 2009. "The Perils of Double Consciousness: The Role of Thought Suppression in Stereotype Threat." *Journal of Experimental Social Psychology* 45(2):299–312.

Lopata, Helena Z., and Barrie Thorne. 1978. "On the Term 'Sex Roles.'" *Signs: Journal of Women in Culture and Society* 3:718–21.

Lorber, Judith. 2005. *Gender Inequality*, third ed. New York: Oxford University Press.

Lott, B., and S. Saxon. 2002. "The Influence of Ethnicity, Social Class, and Context on Judgments about U.S. Women." *Journal of Social Psychology* 142(4):481–99.

Lowe, Roland, and Gary Ritchey. 1973. "Relation of Altruism to Age, Social Class, and Ethnic Identity." *Psychological Reports* 33:567–72.

Lubek, I. 1979. "A Brief Social Psychological Analysis of Research on Aggression in Social Psychology." In *Psychology in Social Context*, edited by A. R. Buss. New York: Irvington.

Luchterhead, Elmer, and Leonard Weller. 1976. "Effects of Class, Race, Sex, and Educational Status on Patterns of Aggression of Lower-Class Youth." *Journal of Youth and Adolescence* 5:59–71.

Lye, Diane N. 1996. "Adult Child-Parent Relationships." *Annual Review of Sociology* 22.

Lye, Diane N., and Daniel H. Klepinger. 1995. "Race and Hispanic Ethnicity, Childhood Living Arrangements and Adult-Child Parent Relations." Unpublished paper, University of Washington, Seattle.

Lye, Diane N., Daniel H. Klepinger, Patricia Davis Hyle, and Anjanette Nelson. 1995. "Child Living Arrangements and Adult Children's Relations with Their Parents." *Demography* 32:261–80.

Lyons, Christopher. 2006. "Stigma or Sympathy: Attributions of Fault to Hate Crime Victims and Offenders." *Social Psychology Quarterly* 69(1):39–59.

McAlister, Alfred, Patrick Sandström, Pekka Puska, Anitta Veijo, Razvan Chereches, and Lenne-Triin Heidmets. 2001. "Attitudes Toward War, Killing, and Punishment of Children Among Young People in Estonia, Finland, Romania, the Russian Federation, and the USA." *Bulletin of the World Health Organization* 79(5).

McArthur, Leslie Zebrowitz, and Linda K. Solomon. 1978. "Perceptions of an Aggressive Encounter as a Function of the Victim's Salience and the Perceiver's Arousal." *Journal of Personality and Social Psychology* 36:1278–90.

McCall, George J., and J. L. Simmons. 1978. *Identities and Interaction: An Examination of Human Associations in Everyday Life*. New York: Free Press.

McGuire, William J., Claire V. McGuire, Pamela Child, and Terry Fujioka. 1978. "Salience of Ethnicity in the Spontaneous Self-Concept as a Function of One's Ethnic Distinctiveness in the Social Environment." *Journal of Personality and Social Psychology* 36:511–20.

McIntosh, Peggy. 1990. "White Privilege: Unpacking the Invisible Knapsack." *Independent School*. Winter:31–36.

McKinley, James C. 2009. "Gay Candidates Get Support That Causes May Not." *New York Times*, December 27.

McKown, C., and R. Weinstein. 2003. "The Development and Consequences of Stereotype-Consciousness in Middle Childhood." *Child Development* 74:498–515.

McNamee, Stephen, and Robert K. Miller, Jr. 2009. *The Meritocracy Myth*. Lanham, MD: Rowman & Littlefield.

Macaulay, J. 1985. "Adding Gender to Aggression Research: Incremental or Revolutionary Change?" Pp. 191–224 in *Women, Gender, and Social Psychology*, edited by V. E. O'Leary, R. K. Unger, and B. Strudler Wallston. Hilldale, NJ: Lawrence Erlbaum.

Maccoby, Eleanor E., and Carol Jacklin. 1974. *The Psychology of Sex Differences.* Stanford, CA: Stanford University Press.

Macy, Michael. 1993. "Backward-Looking Social Control." *American Sociological Review* 58:819–36.

Maddox, K. B., and S. G. Chase. 2004. "Manipulating Subcategory Salience: Exploring the Link Between Skin Tone and Social Perception of Blacks." *European Journal of Social Psychology* 34:533–46.

Maddox, K. B., and S. Gray. 2002. "Cognitive Representation of African Americans: Re-Exploring the Role of Skin Tone." *Personality and Social Psychology Bulletin* 28:250–59.

Maio, G. R., J. M. Olson, M. Bernard, M. A. Luke. 2003. "Ideologies, Values, Attitudes, and Behavior." Pp. 283–308 in *Handbook of Social Psychology*, edited by John DeLamater. New York: Kluwer-Plenum.

Major, Brenda. 1987. "Gender, Justice, and the Psychology of Entitlement." Pp. 124–148 in *Sex and Gender*, vol. 7, edited by P. Shaver and C. Hendrick. Newbury Park, CA: Sage.

———. 1989. "Gender Differences in Comparisons and Entitlement: Implications for Comparable Worth." *Journal of Social Issues* 45:99–115.

———. 1993. "Gender, Entitlement, and the Distribution of Family Labor." *Journal of Social Issues* 49:141–59.

Major, Brenda, R. Gramzow, S. McCoy, S. Levin, T. Schmader, and J. Sidanius. 2002. "Attributions to Discrimination: The Role of Group Status and Legitimizing Ideology." *Journal of Personality and Social Psychology* 82:269–82.

Major, Brenda, W. J. Quinton, and T. Schmader. 2003. "Attributions to Discrimination and Self-Esteem: Impact of Group Identification and Situational Ambiguity." *Journal of Experimental Social Psychology* 39:220–31.

Major, Brenda, and Jeffrey B. Adams. 1983. "Role of Gender, Interpersonal Orientation and Self-Presentation in Distributive-Justice Behavior." *Journal of Personality and Social Psychology* 45:598–608.

Major, Benda, and Kay Deaux 1982. "Individual Differences in Justice Behavior." Pp. 43–76 in *Equity and Justice in Social Behavior*, edited by J. Greenberg and R. L. Cohen. New York: Plenum.

Mamet, David. 1992. *Oleanna.* New York: Vintage.

Manegold, Catherine. 1993. "Women Say Wood Is Victim of Double Standard; Clinton Under Fire." *Seattle Times*, February 7, A6.

Manza, Jeff, and Debbie Van Schnydel. 2000. "Still the Missing Feminist Revolution? Inequalities of Race, Class, and Gender in Introductory Sociology Textbooks." *American Sociological Review* 55(3):468–75.

Margolin, L. 1992. "Beyond Maternal Blame: Physical Child Abuse as a Phenomenon of Gender." *Journal of Family Issues* 13:410–23.

Markus, Hazel, Marie Crane, Stan Bernstein, and Michael Sildai. 1982. "Self-Schemas and Gender." *Journal of Personality and Social Psychology* 42:38–50.

Martin, Patricia Yancey. 2004. "Gender As Social Institution." *Social Forces* 82(4):1249–73.

Martin, Patricia Yancey, and Robert A. Hummer. 1993. "Fraternities and Rape on Campus." Pp. 114–31 in *Violence Against Women: The Bloody Footprints*, edited by P. Bart and E. G. Moran. Newbury Park, CA: Sage.

Martino, W., and B. Meyenn. 2002. "War, Guns and Cool, Tough Things: Interrogating Single-Sex Classes as a Strategy for Engaging Boys in English." *Cambridge Journal of Education* 32(3):303–24.

Martino, W., and M. Pallotta-Chiarolli. 2003. *So What's a Boy?* Maidenhead, UK: Open University Press.

Marvasti, Amir. 2005. "Being Middle Eastern American: Identity Negotiation in the Context of the War on Terror." *Symbolic Interaction* 28(4):525–47.

Marx, Karl, and Friedrich Engels. 1974. *The German Ideology*. New York: International Publishers.

Massey, Douglas S. 2007. *Categorically Unequal: The American Stratification System*. New York: Russell Sage Foundation.

Massey, Douglas S., and Nancy A. Denton. 1993. *American Apartheid: Segregation and the Making of the Underclass*. Cambridge, MA: Harvard University Press.

Mattis, Jacqueline S., Nyasha A. Grayman, Sheri-Ann Cowie, Cynthia Winston, Carolyn Watson, and Daisy Jackson. 2008. "Intersectional Identities and the Politics of Altruistic Care in a Low-Income, Urban Community." *Sex Roles* 59(5/6):418–28.

Mead, George Herbert. 1934. *Mind, Self, and Society*. Chicago: University of Chicago Press.

Meeker, B. F. and P. A. Weitzel-O'Neill. 1977. "Sex Roles and Interpersonal Behavior in Task-Oriented Groups." *American Sociological Review* 42:91–105.

Mehan, Hugh M., and Houston W. Wood. 1975. *The Reality of Ethnomethodology*. New York: John Wiley.

Messerschmidt, James W. 1993. *Masculinities and Crime: Critique and Reconceptualization of Theory*. Lanham, MD: Rowman & Littlefield.

———.1997. *Crime as Structured Action: Gender, Race, Class and Crime in the Making*. Thousand Oaks, CA: Sage.

Messner, Michael A. 2000. "Barbie Girls vs. Sea Monsters: Children Constructing Gender." *Gender and Society* 14:765–84.

Messner, Michael A., and Donald E. Sabo. 1994. *Sex, Violence, and Power in Sports: Rethinking Masculinity*. Freedom, CA: Crossing Press.

Meyers-Whalen, V. N. 2009. "Review and Update: Genomic and Molecular Advances in Sex Determination and Differentiation in Small Animals." *Reproduction in Domestic Animals* 44(2):40–46.

Mezey, Gillian C., and Michael B. King, eds. 2000. *Male Victims of Sexual Assault*, second ed. New York: Oxford University Press.

Mikula, Gerold, ed. 1980. *Justice and Social Interaction*. New York: Springer-Verlag.

Miller, Joan G. 1984. "Culture and the Development of Everyday Social Explanation." *Journal of Personality and Social Psychology* 46:961–78.

Miller, Joan G., D. G. Bersoff, and R. L. Harwood. 1990. "Perceptions of Social Responsibilities in India and in the United States: Moral Imperatives or Personal Decisions?" *Journal of Personality and Social Psychology* 58:33–47.

Mischel, Walter. 1966. "A Social Learning View of Sex Differences in Behavior." Pp. 56–81 in *The Development of Sex Differences*, edited by E. Maccoby. Stanford, CA: Stanford University Press.

Moghaddam, Fathali M., Donald M. Taylor, and Stephen C. Wright. 1993. *Social Psychology in Cross-Cultural Perspective*. New York: W. H. Freeman.

Molm, Linda D. 1981. "The Legitimacy of Behavioral Theory as a Sociological Perspective." *American Sociologist* 16:153–65.

———. 1987. "Power-Dependence Theory: Power Processes and Negative Outcomes." Pp. 171–98 in *Advances in Group Processes*, vol. 4, edited by E. J. Lawler and B. Markovsky. Greenwich, CT: JAI.

———. 1988. "The Structure and Use of Power: A Comparison of Reward and Punishment Power." *Social Psychology Quarterly* 51:108–22.

———. 1989a. "An Experimental Analysis of Imbalance in Punishment Power." *Social Forces* 68:178–203.

———. 1989b. "Punishment Power: A Balancing Process in Power-Dependence Relations." *American Journal of Sociology* 94:1392–1428.

———. 1990. "Structure, Action, and Outcomes: The Dynamics of Power in Social Exchange." *American Sociological Review* 55:427–47.

Molm, Linda D. 1997. "Risk and Power Use: Constraints on the Use of Coercion in Exchange." *American Sociological Review* 62:113–33.

———. 2006. "The Social Exchange Framework." Pp. 24–45 in *Contemporary Social Psychological Theories*, edited by Peter J. Burke. Stanford, CA: Stanford University Press.

Molm, Linda D. and Karen S. Cook. 1995. "Social Exchange and Exchange Networks." 209–35 in *Sociological Perspectives on Social Psychology*, edited by K. S. Cook, G.A. Fine, and J.S. House. Boston: Allyn and Bacon.

Money, J., and Anke Ehrhardt. 1972. *Man and Woman, Boy and Girl*. Baltimore: Johns Hopkins University Press.

Monmaney, Terence. 1995. "The Essence of Maleness May Also Provide Birth Control." *Seattle Times*, July 31, A1.

Moore, Mignon R. 2008. "Gendered Power Relations Among Women: A Study of Household Decision-Making in Lesbian Stepfamilies." *American Sociological Review* 73(2):335–56.

Morgan, Carolyn S., and Alexis J. Walker. 1983. "Predicting Sex Role Attitudes." *Social Psychology Quarterly* 46:148–51.

Morris, Edward. 2005. *An Unexpected Minority*. Piscataway, NJ: Rutgers University Press.

Morris, Jan. 1974. *Conundrum*. New York: Harcourt Brace Jovanovich.

Morrow-Howell, Nancy, Leanne Lott, and Martha Ozawa. 1990. "The Impact of Race on Volunteer Helping Relations among the Elderly." *Social Work* 35:395–402.

Moss, M. K., and R. A. Page. 1972. "Reinforcement and Helping Behavior." *Journal of Applied Social Psychology* 2:360–71.

Muehlenhard, Charlene L. 1988. "Misinterpreted Dating Behaviors and the Risk of Date Rape." *Journal of Social and Clinical Psychology* 6:20–37.

Murphy-Berman, Virginia, John J. Berman, Purnima Singh, Anju Pachauri, and Pramod Kumar. 1984 "Factors Affecting Allocation to Needy and Meritorious Recipients: A Cross-Cultural Comparison." *Journal of Personality and Social Psychology* 46:1267–72.

Murnen, S. K., and M. Kohlman. 2007. "Athletic Participation, Fraternity Membership, and Sexual Aggression: A Meta-Analytic Review." *Sex Roles* 57(1/2):145–57.

Musick, M., J. Wilson, and W. Bynum. 2000. "Race and Formal Volunteering: The Differential Effects of Class and Religion." *Social Forces* 78(4):1539–70.

Myers, Daniel J. 1997. "Racial Rioting in the 1960s: An Event History Analysis of Local Conditions." *American Sociological Review* 62(1):94–112.

Namaste, K. 1996. "Tragic Misreadings: Queer Theory's Erasure of Transgender Subjectivity." Pp. 183–203 in *Queer Studies*, edited by B. Beemyn and M. Eliason. New York: New York University Press.

Newman, Katherine. 1999. *No Shame in My Game: The Working Poor in the Inner City.* New York: Vintage.

New York Times. 1990. "Woman Is Acquitted in Trial For Using the Men's Room." November 3.

Nicholson, Linda. 1994. "Interpreting Gender." *Signs: Journal of Women in Culture and Society* 20:79–105.

Nirenberg, Theodore D., and Jacquelyn W. Gaebelein. 1979. "Third Party Instigated Aggression: Traditional versus Liberal Sex Role Attitudes." *Personality and Social Psychology Bulletin* 5:348–51.

Nobles, Melissa. 2000. *Shades of Citizenship.* Stanford, CA: Stanford University Press.

Olick, Jeffrey K., and Joyce Robbins. 1998. "Social Memory Studies." *Annual Review of Sociology* 24:105–40.

Olson, Toska. 1997. "The Price of Parenting: What Happens When Workers Parent and Parents Work?" PhD dissertation, Department of Sociology, University of Washington, Seattle.

Omi, Michael, and Howard Winant. 1986. *Racial Formation in the United States: From the 1960s to the 1980s.* New York: Routledge and Kegan Paul.

Owens, Timothy J. 2003. "Self and Identity." Pp. 205–32 in *Handbook of Social Psychology*, edited by John DeLamater. New York: Kluwer-Plenum.

Pager, Devah. 2007. *Marked: Race, Crime, and Finding Work in an Era of Mass Incarcerations.* Chicago: University of Chicago.

Parsons, Talcott. 1955. "Family Structure and the Socialization of the Child." In *Family Socialization and Interaction Process*, edited by T. Parsons and R. F. Bales. Glencoe, IL: Free Press.

Pate, Carl Edward. 2006. "Acknowledgment Rituals: Greeting Phenomena between Strangers." Pp. 168–84 in *The Production of Reality*, edited by Jodi O'Brien. Thousand Oaks, CA: Sage.

Peek, Lori. 2005. "Becoming Muslim: The Development of a Religious Identity." *Sociology of Religion* 66(3):215–42.

Penner, Louis A., John F. Dovidio, Jane A. Piliavin, and David A. Schroeder. 2005. "Prosocial Behavior: Multilevel Perspectives." *Annual Review of Psychology* 56:365–92.

Persson, Anna V. and Dara R. Musher-Eizenman. 2005. "College Students' Attitudes Toward Blacks and Arabs Following a Terrorist Attack as a Function of Varying Levels of Media Exposure." *Journal of Applied Social Psychology* 35(9):1879–92.

Peterson, C., and M. E. P. Seligman. 2004. *Character Strengths and Virtues*. New York: Oxford University Press.

Pettit, Becky, and Bruce Western. 2004. "Mass Imprisonment and the Life Course: Race and Class Inequality in U.S. Incarceration." *American Sociological Review* 69:151–60.

Petty, R. E., R. H. Fazio, and P. Briñol, eds. 2009. *Attitudes: Insights From the New Implicit Measures*. New York: Psychology Press.

Phillips, David P. 1983. "The Impact of Mass Media Violence on U.S. Homicides." *American Sociological Review* 48:560–68.

———.1986. "Natural Experiments on the Effects of Mass Media Violence on Fatal Aggression: Strengths and Weaknesses of a New Approach." Pp. 207–50 in *Advances in Experimental Social Psychology*, vol. 19, edited by L. Berkowitz. Orlando, FL: Academic Press.

Phinney, Jean S. 1990. "Ethnic Identity in Adolescents and Adults: Review of Research." *Psychological Bulletin* 108:499–514.

Piliavin, Jane Allyn, and Hong-Wen Charng. 1990. "Altruism: A Review of Recent Theory and Research." *Annual Review of Sociology* 16:27–65.

Piliavin, Jane Allyn, and Rhoda Kesler Unger. 1985. "The Helpful but Helpless Female: Myth or Reality?" Pp. 149–89 in *Women, Gender, and Social Psychology*, edited by Virginia E. O'Leary, Rhoda Kesler Unger, and Barbara Strudler Wallston. Hillsdale, NJ: Lawrence Erlbaum.

Pitchford, Susan. 1992. "Race." Pp. 1615–19 in *The Encyclopedia of Sociology*, vol. 3, edited by E. F. Borgatta and M. L. Borgatta. New York: Macmillan.

Pitt, Richard, and Elizabeth Borland. 2008. "Bachelorhood and Men's Traditional Gender Role Ideology." *Journal of Men's Studies* 16(2).

Pleck, Joseph H., Freya Lund Sonenstein, and Leighton C. Ku. 1993. "Masculinity Ideology and Its Correlates." Pp. 85–110 in *Gender Issues in Contemporary Society*, edited by S. Oskamp and M. Constanzo. Newbury Park, CA: Sage.

Prosser, Jay. 1998. *Second Skins*. New York: Columbia University Press.

Pugh, Meredith D., and Ralph Wahrman. 1983. "Neutralizing Sexism in Mixed-Sex Groups: Do Women Have to be Better Than Men?" *American Journal of Sociology* 88:746–62.

Pyke, S. 1985. "Androgyny: An Integration." *Journal of Women's Studies* 8:529–39.

Quinn, D. M., S. K. Kahng, and J. Crocker. 2004. "Discreditable: Stigma Effects of Revealing a Mental Illness History on Test Performance." *Personality and Social Psychology Bulletin* 30(7):803–15.

Raghubir, Priya, and Ana Valenzuela. 2006. "Center of Inattention: Position Biases in Decision Making." *Organizational Behavior and Human Decision Processes* 99(1):66–80.

Ramos, Reyes. 1979. "Movidas: The Methodological and Theoretical Relevance of Interactional Strategies." *Studies in Symbolic Interaction* 2:141–65.

Rashotte, L. S., and M. Webster, Jr. 2005. "Gender Status Beliefs." *Social Science Research* 34(3):618–33.

Read, Je'nan Ghazal, and John P. Bartkowski. 2000. "To Veil or Not to Veil? A Case Study of Identity Negotiation Among Muslim Women in Austin, Texas." *Gender and Society* 14(3):395–417.

Reid, Pamela Trotman. 1993. "Poor Women in Psychological Research: Shut Up and Shut Out." *Psychology of Women* Quarterly 17:133–50.

Reiman, Jeffrey. 1995. *The Rich Get Richer and the Poor Get Prison*, fourth ed. Boston: Allyn and Bacon.

Renfrow, Daniel G. 2004. "A Cartography of Passing in Everyday Life." *Symbolic Interaction* 27(4):485–506.

———. 2005. *Sexuality as Social Status*. Unpublished dissertation, University of Washington, Seattle.

———. 2008. "Bullying in Our Nation's Schools: Where Do We Go From Here?" In *Agenda for Social Justice*, edited by Robert Perrucci, Kathleen Ferraro, JoAnn Miller, and Glenn W. Muschert. Knoxville, TN: Society for the Study of Social Problems.

Renzetti, Clare. 1988. "Violence in Lesbian Relationships: A Preliminary Analysis of Causal Factors." *Journal of Interpersonal Violence* 3:381–99.

———.1992. *Violent Betrayal: Partner Abuse in Lesbian Relationships*. Newbury Park, CA: Sage.

Reskin, Barbara. 2000. "Getting It Right: Sex and Race Inequality in Work Organizations." *Annual Review of Sociology* 26:707–9.

Rich, Adrienne. 1980. "Compulsory Heterosexuality and Lesbian Existence." *Signs: Journal of Women in Culture and Society* 5:631–60.

Ridgeway, Cecilia. 1982. "Status in Groups: The Importance of Motivation." *American Sociological Review* 47:76–88.

———. 1993. "Gender, Status, and the Social Psychology of Expectations." Pp. 175–97 in *Theory on Gender/Feminism on Theory*, edited by P. England. New York: Aldine de Gruyter.

———. 2000. "The Formation of Status Beliefs: Improving Status Construction Theory." Pp. 77–102 in *Advances in Group Processes*, vol. 17, edited by E. J. Lawler, M. Macy, S. R. Thye, and H. A. Walker. Greenwich, CT: JAI Press.

———. 2009. "Framed Before We Know It: How Gender Shapes Social Relations." *Gender and Society* 23:145–60.

Ridgeway, Cecilia, and Chris Bourg. 2004. "Gender as Status: An Expectation States Approach." Pp. 217–41 in *Psychology of Gender*, second ed., edited by A. H. Eagly, A. Beall, and R. J. Sternberg. New York: Guilford.

Ridgeway, Cecilia, and Lynn Smith-Lovin. 1999. "The Gender System and Interaction." *Annual Review of Sociology* 25:191–216.

Ridgeway, Cecilia L., and Henry A. Walker. 1995. "Status Structures." Pp. 281–310 in *Sociological Perspectives on Social Psychology*, edited by K. S. Cook, G. A. Fine, and J. S. House. Boston: Allyn and Bacon.

Rime, Bernard, and Jacques-Phillipe Leyens. 1988. "Violence dans les Stades: La Réponse des Psycholgues" [Violence in the Stadiums: The Response of Psychologists]. *La Recherche* 19:528–31.

Risman, Barbara. 1998. *Gender Vertigo: American Families in Transition.* New Haven, CT: Yale University Press.

———. 2004. "Gender as Social Structure: Theory Wrestling with Activism." *Gender and Society 18*(4):429–40.

Robinson, Robert V., and Wendell Bell. 1978. "Equity, Success, and Social Justice in England and the United States." *American Sociological Review* 43:125–43.

Rodriquez, S. Fernando, and Veronica A. Henderson. 1995. "Intimate Homicide: Victim-Offender Relationship in Female-Perpetuated Homicide." *Deviant Behavior* 16:45–57.

Rodriguez, S. Fernando, and Martha Smithey. 1999. "Infant and Adult Homicide." *Homicide Studies* 3(2):170–84.

Roff, James D. 1992. "Childhood Aggression, Peer Status, and Social Class as Predictors of Delinquency." *Psychology Reports* 70:31–34.

Romer, Nancy, and Debra Cherry. 1980. "Ethnic and Social Class Differences in Children's Sex-Role Concepts." *Sex Roles* 6:245–63.

Roschelle, Anne. 1997. *No More Kin: Exploring Race, Class, and Gender in Family Networks.* New York: Sage.

Roschelle, Anne, and Peter Kaufman. 2004. "Fitting In and Fighting Back: Stigma Management Strategies Among Homelss Kids." *Symbolic Interaction* 27(1):23–46.

Rose, Robert M., Irwin S. Bernstein, and Thomas P. Gordon. 1975. "Consequences of Social Conflict on Plasma Testosterone Levels in Rhesus Monkeys." *Psychosomatic Medicine* 37:50–61.

Rosenblum, Karen E., and Toni-Michelle C. Travis. 1996. *The Meaning of Difference: American Constructions of Race, Sex and Gender, Social Class, and Sexual Orientation.* New York: McGraw-Hill.

Rosenhan, David L. 1973. "On Being Same in Insane Places." *Science* 179:250–58.

Rosenkrantz, Paul S., Susan R. Vogel, H. Bee, Inge K. Broverman, and Donald M. Broverman. 1968. "Sex-Role Stereotypes and Self Concepts among College Students." *Journal of Consulting and Clinical Psychology* 32:287–95.

Rosenthal, Robert, and Lenore Jacobson. 1968. *Pygmalion in the Classroom: Teacher Expectations and Pupils Intellectual Development.* New York: Holt, Rinehart and Winston.

Rothbaum, F., A. Grauer, and A. Rubin. 1997. "Becoming Sexual: Differences Between Child and Adult Sexuality." *Young Children* 52(6):22–28.

Rothman, Robert A. 1993. *Inequality and Stratification: Class, Color, and Gender.* Englewood Cliffs, NJ: Prentice Hall.

Roumani, Rhoda. 2004. "Flying While Arab." www.beliefnet.com/Faiths/Islam/2004/08/Flying-While-Arab.aspx. Retrieved June 1, 2010.

Routman, Peter. 1995. "Bonded by Adversity—Pair Save a Man and Gain a Friend." *Seattle Times*, November 23, A1.

Rubin, Jeffrey Z., F. J. Provenzano, and Zella Luria. 1974. "They Eye of the Beholder: Parents' Views on Sex of Newborns." *American Journal of Orthopsychiatry* 44:512–19.

Rubin, Lillian. 1976. *Worlds of Pain: Life in the Working Class Family*. New York: Basic Books.

Rudman, Laurie A., and Stephen E. Kilianski. 2000. "Implicit and Explicit Attitudes Toward Female Authority." *Personality and Social Psychology Bulletin* 26(1):1315–28.

Rutter, Virginia, and Pepper Schwartz. Forthcoming. *The Gender of Sexuality*, second ed. Lanham, MD: Rowman & Littlefield.

Salais, D., and R. B. Fischer. 1995. "Sexual Preference and Altruism." *Journal of Homosexuality* 28:185–96.

Sampson, Edward E. 1975. "On Justice as Equality." *Journal of Social Issues* 31(3):45–64.

Sanchez, Laura. 1993. "Women's Power and the Gendered Division of Domestic Labor in the Third World." *Gender and Society* 7:434–59.

Sanders, Clinton. 1999. *Understanding Dogs*. Philadelphia, PA: Temple University Press.

Saperstein, Aliya, and Andrew M. Penner. 2010. "The Race of a Criminal Record." *Social Problems* 57:92–113.

Sapolsky, Robert. 1997. *The Trouble With Testosterone*. New York: Scribner.

Saucier, Donald A., Carol T. Miller, and Nicole Doucet. 2005. "Difference in Helping Whites and Blacks: A Meta-Analysis." *Personality and Social Psychology Review* 9(1):2–16.

Saucier, D. A., S. J. Smith, and J. L. McManus. 2007. "The Possible Role of Discrimination in the Rescue Response After Hurricane Katrina." *Journal of Race and Policy* 3(1):113–21.

Schanzenbach, Max M. and Michael L. Yaeger. 2006. "Prison Time, Fines, and Federal White-Collar Criminals: The Anatomy of a Racial Disparity." *Journal of Criminal Law and Criminology* 96:757–93.

Schope, R. D. and M. J. Eliason. 2004. "Sissies and Tomboys: Gender Role Behaviors and Homophobia." *Journal of Gay and Lesbian Social Services* 16(2):73–97.

Schuman, H., C. Steeh, L. Bobo, and M. Krysan. 1997. *Racial Attitudes in America: Trends and Interpretations*. Cambridge, MA: Harvard University Press.

Schwalbe, M. L., S. Godwin, D. Holden, D. Schrock, S. Thompson, and M. Wolkomir. 2000. "Generic Processes in the Reproduction of Inequality: An Interactionist Analysis." *Social Forces* 79:419–52.

Schwalbe, Michael L. 1991. "Social Structure and the Moral Self." Pp. 281–303 in *The Self-Society Dynamic: Cognition, Emotion and Action*, edited by J. A. Howard and P. L. Callero. New York: Cambridge University Press.

Schwartz, Gary S., Thomas R. Kane, Joanne M. Joseph, and James T. Tedeschi. 1978. "The Effects of Post-Transgression Remorse on Perceived Aggression, Attribution of Intent, and Level of Punishment." *Journal of Social and Clinical Psychology* 17:293–97.

Schwartz, Pepper. 1994. *Peer Marriage: How Love Between Equals Really Works*. New York: Free Press.

Schwartz, Shalom H., and Avi Gottlieb. 1980. "Bystander Anonymity and Reactions to Emergencies." *Social Psychology Quarterly* 39:418–30.

Schwartz, Shalom H., and Judith A. Howard. 1984. "Internalized Values as Motivators of Altruism." Pp. 229–45 in *Development and Maintenance of Prosocial Behavior: In-*

ternational Perspectives on Positive Morality, edited by Ervin Staub, Daniel Bar-Tal, J. Karylowsk, and Janusz Reykowski. New York: Plenum.

Scott, Jean. 1988. *Gender and the Politics of History*. New York: Columbia University Press.

Scott, John P. 1992. "Aggression: Functions and Control in Social Systems." *Aggressive Behavior* 18:1–20.

Scott, Marvin B., and Stanford M. Lyman. 1968. "Accounts." *American Sociological Review* 33:46–62.

Sears, David O. 1988. "Symbolic Racism." Pp. 64–84 in *Eliminating Racism: Profiles in Controversy*, edited by P. A. Katz and D. A. Taylor. New York: Plenum.

Segal, Lynne. 1993. "Does Pornography Cause Violence?" Pp. 5–21 in *Dirty Looks: Women, Pornography, Power*, edited by P. C. Gibson and R. Gibson. London: BFI.

Seligman, Martin E. P. 2002. *Authentic Happiness: Using the New Positive Psychology to Realize Your Potential for Lasting Fulfillment*. New York: Free Press.

Settles, Isis H. 2006. "Use of An Intersectional Framework to Understand Black Women's Racial and Gender Identities." *Sex Roles* 54:589–601.

Settles, Isis H., Jennifer S. Pratt-Hyatt, and NiCole T. Buchanan. 2008. "Through the Lens of Race: Black and White Women's Perceptions of Womanhood." *Psychology of Women Quarterly* 32(4):454–68.

Shaw, Jerry I., Hans W. Borough, and Matthew I. Fink. 1994. "Perceived Sexual Orientation and Helping Behavior by Males and Females: The Wrong Number Technique." *Journal of Psychology and Human Sexuality* 4:73–81.

Shelton, Beth A., and Daphne John. 1993. "Does Marital Status Make a Difference? Housework Among Married and Cohabiting Men and Women." *Journal of Family Issues* 14:401–20.

Shields, Stephanie. 2002. *Speaking From the Heart: Gender and the Social Meaning of Emotion*. Cambridge, UK: Cambridge University Press.

Shields, Stephanie. 2007. "Passionate Men, Emotional Women: Psychology Constructs Gender Difference in the Late 19th Century." *History of Psychology* 10(2):92–110.

Shinnar, Rachel S. 2008. "Coping with Negative Social Identity: The Case of Mexican Immigrants." *Journal of Social Psychology* 148(5):553–76.

Shotland, R. Lance, and Jane M. Craig. 1988. "Can Men and Women Differentiate Between Friendly and Sexually Interested Behavior?" *Social Psychology Quarterly* 51:66–73.

Shotland, R. Lance, and Margaret K. Straw. 1976. "Bystander Response to an Assault: When a Man Attacks a Woman." *Journal of Personality and Social Psychology* 34:990–99.

Sidanius, J., and F. Pratto. 1999. *Social Dominance Theory*. New York: Cambridge University Press.

Sigelman, Lee. 2001. "The Presentation of Self in Presidential Life: Onstage and Backstage with Johnson and Nixon." *Political Communication* 18:1–22.

Signorella, Margaret L., and Irene Hanson Frieze. 2008. "Interrelations of Gender Schemas in Children and Adolescents: Attitudes, Preferences, and Self-Perceptions." *Social Behavior and Personality: An International Journal* 36(7):941–54.

Simpson, Brent, Kyle Irwin, and Peter Lawrence. 2006. "Does a 'Norm of Self-Interest' Discourage Prosocial Behavior? Rationality and Quid Pro Quo in Charitable Giving." *Social Psychology Quarterly* 69:3296–3306.

Simon, Rita J., and J. Landis. 1991. *The Crimes Women Commit, the Punishments They Receive*. Lexington, MA: D.C. Heath.

Skinner, B. F. 1938. *The Behavior of Organisms*. New York: Appleton-Century-Crofts.

———. 1974. *About Behaviorism*. New York: Knopf.

Skrypnek, Berna J., and Mark Synder. 1982. "On the Self-Perpetuating Nature of Stereotypes about Men and Women." *Journal of Experimental Social Psychology* 18:277–91.

Smedley, Audrey. 1993. *Race in North America: Origin and Evolution of a Worldview*. Boulder, CO: Westview.

Smedley, Joseph W., and James A. Bayton. 1978. "Evaluative Race-Class Stereotypes by Race and Perceived Class of Subjects." *Journal of Personality and Social Psychology* 36:530–35.

Smeser, Neil. 1999. "Looking Back at 25 Years of Sociology and the Annual Review of Sociology." *Annual Review of Sociology* 25(1):1–18.

Smith, Patricia A., and Elizabeth Midlarsky. 1985. "Empirically Derived Conceptions of Femaleness and Maleness: A Current View." *Sex Roles* 12:313–28.

Smith, Elizabeth S., Ashleigh Smith Powers, and Gustavo A. Suarez. 2005. "If Bill Clinton Were a Woman: The Effectiveness of Male and Female Politicians' Account Strategies Following Alleged Transgressions." *Political Psychology* 26(1):115–34.

Smith-Lovin, Lynn. 1995. "The Sociology of Affect and Emotion." Pp. 118–48 in *Sociological Perspectives on Social Psychology*, edited by Karen S. Cook, Gary Alan Fine, and James S. House. Boston: Allyn and Bacon.

Sneed, Joel R., Jeffrey G. Johnson, Patricia Cohen, Carol Gilligan, Henian Chen, Thomas N. Crawford, and Stephanie Kasen. 2006. "Gender Differences in the Age-Changing Relationship Between Instrumentality and Family Contact in Emerging Adulthood." *Developmental Psychology* 42(5):787–97.

Snow, David A., and Leon Anderson. 1987. "Identity Work among the Homeless: The Verbal Construction and Avowal of Personal Identities." *American Journal of Sociology* 92:1336–71.

———. 1993. *Down on Their Luck: A Study of Homeless Street People*. Berkeley: University of California Press.

Snyder, Mark. 1984. "When Belief Creates Reality." Pp. 248–305 in *Advances in Experimental Social Psychology*, vol. 18, edited by L. Berkowitz. Orlando, FL: Academic Press.

Synder, Mark, and Berna J. Skrypnek. 1981. "Testing Hypotheses about the Self: Assessment of Job Suitability." *Journal of Personality* 49:193–211.

Snyder, Mark, Elizabeth Decker Tanke, and Ellen Berscheid. 1977. "Social Perception and Interpersonal Behavior: On the Self-Fulfilling Nature of Social Stereotypes." *Journal of Personality and Social Psychology* 35:656–66.

Snyder, Mark, and Seymour W. Uranowitz. 1978. "Reconstructing the Past: Some Cognitive Consequences of Person Perception." *Journal of Personality and Social Psychology* 36:941–50.

South, Scott J., and Glenna Spitze. 1994. "Housework in Marital and Nonmarital Households." *American Sociological Review* 59:327–47.

Spalter-Roth, Roberta, and Janene Scelza. 2008. "How Does Our Membership Grow? Indicators of Change by Gender, Race and Ethnicity, and Degree Type, 2001-2007." *ASA Research Brief.* Washington, DC: American Sociological Association.

Spence, J., and C. Buckner. 2000. "Instrumental and Expressive Traits, Trait Stereotypes, and Sexist Attitudes: What Do They Signify?" *Psychology of Women Quarterly* 24:44–63.

Spence, Janet T., Kay Deaux, and Robert L. Helmreich. 1985. "Sex Roles in Contemporary American Society." Pp. 149–78 in *The Handbook of Social Psychology*, third ed., edited by G. Lindzey and E. Aronson. New York: Random House.

Spence, Janet T., and Robert L. Helmreich. 1972. "The Attitudes Toward Women Scale: An Objective Instrument to Measure Attitudes Toward the Rights and Role of Women in Contemporary Society." *JSAS Catalog of Selected Documents in Psychology* 2:66.

———. 1978. *Masculinity and Femininity: Their Psychological Dimensions, Correlates and Antecedents.* Austin: University of Texas Press.

Spence, Janet T., Robert L. Helmreich, and Joy Stapp. 1974. "The Personal Attributes Questionnaire: A Measure of Sex-Role Stereotypes and Masculinity-Femininity." *JSAS Catalog of Selected Documents in Psychology* 4:43–44.

Spence, Janet T., and Linda L. Savin. 1985. "Images of Masculinity and Femininity." Pp. 35–66 in *Women, Gender, and Social Psychology*, edited by V. E. O'Leary, R. K. Unger, and B. S. Wallston. Hillsdale, NJ: Lawrence Erlbaum.

Spencer, S. J., C. M. Steele, and D. M. Quinn. 1999. "Stereotype Threat and Women's Math Performance." *Journal of Experimental Social Psychology* 35:4–28.

Spitze, Glenna. 1988. "Women's Employment and Family Relations: A Review." *Journal of Marriage and the Family* 50:595–618.

Spitze, Glenna, and John R. Logan 1990. "Sons, Daughters and Intergenerational Social Support." *Journal of Marriage and the Family* 52:420–30.

Sprafkin, J. N., R. M. Liebert, and R. W. Poulos. 1975. "Effects of Prosocial Televised Examples on Children's Helping." *Journal of Experimental Child Psychology* 20:119–26.

Sprague, Joey. 1995. "Self-Determination and Empowerment: Making the Connection." Unpublished paper, University of Kansas.

Sprague, Joey, and Kelley Massoni. 2005. "Student Evaluations and Gendered Expectations: What We Can't Count Can Hurt Us." *Sex Roles* 53(11/12):779–93.

Sprecher, Susan. 1998. "Insiders' Perspectives on Reason for Attraction to a Close Other." *Social Psychology Quarterly* 61:287–300.

Sprecher, Susan, and Maura Toro-Morn. 2002. "A Study of Men and Women From Different Sides of Earth to Determine If Men Are From Mars and Women Are From Venus in Their Beliefs About Love and Romantic Relationships." *Sex Roles* 46(5/6).

Stacey, Judith, and Barrie Thorne. 1985. "The Missing Feminist Revolution in Sociology." *Social Problems* 32:301–16.

Stack, Carol. 1974. *All Our Kin: Strategies for Survival in the Black Community.* New York: Harper and Row.

Stangor, Charles, Laure Lynch, Changming Duan, and Beth Glass. 1992. "Categorization of Individuals on the Basis of Multiple Social Features." *Journal of Personality and Social Psychology* 62:207–18.

Stanko, Elizabeth. 1990. *Everyday Violence.* London: Pandora.

Stansell, Christine. 2008. "Like a Natural Woman." *New York Times Magazine,* June 15.

Staples, Brent. 1994. "Black Men and Public Space." Pp. 156–58 in *The Production of Reality: Essays and Readings in Social Psychology,* edited by P. Kollock and J. O'Brien. Thousand Oaks, CA: Pine Forge Press.

Steele, Claude M., and Joshua Aronson. 1995. "Stereotype Threat and the Intellectual Performance of African Americans." *Journal of Personality and Social Psychology* 69:797–811.

Steinmetz, Suzanne K. 1977/1978. "The Battered Husband Syndrome." *Victimology* 2:499–509.

Stephan, Walter G., and David Rosenfield. 1982. "Racial and Ethnic Stereotypes." Pp. 92–136 in *In the Eye of the Beholder: Contemporary Issues in Stereotyping,* edited by A. G. Miller. New York: Praeger.

Stets, Jan E., and Peter J. Burke. 2005. "Identity Verification, Control, and Aggression in Marriage." *Social Psychology Quarterly* 68:160–78.

Stewart, A.J., and A. L. Dottolo. 2006. "Feminist Psychology." *Signs: A Journal of Women in Culture and Society* 31(2):493–509.

Stolte, John F. 1987. "The Formation of Justice Norms." *American Sociological Review* 52:774–84.

Stolte, John F., Gary Alan Fine, and Karen S. Cook. 2001. "Sociological Miniaturism: Seeing the Big Through the Small in Social Psychology." *Annual Review of Sociology* 27:387–413.

Stone, Jeff, Christian I. Lynch, Mike Sjomeling, and John M. Darley. 1999. "Stereotype Threat Effects on Black and White Athletic Performance." *Journal of Personality and Social Psychology* 77(6):1213–27.

Straus, Murray A. 1990. *Physical Violence in American Families.* New Brunswick, NJ: Transaction Books.

———. 1991. "Discipline and Deviance: Physical Punishment of Children and Violence and Other Crime in Adulthood." *Social Problems* 38:133–54.

Straus, Murray A., and Richard J. Gelles. 1986. "Societal Change and Change in Family Violence from 1975 to 1985 as Revealed by Two National Surveys." *Journal of Marriage and the* Family 48:465–79.

Straus, Murray A., Richard.J. Gelles, and Suzanne K. Steinmetz. 2006. *Behind Closed Doors: Violence in the American Family.* New York: Transaction Publishers.

Stryker, Sheldon. 1980. *Symbolic Interactionism: A Social Structural Version.* Menlo Park, CA: Benjamin-Cummings.

Stryker, Sheldon, and Anne Statham. 1985. "Symbolic Interactionism and Role Theory." Pp. 311–78 in *The Handbook of Social Psychology,* vol. 1, edited by G. Lindzey and E. Aronson, third ed. New York: Random House.

Stryker, Sheldon, and Kevin D. Vryan. 2003. "The Symbolic Interactionist Frame." Pp. 3–28 in *Handbook of Social Psychology*, edited by John DeLamater. New York: Kluwer-Plenum.

Stryker, Susan. 1994. "My Words to Victor Frankenstein Above the Village of Chamounix—Performing Transgender Rage." *GLQ: A Journal of Lesbian and Gay Studies* 1(3):227–54.

———. 2006. "(De)Subjugated Knowledges: An Introduction to Transgender Studies." Pp. 1–18 in *The Transgender Studies Reader*, edited by Susan Stryker and Stephen Whittle. New York: Routledge.

Sullivan, Maureen. 2004. *The Family of Woman: Lesbian Mothers, Their Children, and the undoing of Gender*. Los Angeles: University of California Press.

Sullivan, Christopher. 1995. "Judge Refuses to Declare Mistrial; Sentencing Begins: Jury Must Decide If Smith Deserves Death Penalty." *Seattle Times*, July 24, A2.

Suls, J., and P. J. Green. 2003. "Pluralistic Ignorance and College Student Perceptions of Gender-Specific Alcohol Norms." *Health Psychology* 22:479–86.

Tajfel, Henri. 1981. *Human Groups and Social Categories: Studies in Social Psychology*. Cambridge: Cambridge University Press.

———. 1982. *Social Identity and Intergroup Relations*. London: Cambridge University Press.

Tarman, C., and D. O. Sears. 2005. "The Conceptualization and Measurement of Symbolic Racism." *The Journal of Politics* 67:731–61.

Tavris, Carol. 1989. *Anger: The Misunderstood Emotion*. New York: Touchstone.

Taylor, Yvette. 2009. "Interesting Intersections? Researching Class, Gender, and Sexuality." Pp. 193–209 in *The Intersectional Approach: Transforming the Academy through Race, Class, and Gender*, edited by Michele Berger and Kathleen Guidroz. Chapel Hill: University of North Carolina Press.

Taylor, Donald M., and Vaishna Jaggi. 1974. "Ethnocentrism and Causal Attribution in a South Indian Context." *Journal of Cross-Cultural Psychology* 5:162–71.

Taylor, Shelley E., Susan T. Fiske, Nancy L. Etcoff, and Audrey J. Ruderman. 1978. "Categorical Bases of Person Memory and Stereotyping." *Journal of Personality and Social Psychology* 36:778–93.

Taylor, Shelley E., Anne Peplau, and David O. Sears. 1994. *Social Psychology*, eighth ed. Englewood Cliffs, NJ: Prentice Hall.

Taylor, Stuart P., and James D. Sears. 1988. "The Effects of Alcohol and Persuasive Social Pressure on Human Physical Aggression." *Aggressive Behavior* 14:237–43.

Tedeschi, J. T., ed. 1981. *Impression Management Theory and Social Psychological Research*. New York: Academic Press.

Terman, Lewis M., and Catherine Cox Miles. 1936. *Sex and Personality: Studies in Masculinity and Femininity*. New York: McGraw-Hill

Tetlock, P. E. 1981. "Pre to Postelection Shifts in Presidential Rhetoric: Cognitive Adjustment or Impression Management." *Journal of Personality and Social Psychology* 41:207–13.

Thibaut, John W., and Harold H. Kelley. 1959. *The Social Psychology of Groups*. New York: John Wiley.

Thomas, Jeannie B. 1999. "Dumb Blondes, Dan Quayle, and Hillary Clinton: Gender, Sexuality, and Stupidity in Jokes." *Journal of American Folklore* 110(437):277–313.

Thomas, A. J., K. M. Witherspoon, and S. L. Spreight. 2004. "Exploring Internalized Oppression of African American Women." In *The Psychology of Prejudice and Discrimination*, edited by J. L. Chin. Westbrook, CT: Praeger Press.

Thompson, Linda. 1991. "Family Work: Women's Sense of Fairness." *Journal of Family Issues* 12:181–96.

Thompson, Linda, and Alexis J. Walker. 1989. "Gender in Families: Women and Men in Marriage, Work, and Parenthood." *Journal of Marriage and the Family* 51:845–71.

Thorne, Deborah, and Leon Anderson. 2006. "Managing the Stigma of Personal Bankruptcy." *Sociological Focus* 39(2):77–97.

Thorne, Barrie. 1993. *Gender Play: Girls and Boys in School.* New Brunswick, NJ: Rutgers University Press.

Thorne, Barrie, Cheris Kramarae, and Nancy Henley. 1983. *Language, Gender, and Society.* Rowley, MA: Newbury House.

Tichenor, Veronica. 2005. "Maintaining Men's Dominance: Negotiating Identity and Power When She Earns More." *Sex Roles* 53(3/4):191–205.

Timmer, Susan G., Jacquelynne Eccles, and Keith O'Brien. 1985. "How Children Use Time." Pp. 353–82 in *Time, Goods, and Well-Being*, edited by F. T. Juster and F. P. Stafford. Ann Arbor: University of Michigan Institute for Social Research.

Towson, Shelagh M., and Mark P. Zanna. 1982. "Toward a Situational Analysis of Gender Differences in Aggression." *Sex Roles* 8:903–14.

Trebay, Guy. 2008. "He's Pregnant. You're Speechless." *New York Times*, June 22.

Triandis, Harry C. 1976. "The Future of Pluralism." *Journal of Social Issues* 32(4):179–207.

Tsang, Ellen. 1994. "Investigating the Effects of Race and Apparent Lesbianism upon Helping Behaviour." *Feminism and Psychology* 4:469–71.

Turk, James L., and Norman W. Bell. 1972. "Measuring Power in Families." *Journal of Marriage and the Family* 34:215–23.

Turner, Jonathan H. 1982. *The Structure of Sociological Theory.* Homewood, IL: Dorsey.

Turner, Kelly L., and Christia Brown. 2007. "The Centrality of Gender and Ethnic Identities Across Individuals and Contexts." *Social Development* 16(4):700–19.

Tversky, A., and D. Kahneman. 1982. "Judgment Under Uncertainty." Pp. 3–22 in *Judgment Under Uncertainty*, edited by D. Kahneman, P. Slovic, and A. Tversky. New York: Cambridge University Press.

Twenge, J. M., and J. Crocker. 2002. "Race and Self-Esteem: Meta-Analyses Comparing Whites, Blacks, Hispanics, Asians, and American Indians and Comment on Gray-Little and Hafdahl (2000)." *Psychology Bulletin* 128(3):371–408.

Unger, Rhoda K. 1976. "Male Is Greater Than Female: The Socialization of Status Inequality." *The Counseling Psychologist* 6:2–9.

———. 1978. "The Politics of Gender: A Review of Relevant Literature." In *Psychology of Women: Future Directions of Research*, edited by J. Sherman and F. Denmark. New York: Psychological Dimensions.

———. 1998. *Resisting Gender: Twenty-Five Years of Feminist Psychology.* London: Sage.

Unger, Rhoda, and Mary Crawford. 1992. *Women and Gender: A Feminist Psychology.* New York: McGraw-Hill.

United Nations Crime and Justice Information Network. 2002. *Survey on Crime Trends and the Operations of Criminal Justice Systems.* New York: United Nations.

United Nations Development Fund for Women. 2005. "Women, Work & Poverty." *Progress of the World's Women 2005.* New York: United Nations Development Fund for Women.

Vander Zanden, James W. 1990. *The Social Experience: An Introduction to Sociology.* New York: McGraw-Hill.

Verser, R., and R.H. Wicks. 2006. "Managing Voter Impressions: The Use of Images on Presidential Candidate Web Site During the 2000 Campaign." *Journal of Communication* 56:178–97.

Visher, Christy A. 1983. "Gender, Police Arrest Decisions, and Notions of Chivalry." *Criminology* 21(1):5–28.

Voicu, Mălina, Bogdan Voicu, and Katarina Strapcova. 2008. "Housework and Gender Inequality in European Countries." *European Sociological Review* 25(3):365–77.

von Baeyer, Carl L., Debbie L. Sherk, and Mark P. Zanna. 1981. "Impression Management in the Job Interview: When the Female Applicant Meets the Male (Chauvinist) Interviewer." *Personality and Social Psychology Bulletin* 7:45–51.

Vonk, Roos, and Richard D. Ashmore. 2003. "Thinking about Gender Types: Cognitive Organization of Female and Male Types." *British Journal of Social Psychology* 42(2).

Vorauer, J. D., A .J. Hunter, K. J. Main, and S. Roy. 2000. "Meta-Stereotype Activation: Evidence from Indirect Measures for Specific Evaluative Concerns Experienced by Members of Dominant Groups in Intergroup Interaction." *Journal of Personality and Social Psychology* 78:690–707.

Vorauer, J. D., K. J. Main, and G. B. O'Connell. 1998. "How Do Individuals Expect to Be Viewed by Members of Lower Status Groups?" *Journal of Personality and Social Psychology* 75:917–37.

Wagner, David G., Rebecca S. Ford, and Thomas W. Ford. 1986. "Can Gender Inequalities Be Reduced?" *American Sociological Review* 51:47–61.

Watson, John B. 1924. *Behaviorism.* Chicago: University of Chicago Press.

Watts, Barbara L., Lawrence A. Messe, and Robin R. Vallacher. 1982. "Toward Understanding Sex Differences in Pay Allocation: Agency, Communion, and Reward Distribution Behavior." *Sex Roles* 8:1175–81.

Webster, Murray, Jr., and James E. Driskell, Jr. 1983. "Beauty as Status." *American Journal of Sociology* 89(1):140–65.

Webster, Murray, Jr., Stuart J. Hysom, and Elise M. Fullmer. 1998. "Sexual Orientation and Occupation as Status." Pp. 1–21 in *Advances in Group Processes*, edited by J. Skvoretz and J. Szmatka, vol. 15. New York: JAI Press.

Weeks, M., and M.B. Lupfer. 2004. "Complicating Race: The Relationship Between Prejudice, Race and Social Class Categorizations." *Personality and Social Psychology Bulletin* 30:972–84.

Wegner, Daniel. 1986. "Transactive Memory: A Contemporary Analysis of the Group Mind." Pp. 185–208 in *Theories of Group Behavior,* edited by B. Mullen and G. R. Goethals. New York: Springer-Verlag.

Wegner, Daniel M., and William D. Crano. 1975. "Racial Factors in Helping Behavior: An Unobtrusive Field Experiment." *Journal of Personality and Social Psychology* 32:901–5.

Weisstein, Naomi. 1970. "'Kinder, Kuche, Kirche' as Scientific Law: Psychology Constructs the Female." Pp. 205–20 in *Sisterhood Is Powerful,* edited by R. Morgan. New York: Vintage.

Weitz, Rose, and Leonard Gordon. 1993. "Images of Black Women Among Anglo College Students." *Sex Roles* 28:19–34.

West, Candace, and Sarah Fenstermaker. 1995. "Doing Difference." *Gender and Society* 9:8–37.

West, Candace, and Don H. Zimmerman. 1987. "Doing Gender." *Gender and Society* 1:125–51.

———. 2009. "Accounting for Doing Gender." *Gender and Society* 23(1):112–22.

West, Stephen G., Glayde Whitney, and Robert Schnedler. 1975. "Helping a Motorist in Distress: The Effects of Sex, Race and Neighborhood." *Journal of Personality and Social Psychology* 31:691–98.

Wexler, Phil. 1983. *Critical Social Psychology.* Boston, MA: Routledge and Kegan Paul.

White, Deborah Gray. 1999. *Too Heavy a Load: Black Women in Defense of Themselves 1894–1994.* New York: W. W. Norton.

White, Jacquelyn W., and Robin M. Kowalski. 1994. "Deconstructing the Myth of the Nonaggressive Woman." *Psychology of Women Quarterly* 18:487–508.

White, Jacquelyn W., and Susan B. Sorenson. 1992. "A Sociocultural View of Sexual Assault: From Discrepancy to Diversity." *Journal of Social Issues* 48(1):187–95.

Whiting, Beatrice B., and C. P. Edwards. 1988. *Children of Different Worlds: The Foundation of Social Behavior.* Cambridge, MA: Harvard University Press.

Whiting, Beatrice B., and John W. M. Whiting. 1975. *Children of Six Cultures: A Psychocultural Analysis.* Cambridge, MA: Harvard University Press.

Wicker, Alan W. 1969. "Attitudes Versus Actions: The Relationship of Verbal and Overt Behavioral Responses to Attitude Objects." *Journal of Social Issues* 25(4):41–78.

Widmer, Ted. 2005. *Martin Van Buren.* New York: Henry Holt and Company.

Wilcox, W. Bradford, and Steven L. Nock. 2006. "What's Love Got To Do With It? Equality, Equity, Commitment and Women's Marital Quality." *Social Forces* 84(3).

Wilkie, J. R., M. M. Ferree, and K. S. Ratcliff. 1998. "Gender and Fairness: Marital Satisfaction in Two-Earner Couples." *Journal of Marriage and the Family* 60:577–94.

Wilson, Sandra R., Nancy L. Brown, Carolina Mejia, and Philip W. Lavori. 2002. "Effects of Interviewer Characteristics on Reported Sexual Behavior of California Latino Couples." *Hispanic Journal of Behavioral Sciences* 24(1):38–62.

Winther, Paul. 2007. "The 'Killing' of Neni Bai." Pp. 106–11 in *The Sociological Outlook,* edited by Reid Luhman. Lanham, MD: Rowman & Littlefield.

Wispe, L. G., and H. B. Freshley. 1971. "Race, Sex, and Sympathetic Helping Behavior: The Broken Bag Caper." *Journal of Personality and Social Psychology* 17:59–65.

Wittenbrink, B., and N. Schwarz, eds. 2007. *Implicit Measures of Attitudes*. New York: Guilford Press.

Wittig, Michelle A., Gary Marks, and Gary A. Jones. 1981. "Luck Versus Effort Attributions: Effect on Reward Allocations to Self and Other." *Personality and Social Psychology* 7:71–78.

Wood, Wendy, and Steven J. Karten. 1986. "Sex Differences in Interaction Style as a Product of Perceived Sex Differences in Competence." *Journal of Personality and Social Psychology* 50:341–47.

Wooley, Helen Thompson. 1910. "Psychological Literature: A Review of the Most Recent Literature on the Psychology of Sex." *Psychological Bulletin* 7:335–42.

Word, Carl O., Mark P. Zanna, and Joel Cooper. 1974. "The Nonverbal Mediation of Self-Fulfilling Prophecies in Interracial Interaction." *Journal of Experimental Social Psychology* 10:109–20.

Wright, David, and Sunleen Miller. 2007. "Obama Dropped Flag Pin in War Statement." *ABC News*, October 4. abcnews.go.com/Politics/story?id=3690000&page=1. Retrieved June 3, 2010.

Wright, Erik O., Karen Shire, Shu-ling Hwang, Maureen Dolan, and Janeen Baxter. 1992. "The Non-Effects of Class on the Gender Division of Labor in the Home: A Comparative Study of Sweden and the United States." *Gender and Society* 6:252–82.

Wunderlich, Elizabeth, and Frank N. Willis. 1977. "The Youth of Victims as a Factor Affecting the Probability of Receiving Aid." *Journal of Psychology* 97:93–94.

Yamagishi, Toshio, Mary R. Gillmore, and Karen S. Cook. 1988. "Network Connections and the Distribution of Power in Exchange Networks." *American Journal of Sociology* 93:833.

Yaniv, Oren. 2009. "Caster Semenya, Forced to Take Gender Test, Is a Woman . . . and a Man." *New York Daily News*, September 10.

Yarrow, Marian R., Phyllis M. Scott, and Carolyn Z. Waxler. 1973. "Learning Concern for Others." *Developmental Psychology* 8:240–60.

York, Richard, and Brett Clark. 2007. "Gender and Mathematical Ability: The Toll of Biological Determinism." *Monthly Review* 59(6):7–15.

Zavis, Alexandra. 2008. "Grooming a Female Suicide Bomber." *Los Angeles Times*, August 21.

Zerubavel, Eviatar. 1996. "Lumping and Splitting: Notes on Social Classification." *Sociological Forum* 11(3):421–33.

Index

accounts: as excuse, 142; for impression management repair, 142; as justification, 142; as variable, 145

actors, social: as activated, 89–90; cultural competence of, 145; for expectation states theory, 141; identities of, 151; perceptions/response by, 2, 3, 139; race of, 3; for social cognition, 89–90; social exchange theory for, 6; social schemas for, 8, 145–46, 151. *See also* social cognition, theory/process of

African Americans: in academia, 54, 85; acknowledgment rituals among, 49; attitudes toward, 92–93; class and, 40, 78; competence among, 40, 54, 85; discrimination against, 49, 99, 172–73; domestic labor by, 40, 73; family aid by, 190; as helping blacks, 178–79; images of, as women, 40, 99; intellectualism of, 35–36, 138; oppression of, 40; stereotypes for, 102–3, 138–39, 148; subtypes for, 103–4; volunteerism by, 178–79; during World War II, 41

age: gender and, 3–4, 101, 208; of population, 189; stratification in, 65, 99–100

aggression: alcohol and, 162; altruism and, 30, 55, 196; attribution and, 170; as biological, 161–62; against children, 158, 159, 164, 182–83, 192; in children, 61, 164, 181, 188; coercion as, 74–75, 167–68, 175; context for, 181–82; cost *v.* benefit for, 167–68; cues for, 162, 170, 188; culture and, 163; definition of, 158; as direct *v.* indirect, 181; essentialist/biological perspectives of, 161–63, 180; ethnicity and, 184–85; as evolutionary, 161–62; as expressive, 159, 194; feelings *v.* behavior and, 165; frustration-aggression theory for, 162–63, 180, 184; gender and, 30, 58–59, 159, 191; homophobia and, 174, 187; hormones for, 162, 194; identity and, 135; impression management of, 173; inaction and, 175; as indirect, 159; as instrumental, 159, 194; intent of,

bias: attribution for, 113–14, 146; by
    class, 177; in criminal justice system,
    183, 184, 197n3; dehumanization
    and, 186; in social exchange theory,
    66, 83; in social psychology, 16, 115
bisexuals, rights for, 23
Black, Stephen L., 165
Black Caucus, 144
black liberation theology, 132, 144
Black Panthers, 144
blacks. *See* African Americans
Blair, C. A., 169
Blumstein, Philip, 73, 135
Bobbitt, John/Lorena, 182
Bornstein, Kate, 20
Braly, Kenneth W., 102
Breines, Winnie, 159–60
Brewer, Marilynn B., 101
Brines, Julie, 48, 69–71, 74–75, 80–81,
    83
Brown, Kathleen, 74
Bryson, Seymour, 93
BSRI. *See* Bem Sex Role Inventory
Buchanan, NiCole T., 103
bullying, in school, 192
Bush, George W., 74, 130, 131

Calabrese, Raymond L., 176
Cammermeyer, Grethe, 109–10
Campbell, Donald T., 103
Cantor, Muriel G., 21
Carlsmith, J. M., 89
Carpenter, Sandra, 100
Carr, Joetta L., 165
Carrigan, Tim, 17
Carrington, Christopher, 72, 73
categorization: errors in, 100; of
    information, 7, 90–91, 99–100, 109;
    of sexes, 12–13; stereotype for, 102
Census, U.S., 25
charity, donation to, 166, 177, 196
Charon, Joel M., 19
Chavez, Linda, 73, 74
cheating, 176
Cherry, Debra, 40

children: abuse of, 158, 159, 164,
    182–83, 192; aggression in, 61,
    164, 181, 188; altruism in, 163–64,
    190; bullying of, 192; cross-cultural
    help by, 190–91; developmental
    psychology for, 59; gender identity/
    polarization by, 15, 20, 38; imitation
    by, 36; of lesbians, 209; modeling for,
    36, 60, 61, 163–64, 181; punishment
    of, 158, 164; reinforcement for, 60,
    61–62, 163–64; sexual play by, 23;
    socialization of, 36, 39, 124; social
    learning theory for, 61; women's help
    for, 176, 189, 190
Chisholm, Shirley, 144
chivalry, 173
Chow, Esther Ngan-Ling, 40–41
Clark, R., 42
class, social: as achieved, 27, 78,
    105–6; African Americans and,
    40, 78; altruism and, 167, 176–77;
    attribution and, 114; behavioral
    confirmation and, 136; bias by, 177;
    body shape and, 12; crime by, 183;
    discrimination by, 177; domestic
    labor and, 73–74; equality and,
    105; essentialist perspective on, 53;
    gender and, 3–4, 28, 50, 58, 128, 208;
    hierarchy of, 29, 52, 58, 65, 99–100,
    112; identity with, 20; importance
    of, 27–28; interaction with, 9;
    justice/equity and, 42, 43, 53, 77–78,
    116; personality traits and, 105–6;
    power and, 7, 77–78, 136; privilege
    according to, 28–29; race and, 23,
    28, 58, 104; resource distribution by,
    77–78; schemas for, 104–6; shift in,
    25, 128; social psychology and, 54; as
    socioeconomic, 3–4, 6, 23, 27, 105;
    stereotypes for, 40, 184; in U.S., 105;
    variation in, 104; victimization and,
    185, 187; of witness, 3–4; for women,
    17, 28, 44, 51, 71, 140, 193
Clinton, Hillary Rodham, 130, 146, 208
Clinton, William J., 73–74

exchange theory for, 5–7, 9–10; sociological approach to, 4, 211; structure of, 16; symbolic interaction and, 5, 9, 10, 121, 154

social structure: aggression and, 193; context for, 3–4; gender within, 14, 50–51, 74, 127; interaction and, 145, 172; negotiation with, 51; relationship with, 8, 51; social cognition theory and, 169; social exchange theory and, 63, 74, 85, 203. *See also* institutions, social; society

society: aggression by, 196; alienation from, 2; altruism within, 166, 176–77, 196; developmental psychology for, 59; face of, 42–43, 69–70, 179–80, 197n2; gendered roles for, 42–43, 69–70; inequality within, 21–22, 33, 42, 43, 53, 67, 197n2; prosocial behavior of, 158, 163, 190; role of, 42–43, 69–70

solidarity, intragroup, 190

Solomon, Linda K., 110

South, Scott J., 71

Spence, Janet T., 43

Spitze, Glenna, 71

Sprague, Joey, 195

Spreight, S. L., 40

Stacey, Judith, 43

Stangor, Charles, 101

Staples, Brent, 148, 150

Statham, Anne, 152

status, social: characteristics for, 140; domestic labor and, 73–74; for men *v.* women, 17, 44, 51, 71, 140, 193. *See also* class

Steele, Claude M., 138

Steffen, Valerie J., 181, 192

Stephan, Walter G., 184

stereotype(s): for African Americans, 102–3, 138–39, 148; for aggression, 169, 170–71; for Asian Americans, 40–41; categorization of, 102; for class, 40, 184; as consensual, 107; context for, 35; in culture, 19, 40–41,

102–3, 106, 138–39, 148, 185, 196, 201; for disability, 40; ethnicity and, 40, 106; for gender, 7, 11, 15, 17, 19, 34–35, 37–40, 42–45, 69–70, 73, 96, 102–3, 113–14, 137, 143, 147–48, 169, 170–71, 174–75, 176, 180, 182–86, 193–94, 196, 201–2, 209; impression management and, 147–48, 150; within interview, 17, 48, 138; in media, 41; memory and, 111; as meta-stereotypes, 4, 102, 106; perception of, 17; personality and, 37, 115; polarization of, 15, 20, 38; power of, 37; prescriptions as, 42–45; as racial, 40, 102–3, 138; schema for, 7; self-esteem and, 40; sexual orientation and, 40; as threat, 35, 138–39, 148, 150; types of, 19, 37. *See also* schemas

Stereotypic Roles for Black Women Scale (Spreight, Thomas, Witherspoon), 40

Stets, Jan E., 135

Stolte, John F., 84

stratification, social: by age, 65, 99–100; by class, 65, 99–100; equity *v.* equality in, 80; through gender, 52, 99–100, 128; legitimacy of, 107; for men/women, 52, 140; by race, 65, 99–100; self-evaluation and, 107; social exchange theory and, 65; symbolic interaction and, 152. *See also* class, social

Straw, Jane M., 168

Stryker, Sheldon, 125, 152

Studs (television), 46

symbolic interaction: aggression and, 173–75, 193; altruism and, 171–73; behavior for, 5, 9, 10, 50; cognition and, 114–15, 117, 151; expectation states theory and, 139; goals for, 132; identity for, 125, 151, 153–54; impression management for, 128–35, 151; inference for, 123; other's perspective in, 172; perception for, 5, 9, 10, 50; power and, 152;

About the Authors

Jocelyn A. Hollander is a faculty member at the University of Oregon. Her research focuses on gender, particularly how people resist gender expectations and change understandings of gender. She teaches courses on gender, microsociology, pedagogy, and the sociology of food.

Daniel G. Renfrow is an assistant professor of sociology at Wells College. He completed his PhD in sociology at the University of Washington in 2005. His research examines the microfoundations of inequalities associated with sexuality, gender, and, more recently, species. He regularly teaches courses in sociological theory and methods, masculinities, and human-animal interaction.

Judith A. Howard is professor of sociology and divisional dean of social sciences at the University of Washington. Her research focuses on social cognition and the microsocial study of gender dynamics in their immersions with other dimensions of societal inequalities. She is a former coeditor (with Carolyn Allen) of *Signs: Journal of Women in Culture and Society.*